Helping People Grow

Practical Approaches to Christian Counseling

Edited By

Gary R. Collins

Vision House

Santa Ana, California 92705

❖

To
Vernon C. Grounds

Educator and Leader
in the field of
Christian Counseling
on the occasion of his
sixty-fifth birthday

❖

Preface

At a recent meeting of the American Psychological Association, a speaker commented that "there is no such thing as a Christian theory of counseling." He went on to suggest that every current approach to counseling is based on humanistic, naturalistic, non-Christian presuppositions.

When I heard that statement my hand reached for a pen, and I began to write the names of those Christians who, in recent years, have attempted to develop Christian approaches to counseling. Before the conference speaker had finished his talk, I had a rough outline in mind for the book which you now hold in your hands, although it took almost two years for the manuscript to be completed.

As an editor, I make no claim to have included all of the Christian approaches to counseling, nor do I claim that the approaches which are included necessarily represent the most highly developed or the best ones. In general, I have not contacted major representatives of the Clinical Pastoral Education movement, primarily because their positions are well-known and clearly elaborated elsewhere. Their omission in no way implies that their contributions are unimportant or non-Christian.

Furthermore, I have not tried to limit inclusion in this volume to people with whom I am in agreement psychologically or to people whose approaches are highly sophisticated. Some of the authors have seemingly simple positions, but they are included because of their wide influence in the field of Christian counseling. As a Protestant evangelical writing for readers who would tend to share my theological position, I have selected authors who (perhaps with two or three exceptions) assume that the Bible is the Word of God and that the Scriptures must be the basis for our Christian counseling positions.

It is my hope that this volume will be helpful to pastoral counselors, to students, to professionals (including those who make no claim to be Christian) and to interested laymen, all of whom might want to know more completely what is happening in the area of Christian counseling, especially in the more conservative Protestant segments of Christianity.

Although most of the following chapters have been written specifically for this book, other chapters are reprints or adaptations from previously published works. This book, therefore, summarizes material that until now has appeared in a scattered variety of publications. Hopefully, this book will encourage readers to turn to the more lengthy and detailed writings of those authors whose work is included or discussed in the following pages.

I deeply appreciate all of those authors who took time from busy schedules to prepare the following chapters, and I appreciate the practical assistance of Marlene Terbush, James Beesley, and Raymond Oehm. It is my hope that this volume will provide useful information and will serve as a stimulus both for continued discussion and for the further development and elaboration of Christian approaches to the helping relationship.

—Gary R. Collins

Contents

1

INTRODUCTION: APPROACHES TO CHRISTIAN COUNSELING

Gary R. Collins

Within recent years, books and articles on Christian counseling have appeared with increasing frequency. Some of these publications present sophisticated explanations of human behavior, detailed counseling techniques, and convincing case histories, many of which are presented as the Christian (or biblical) way to counsel.

In the midst of this avalanche of information, it is easy to become inundated with names and theories, uncertain about how the different writers relate to each other, unable to evaluate which of these approaches is effective, and frustrated in our attempts to determine the theological assumptions of the authors. This book is designed to clarify some of these issues, beginning with this first chapter, which is written as an overview of the exciting, rapidly growing field of Christian counseling.

This chapter is an updated and expanded revision of an article entitled "The Pulpit and the Couch," which appeared in the August 27, 1975, issue of *Christianity Today* (volume 19, number 23, pp. 5-9). (Copyright © 1975 by *Christianity Today*. Used by permission.)An earlier draft of the chapter was presented as an invited paper at the 26th Annual Convention of the Evangelical Theological Society, in Dallas, Texas, December 1974.

Gary R. Collins holds the Ph.D. degree from Purdue University, and is currently Professor of Pastoral Counseling and Psychology at Trinity Evangelical Divinity School, in Deerfield, Illinois. He has written several books in the area of Christian counseling and is the editor of this volume.

Several years ago (on July 28, 1955, to be exact) the United States Congress passed legislation known as the "Mental Health Study Act."[1] Concerned over an apparent increase in "mental illness" and spiraling treatment costs, the Congress authorized expenditure of more than one million dollars for an in-depth research program designed to study current "resources, methods, and practices for diagnosing, treating, caring for and rehabilitating" the emotionally disturbed. A forty-five-member panel, known as the Joint Commission on Mental Illness and Health, distributed the research money, supervised the publication of ten book-length research summaries, and made a number of recommendations for a national mental health program.[2]

Among the many interesting findings of the Joint Commission research was the discovery that when people had personal problems, only 28 percent of them went to professional counselors or clinics. Approximately 29 percent consulted their family physician, and 42 percent sought help from a clergyman.[3] There are probably some good reasons for this tendency to seek help from religious leaders. The clergyman is readily available, his or her services are free, and it is probably less threatening for people to talk to a priest or minister than to visit a psychiatrist. The Joint Commission recommended, therefore, that

> A host of persons untrained or partially trained in mental health principles and practices— clergymen, family physicians, teachers . . . and

others—are already trying to help and to treat the
mentally ill in the absence of professional
resources. . . . With a moderate amount of training through short courses and consultation on the
job, such persons can be fully equipped with an
additional skill as mental health counselors. . . .
Teaching aid must be provided to teachers' colleges, schools of theology, schools of social work,
and others so that they may have part-time or full-
time faculty members (physicians, clinical
psychologists, psychiatric social workers, for example) who will integrate mental health information
into the training programs of these professions.*[4]

It is very probable that the research figures of the Joint
Commission are no longer accurate. Today, perhaps more or
less than 42 percent of people with problems seek help from a
clergyman, but several conclusions remain. First, people in
need of help have a strong desire for counseling that is based
on and sympathetic to the fundamental teachings of Christianity. Second, the pastor is still called upon to do much,
perhaps most, of the conseling that is done in this country.
And third, the theological seminary has a responsibility to
equip men and women for this important phase of their
ministry.

In one sense, Christian counseling has been with us for
centuries. The Old Testament is filled with examples of godly
men and women who were used by the Holy Spirit to encourage, guide, support, confront, advise, and in other ways
help those in need. Jesus was described as a ''wonderful
Counselor,'' and His followers were appointed not only to

---

*Used by permission of Basic Books.
See footnote 4.

preach but to deal with the spiritual and psychological needs of individuals (Matthew 10:7,8). Later, the New Testament epistles gave great insight into the counseling techniques of their inspired writers. Throughout the Christian era, church leaders have engaged in what have been called the four pastoral functions: healing, sustaining, guiding, and reconciling.[5]

What we now know as the pastoral counseling movement, however, was begun by some pastors and physicians about fifty years ago. Perhaps the best-known of the founding fathers was Anton T. Boisen, a minister and writer who during the first sixty years of his long life experienced a number of psychotic breakdowns, three of which led to confinement in mental institutions. Boisen became convinced of the need to train seminary students for work with the mentally ill. Beginning with only a few students, he began a loosely organized training program for seminarians at Worcester State Hospital in Massachusetts.

From this simple beginning, "Clinical Pastoral Education" (CPE) has developed into a highly organized movement. Much of its work has been admirable: providing standards for the training of pastoral counselors; convincing hospital personnel of the importance of involving pastors in treatment of the physically and mentally ill; investigating ways in which theology and the psychological sciences can be related; showing the importance of training in counseling for seminarians; demonstrating that the personal and spiritual development of the seminarian is at least as important as his or her intellectual training for the ministry.[6]

In the 1930s and 1940s, when many seminaries were adding clinical pastoral training to their curricula, theologically conservative schools were skeptical. CPE appeared to be a theologically liberal movement, and this, coupled with a general distrust of psychology, undoubtedly caused evangelicals to stay apart from the CPE movement.

While in no way endorsing CPE theology, Christian psychologists Clyde Narramore and Henry Brandt showed that a biblical approach to counseling was possible, and some evangelicals began to see the relevance of psychology to theological education. Now most seminaries and Bible schools have courses in pastoral counseling, and some even have highly developed departments of pastoral psychology and counseling. Evangelical contact with the CPE movement remains minimal, but some evangelicals have attempted to develop more biblical approaches to the counseling process. These approaches, coupled with the orientations of liberal Protestant and Catholic writers, have given us the beginnings of a growing and potentially valuable body of literature in Christian counseling.

Christian counseling can be divided into five overlapping categories that might be labeled the mainstream, the evangelical pastoral counselors, the Christian professionals, the theoretician-researchers, and the popularizers.

THE MAINSTREAM

Much of the current training in Christian counseling takes place within the guidelines of the CPE movement. Numerous hospitals have CPE training programs with carefully planned curricula and certified instructors. Many seminaries make one quarter of CPE training a requirement for graduation. People in the field follow CPE-oriented publications such as the *Journal of Pastoral Care* or the *Journal of Pastoral Counseling*. Supervised counselor training and exposure to hospital settings can be a valuable experience, which CPE clearly provides, but the training raises several problems for theologically conservative people.

First, following the leadership of Princeton's Seward Hiltner, CPE tends to consider personal experience rather than Scripture the foundation of training. Thomas Oden describes the method this way:

> The overwhelming weight of authority for theological knowledge is given to experience, and in this sense the American pastoral care movement belongs essentially to the tradition of a liberalizing, pragmatizing pietism. One first does certain things and experiences certain relationships, like shepherding the flock, and only then draws valid theological conclusions.**[7]

Oden makes this perceptive comment:

> Although we hardly wish to challenge the validity of interview analysis in pastoral care, we seriously question whether this alone is adequate as a vantage point for drawing theological conclusions without the theological equilibrium that comes from the sustained study of Scripture and tradition and the struggle for rational systematic self-consistency.**[8]

A second problem is that the CPE movement tends to borrow uncritically from humanistic secular psychology. In a book on the clinical training of ministers, Hiltner has written:

> In terms of basic attitude, approach, and method, pastoral counseling does not differ from effective counseling by other types of counselors. It differs in terms of the setting in which counseling is done, the religious resources which are drawn upon, and the dimension at which the pastor must view all

---

**Used by permission of Thomas Oden.
See footnotes 7 and 8.

human growth and human problems.***[9]

The "religious resources" and "dimension" about which Hiltner speaks are not very well-defined, but one gets the impression in another of his books, *Pastoral Counseling,*[10] that prayer, Bible reading, and references to Christian doctrine are merely a part of the pastoral counselor's collection of techniques.

Third, people in the CPE movement appear to have little tolerance for conservative theological positions. Certainly in the past and perhaps in the present, evangelicals have tended to be directive, authoritarian counselors, insensitive to the needs and feelings of counselors. CPE leaders have resisted this approach and have been quick to notice the rigidities and insecurities that are often found among conservative Christians. Evangelicals also present a biblically based theology that to many critics appears to be narrow-minded and inflexible. As a result of these observations and the failure of evangelicals to show that a theologically conservative approach to counseling is more effective than the work done by CPE-trained counselors, theologically liberal counselors have tended to develop an inflexibility of their own in which they fail to take conservatives seriously.

Of course, pastoral counselors, like theologians, cover a broad theological spectrum. Some of the most familiar persons in the mainstream movement—William Hulme, Wayne Oates, Carroll Wise, and John Sutherland Bonnell,[11] for example—take a more sympathetic view of conservative protestant theology than would such others as Seward Hiltner, Ernest Bruder, Edward Thornton, or Russell Dicks.[12]

***Used by permission of Abingdon Press.
See footnote 9.

EVANGELICAL PASTORAL COUNSELORS

Currently the most outspoken and lucid opponent of the CPE mainstream is Jay E. Adams, former professor of practical theology at Westminster Theological Seminary in Philadelphia. In several controversial but widely influential volumes[13] Adams criticizes counseling which is not based on Scripture and proposes a directive approach which he terms "nouthetic counseling" (see chapter 8).

Adams is clearly familiar with the contemporary psychological literature. Many of his criticisms of the mainstream are well-founded, and more than anyone else he has attempted to develop an approach to counseling which is consistent with the truths of Scripture. In the opinion of many, however, Adams' lack of formal training in psychology has led him to oversimplify and thus to reject too quickly the arguments of his opposition. His confrontational approach to counseling is clearly based on Scripture, but he appears to overlook other Bible passages which show the equal importance of supportive, referral, and insight counseling. Adams also has had a tendency to attack psychological writers, Christian and non-Christian alike, in a combative, name-calling manner. This has undermined some of his arguments and detracted from what might be taken as a more serious approach if it were presented in a more gracious manner.

Less influential than Adams are several other evangelical pastors-turned-counselor. Bob Smith, William E. Crane, Maurice Wagner, and Paul D. Morris[14] (see chapter 12), for example, have each written books on pastoral counseling from an evangelical perspective. In addition to pastoral training, some of these men have had formal training in psychology. They lack the abrasive character of Adams' writing, but as yet none has published an approach which is as well-developed as Adams' "nouthetic counseling."

THE CHRISTIAN PROFESSIONALS

As might be expected, much of the biblically oriented writing in the field of Christian counseling has been done by people with formal training in psychology, psychiatry, and related disciplines. Professionals, such as Paul Tournier (see chapter 3), Donald Tweedie, James Dobson, Bruce Narramore, Millard Sall, Quentin Hyder, Frank Minirth, and James Mallory[15] have directed their writings primarily to lay readers. Others, such as Clyde Narramore, Charles Solomon, Lawrence Crabb (see chapter 9), and Gary Collins[16] have also written books and papers that deal with counseling from both a pastoral and professional perspective. In addition, there are several religiously oriented writers (such as Gerard Egan and Eugene Kennedy)[17] who are trained professionals but whose writings make no attempt to combine theology with counseling principles.

The quality and theological sophistication of these works varies, of course, and most of the writers who do take a theological stand risk ostracism from their professional colleagues for even daring to take religion seriously. It is not surprising, therefore, that these authors proceed cautiously in their criticisms of psychology or in their attempts to combine psychology and theology. More than any others, however, these people understand the professional literature and intricacies of the counseling process. It is from them, and others like them, that the most creative work in this field must come.

Based on casual observations at professional meetings and at conventions of groups such as the Christian Association for Psychological Studies, one gets the impression that many unknown evangelicals are in the field of counseling. Most of these unsung heroes do not write (and hence are not widely known), but in their day-to-day work they are individually attempting to integrate biblical teachings with counseling techniques and concepts. The Evangelical *Journal of*

Psychology and Theology has given many of these counselors a forum for expressing their ideas and conclusions about pastoral psychology and counseling.

THE THEORETICIAN-RESEARCHERS

For one involved in Christian counseling it might be easy to conclude that research and theory are of minor importance. On the contrary, these areas are of crucial significance: first, in that they add professional and intellectual support to the conclusions of Christian counselors, and second, in that they provide an apologetic for facing the anti-Christian challenges that are constantly being raised in university psychology classes.

Many years ago, Freud dismissed religion as an illusion, a "universal obsessional neurosis" which serves as a narcotic to help potentially troubled people maintain their personal stability. B.F. Skinner's behaviorism, Ellis's rational-emotive therapy, Rogers' humanistic approach to counseling, Maslow's third-force psychology—all attack the very basis of Christianity and present the church with what may be one of its greatest current intellectual challenges.

Regretfully, Christians for the most part have avoided this battleground and allowed psychology to cut the theological moorings of numerous students and psychologists-in-training. Several years ago Vernon Grounds wrote a series of articles in this area, and in 1973 Bruce Narramore outlined some of the problems that must be tackled in this work.[18] In addition, several books have attempted to discuss psychology and religion from a biblical perspective.[19] Among the most influential volumes are *What, Then, Is Man?* by a group of Lutheran writers; books on the psychology of religion by Wayne Oates, Mansell Pattison, and Newton Malony (see chapter 5); and two recent books by Malcolm Jeeves and Gary Collins.[20]

THE EVANGELICAL POPULARIZERS

Any survey of the current status of pastoral psychology and counseling would be incomplete without some reference to the popular speakers who currently crisscross the country dispensing practical advice on daily living. The best-known of these is Bill Gothard, with his "Institute of Basic Youth Conflicts" seminars, but there are others: Keith Miller, Bruce Larson, Tim LaHaye, Ruth Carter Stapleton, Howard Hendricks, J. Allan Petersen, and Norman Wright. Some, like Bill Gothard, are best-known as speakers; others, like Paul Tournier, Keith Miller, Charlie Shedd, and Marabel Morgan, are best-known through their books; still others, (like LaHaye and Petersen) are primarily trained in theology, with little or no formal background in psychology.

Professional psychologists and social observers view these people with amazement. They often come on the scene suddenly, attract large followings, and have a significant impact on their followers. The reasons for the popularity of these people have been summarized elsewhere,[21] but the popularizers appear to have several characteristics in common. All deal with practical, down-to-earth subjects, give simple explanations for problems, provide viable formulas for success and problem-solving, communicate effectively without psychological jargon, are attractive personalities, are at least somewhat biblically oriented, and say something that is in some way unique. In an age of economic and political instability, declining morals, and increasing crime, these popularizers proclaim a message of hope, stability, and the promise of success. People follow these leaders like sheep looking for a shepherd, much to the amazement and probable distress of many of the leaders themselves.

Professional counselors complain that the popularizers are overly simplistic and in danger of doing harm by their "self-help" formulas for psychological stability and principles for spiritual growth. It cannot be denied, however, that many people are helped by these popular Christian psychologies. Professionals who are disturbed by the simplicity of some of the popular approaches surely have an obligation to follow up their criticisms with the development of approaches which are more balanced, less grandiose in their claims of success, and more valid biblically and psychologically.

THE FUTURE

Compared with the less conservative segments of the church, evangelicals have been slow to enter the fields of pastoral psychology and Christian counseling. Pockets of skepticism, mistrust of psychology, and acceptance of the naive view that commitment to Christ will automatically eliminate all problems still exist throughout the Christian world.

Now, however, this is changing. The development of Christian graduate schools of psychology, seminary degree programs in pastoral psychology and counseling, commendable undergraduate psychology programs at Christian colleges; the emergence of new Christian counseling centers; the appearance of the *Journal of Psychology and Theology;* the influence of popularizers; the willingness of mission boards to have psychologists assist in the selection and counseling of missionaries; and the psychological research on religious experience — developments like these all point to an explosion of interest in this area. There is no one geographical or academic center for all of this activity, and as yet there are few established leaders, although several are emerging.

To predict where this whole field will go in the next few years is probably impossible, but it would seem that our efforts should be focused on five major areas.

1. *Christian counseling.* What, if anything, is unique about counseling from a biblical perspective? Is Christian counseling simply a Rogerian, Freudian, or behavioristic ap-

proach with occasional prayer and reading of Bible verses tacked on, or it counseling based on biblical assumptions that are in some way unique?

It is unrealistic to expect that we will ever arrive at a single biblical approach to counseling, any more than we have discovered a single biblical approach to missions, evangelism, or preaching. To a large extent, counseling techniques depend on the personality of the counselor and the nature of the counselee's problems, but we should seek to uncover the various techniques and several counseling approaches which arise out of or are clearly consistent with the teachings of Scripture. Then we should try out these techniques and test their effectiveness, not using subjective feeling as proof that we are "really helping people," but employing carefully controlled evaluation and assessment techniques.

2. *Training and education.* How do we train people to be effective counselors? This is a problem which has concerned secular psychologists and mainstream pastoral counselors for several years. Only now are researchers learning how to select sensitive people and mold them into perceptive counselors. Much of this work can be applied to training Christian counselors, but in addition we must be alert to the spiritual qualifications for counselors that are mentioned in Galatians 6:1 and elsewhere.

The training of Christian counselors must take place on three fronts. First, there must be concern about training the professionals. This training most often occurs in graduate schools of psychology and in counseling centers where students get practical experience to prepare for professional counseling careers. Second, Christians (especially evangelicals) must give special attention to the training of pastors and other church leaders. This is the major responsibility of the seminaries, whose task is not only to train students but to give continuing education to missionaries, ministers, and other Christian workers.

A third area of training is much newer but sure to be of increasing significance in the coming decade. This is the training of laymen for what has come to be termed "peer counseling." Nobody knows how many people turn to relatives, neighbors, friends, or fellow church members in times of psychological and spiritual need, but it may be that this is where most counseling takes place. Training programs must be developed to consider such questions as how we select and train lay counselors, how they should be supervised, what kinds of problems they can handle best, how they can be trained to make referrals, and even whether such people should be doing counseling at all. It is possible that a little counseling knowledge can be a dangerous thing, but no knowledge might be worse.

3. *Preventive psychology.* According to the well-known proverb, an ounce of prevention is worth a pound of cure, but this has not been applied to the field of counseling until recently. In the secular world, Caplan's *Principles of Preventive Psychiatry,*[22] published in 1964, did much to alert counselors to the importance of helping people to avoid problems or to stop existing difficulties form getting worse. Two books by Clinebell and one by a writer named Gl..n Whitlock[23] have pointed to the need for preventive pastoral psychology, but these books take no real biblical stance. In a sense, premarital counseling[24] is a form of prevention that has been widely used by Christians and non-Christians alike, and the books and speeches by the popularizers help many people to avoid problems. Apart from this, however, very little has been done in the area of preventive psychology. It is a wide-open and vitally important field, especially for people who believe that a commitment to Christ can have a practical influence on how one prepares for and copes with the problems of life.

4. *Theory and psychological apologetics.* There appear to be two overlapping concerns for Christians in this area. First

we must help Christian students and psychologists to see that in spite of the analyses of Freud, Skinner, and others, Christianity and psychology need not be antithetical. The Christian in the field of psychology is in a unique position to study such issues as the meaning of life, the effect of belief on psychological functioning, and the ways in which psychological science and Christian faith can be integrated to bring a fuller understanding of human behavior. Christians in psychology must not abandon the field of personality theory, philosophy of science, or psychology of religion. In these fields evangelicals can make a special contribution, and young Christians in psychology must be helped to see this. They must also be helped to see that psychological analyses of faith healing and conversion, as well as of Christian behavior, persuasion techniques, beliefs, attitudes, and religious experience, need not undercut the Christian's belief system. There are good answers and counterarguments to the challenges that come to Christianity from psychology. The Christian must be helped to understand these counterarguments and learn how to present them.

Closely related to this should be a clear and concise outreach to nonbelievers who are in the psychological disciplines and to laymen who are sophisticated psychologically. The non-Christian, while criticizing and rejecting religious presuppositions, may uncritically and religiously accept a whole group of philosophical assumptions as a basis for his or her own psychological conclusions. This inconsistency should be pointed out. In addition, the relevance and intellectual bases of Christianity need to be presented to people who are discovering that psychology, while powerful, does not have all the answers to human problems. Like the young student, the professional who offers anti-Christian psychological analyses should be shown his or her errors and faulty conclusions.

This theoretical and apologetical emphasis in the field of

pastoral psychology is one of the most difficult tasks. Psychologists are remarkably resistant to anything philosophical or theological, and their students are easily swayed by psychological analyses. To perform useful work in this area, one must be thoroughly familiar with both theology and psychology, must be a skilled communicator, and must be astute in observing the changing psychological scene.

5. *Research.* Good research is difficult, time-consuming, frustrating, and expensive. Christian professors are often too busy with course work to engage in extensive research, the universities do not encourage research in the area of religious experience, and money for such projects is difficult to raise. Furthermore, such variables as Christian maturity, faith in God, and counseling effectiveness are very hard to investigate empirically. Perhaps these obstacles have dissuaded many from entering the field of psychological research, but this work must be done if the counseling, training, preventing, and theorizing that we have described above is to be done with maximum efficiency.

IS THEORY IMPORTANT?

The following pages present a variety of theoretical approaches to Christian counseling. Paul Tournier, Jay Adams, Lawrence Crabb, and others who are presented in this book may not be thought of as counseling theorists, but theirs are as much theoretical positions as are the theories of Freud, Rogers, Glasser, or Ellis. The latter are counseling theories based on humanistic presuppositions; the former base their approaches on the foundational tenets of Christianity. At present, Christian theories are neither as well-developed nor as sophisticated as the secular theories, but Christian approaches are developing in complexity, and this book attempts to summarize the approaches of those Christians who are doing the most significant writing in this field.

Defined somewhat formally, a theory is a logically and systematically organized set of definitions, assumptions, hypotheses, facts, and empirically demonstrated laws, all of which are put forth for the purpose of explaining behavior, making predictions, and guiding both research and counseling activities. A theory ties known facts together in a meaningful way. In the field of counseling the theory summarizes what we know about the way people act and the way problems develop. The theory describes how people change and grow. It includes an elaboration of the assumptions on which the theorist works—assumptions which in the case of a Christian counselor must be built on biblical revelation and (in some cases) religious tradition.

A good theory is clear, comprehensive, explicit, simple, and useful in enabling us to discover truth and help people grow. Good counseling theories include statements about the goal of counseling as well as descriptions of the techniques by which effective counseling is accomplished. Such theories influence our work at four different levels.

First, *the counselee*—the person who comes for counseling —is influenced by his or her own theories.[25] The counselee has some ideas about how the counselor will proceed, what will happen within the counseling relationship, and whether counseling is likely to be effective. If the counselee's expectations differ from what the counselor does, there is a conflict which must be resolved before counseling can be successful. Consider what might happen, for example, if a non-Christian counselee comes to a Christian counselor, expecting that the counseling will be Freudian and that the counselee will be required to lie down on a couch. If there is no couch in the office, and if the counselor quotes from the Scriptures, and if there is no reference to Freud, the counselee might at first be confused because his or her theory differs from that of the counselor.

By now it should be clear that *the counselor's* theory is also important in the counseling relationship. Some counselors work primarily to give insight to their counselees. Others have a theoretical approach which encourages people to change their behavior. Still others are concerned about bringing people into a growing relationship with Jesus Christ, on the assumption that this in itself will bring an automatic solution to problems. Christian counselors who may agree on the biblical and theological truths may nevertheless approach counseling in different ways, each of which is presented as a biblically based theory of counseling.

As we grow up, each of us develops a number of assumptions which guide our thinking and largely determine how we behave. Our assumptions about the universe, human nature, right and wrong, and what will and will not work all determine how we think or act. This is certainly true in the area of counseling. For example, the counselor who does not believe in the existence of God is certain to approach his or her counselees differently from the person who believes that God created the universe, currently holds it all together, and is vitally interested in even the minor problems of the people who inhabit the earth. The counselor who assumes that our main purpose in life is to satisfy and enjoy ourselves will think and counsel differently from the counselor who agrees with the Apostle Paul that our task in life is ultimately to "proclaim him [Christ], counseling and teaching everyone with all wisdom, so that we may present everyone perfect in Christ" (Colossians 1:28 NIV).

Counselor education is also influenced by theory. Tournier's approach differs from that of Jay Adams, whose approach in turn differs from that of Charles Solomon. Each of these people, therefore, would train others to move toward different goals and to use different techniques, and the training itself would differ according to the trainer's theory of teaching.

Finally, *research* in Christian counseling is affected by theory. This has been seen very clearly in the secular world, where client-centered theorists, psychoanalyists, and behavioral counselors each approach research in a unique way, with different methods for measuring outcomes or defining success.

Counseling theory, therefore, influences the counselee, the counselor, the counselor-educator, and the researcher. For the reader who is trying to become more proficient in "helping people grow," it is important to realize that there is considerable overlap between the Christian theorists' assumptions, goals, and techniques. But there are also differences, and in the following chapters these will be summarized. The concluding two chapters summarize the similarities between theories, present guidelines for evaluating theories, and make some suggestions for the future. Hopefully, all of this will be of personal interest and practical value to the Christian counselor.

CONCLUSION

Psychology and counseling present the Christian with an exciting and potentially rewarding challenge. In many respects this is still a new field within the world of Christian scholarship (as opposed, for example, to more established areas of study, such as systematic theology, biblical studies, or homiletics). It is a field which needs creative thinkers who are willing to become pioneers. If they are to make a significant contribution, however, these pioneers must be products of solid psychological and theological training, and they must be deeply committed to the authority of Scripture and to the Lordship of Jesus Christ. Like all pioneers, people in this expanding field will find the way rough and uncharted at times, but the rewards are deeply satisfying, for they count not only toward helping people in the present, but also for preparing people for eternity.

FOOTNOTES

1. Public Law 182, 84th Congress, Chapter 417, 1st Session, H.J. Res. 256.
2. For a summary of the Joint Commission report, including a listing of the ten book-length monographs, see Joint Commission on Mental Illness and Health, *Action for Mental Health* (New York: Science Editions, 1961).
3. Ibid., p. 103.
4. Excerpted from *Action for Mental Health,* by the Joint Commission on Mental Illness and Health, © 1961 by Basic Books, Inc., Publishers, New York.
5. For a discussion of these four functions see W.A. Clebsch and C.R. Jackle, *Pastoral Care in Historical Perspective* (Englewood Cliffs, NJ: Prentice-Hall, 1964).
6. For an excellent overview of the CPE movement see E.E. Thornton, *Professional Education for Ministry: A History of Clinical Pastoral Education* (Nashville: Abingdon, 1970).
7. T.C. Oden, *Contemporary Theology and Psychotherapy* (Philadelphia: Westminster, 1967), p. 89.
8. Ibid., p. 90.
9. S. Hiltner, *The Counselor in Counseling* (New York: Abingdon, 1950), p. 11.
10. S. Hiltner, *Pastoral Counseling* (New York: Abingdon, 1949), pp. 137-226. For a brief critique of Hiltner's use of religious resources see Oden, op. cit., p. 87.
11. For a consideration of the works of these men, one might see the following sample writings: W.E. Hulme, *How to Start Counseling* (Nashville: Abingdon, 1955); W.E. Oates, *Protestant Pastoral Counseling* (Philadelphia: Westminster, 1962); C. Wise, *Pastoral Counseling, Its Theory and Practice* (New York: Harper, 1951); and J.S. Bonnell, *Psychology for Pastor and People* (New York: Harper, 1948).
12. Representative works include Hiltner, op. cit.; E.E. Bruder, *Ministering to Deeply Troubled People* (Englewood Cliffs, NJ: Prentice-Hall, 1963); E.E. Thornton, *Theology and Pastoral Counseling* (Englewood Cliffs, NJ: Prentice-Hall, 1964); R.L. Dicks, *Pastoral Work and Pastoral Counseling* (New York: Macmillan, 1949).
13. The best-known of these books are *Competent to Counsel* (Grand Rapids: Baker, 1970) and its "sequel and companion volume," *The Christian Counselor's Manual* (Nutley, NJ: Presbyterian and Reformed, 1973).

14. B. Smith, *Dying to Live: An Introduction to Counseling That Counts* (Waco, TX: Word, 1976); W.E. Crane, *Where God Comes In: The Divine "Plus" in Counseling* (Waco: Word, 1970); M.E. Wagner, *Putting It All Together* (Grand Rapids: Zondervan, 1974); and P.D. Morris, *Love Therapy* (Wheaton: Tyndale, 1974).

15. Sample writings include Tournier, *A Place for You* (New York: Harper and Row, 1968); D.F. Tweedie Jr., *The Christian and the Couch* (Grand Rapids: Baker, 1963); J.C. Dobson, *Dare to Discipline* (Wheaton: Tyndale, 1970); B. Narramore, *Help! I'm a Parent* (Grand Rapids: Zondervan, 1972); O.Q. Hyder, *The Christian's Handbook of Psychiatry* (Old Tappan, NJ: Revell, 1971); J. Mallory, *The Kink and I* (Wheaton: Victor Books, 1973); M.J. Sall, *Faith, Psychology and Christian Maturity* (Grand Rapids: Zondervan, 1975); and F.B. Minirth, *Christian Psychiatry* (Old Tappan, NJ: Revell, 1977).

16. C.M. Narramore, *The Psychology of Counseling* (Grand Rapids: Zondervan, 1960); C.R. Solomon, *Counseling with the Mind of Christ* (Old Tappan, NJ: Revell, 1977); L.J. Crabb, *Effective Biblical Counseling* (Grand Rapids: Zondervan, 1977); and G.R. Collins, *Effective Counseling* (Creation House, 1972) and *How to Be a People Helper* (Santa Ana: Vision House, 1976).

17. G. Egan, *The Skilled Helper* (Monterey: Brooks/Cole, 1975); and E. Kennedy, *On Becoming a Counselor* (New York: Seabury, 1977).

18. The Grounds articles appeared in *His* Magazine in 1963. See also B. Narramore, "Perspectives on the Integration of Psychology and Theology" in *Journal of Psychology and Theology*, Vol. 1, January 1973, pp. 3-18.

19. See, for example, P. Tournier, *The Person Reborn* (New York: Harper and Row, 1966); R.O. Ferm, *The Psychology of Christian Conversion* (Westwood, NJ: Revell, 1959); P.F. Barkman, *Man in Conflict* (Grand Rapids: Zondervan, 1965); H.W. Darling, *Man in Triumph: An Integration of Psychology and Biblical Faith* (Grand Rapids: Zondervan, 1969); and B. Narramore and B. Counts, *Guilt and Freedom* (Santa Ana: Vision House, 1974).

20. P. Meehl, et. al., *What, Then, Is Man?* (St. Louis: Concordia, 1958); W.E. Oates, *Psychology of Religion* (Waco: Word, 1973); E.M. Pattison, ed., *Clinical Psychology and Religion* (Boston: Little, Brown, 1969); H.N. Malony, ed., *Current Perspectives in the Psychology of Religion* (1977); M. Jeeves, *Psychology and Religion: The View Both Ways* (Downers Grove: InterVarsity, 1976); and G.R. Collins, *The Rebuilding of Psychology: An Integration of*

Psychology and Christianity (Wheaton: Tyndale, 1977). See also G.R. Collins, *Search for Reality: Psychology and the Christian* (Santa Ana: Vision House, 1969).

21. G.R. Collins, "Popular Christian Psychologies: Some Reflections" in *Journal of Psychology and Theology,* Vol. 3, Spring 1975, pp. 127-32.

22. Published in New York by Basic Books.

23. H.J. Clinebell, Jr., *Mental Health Through Christian Community* (New York: Abingdon, 1965); H.J. Clinebell, Jr., ed., *Community Mental Health: The Role of Church and Temple* (New York: Abingdon, 1970); and G.E. Whitlock, *Preventive Psychology and the Church* (Philadelphia: Westminster, 1973).

24. An excellent recent volume in this area is by H.N. Wright, *Premarital Counseling* (Chicago: Moody, 1977).

25. The ideas in this section are adapted from B. Stefflre and K. Matheny, *The Function of Counseling Theory* (New York: Tym Shore Corp., 1968).

2

RELATIONSHIP COUNSELING

David Carlson

Recent writers in the field of counseling have emphasized that people helping involves a meaningful relationship between the counselor and counselee. Without this relationship, counseling is rarely effective.

David Carlson carries this theme into the current chapter, but he goes much farther. He begins with a discussion of the relationship between psychology and theology. He considers the counseling relationships described in the Bible and proposes an "integrated biblical model of counseling" based on Jesus' style of relating to others. At times He was prophetic and confrontational, but at other times He was more priestly, encouraging confession while the helper listened. The result is a realistic, practical, biblically oriented approach to the helping relationship.

David Carlson is a clinical social worker with graduate degrees in social work, sociology, and theology from University of Chicago, Northern Illinois University, and Trinity Evangelical Divinity School. He is codirector of Barrington Counseling Associates, a group practice of Christian psychotherapists in Lake Zurich, Illinois, and he is associate professor and Chairman of the Department of Sociology, Trinity College, Deerfield, Illinois.

This chapter is a revision of a paper entitled "Jesus' Style of Relating: The Search for a Biblical View of Counseling," which appeared in the Summer 1976 issue of the *Journal of*

Psychology and Theology. Copyright 1976 by the Rosemead Graduate School of Psychology. Used by permission.

From a poverty of positive Christian writing on counseling twenty years ago, the layman and professional is bombarded with a current plethora of material. While the availability of material and perspectives is desirable, they pose a formidable set of claims with which to deal. In many ways, the reader is often overwhelmed when confronted with the various Christian approaches to counseling. This chapter will provide some guidelines for choosing a Christian style of counseling, and will then suggest a model which integrates the Christian counseling maze.

STEPS TO CHOOSING A STYLE OF COUNSELING

Choosing a style of Christian counseling is accomplished and aided when one understands what the issues are. A first step to choosing a style of counseling is to recognize that currently there is *no one school of thought* that can claim exclusive rights to the label "Christian" or "biblical." This declaration will come as a surprise to many, who assume that Christians have reached a consensus on counseling. By the time you have reached this chapter, you should be convinced that there are many claims to the title "Christian" or "biblical" counseling. Later in this discussion I will give you a sampler of their approaches and try to organize them into an understandable framework.

A second step to choosing a style of Christian counseling is to understand that there is *no recognized set of techniques* that are exclusively Christian or biblical. It is true that several writers have claimed their selected list of techniques to be biblical, yet we do not have a consensus on this issue either. Christian counseling principles are still being researched. A third step to choosing a style of Christian counseling is to understand that there is currently *no list of principles* upon which all Christian counselors agree. Yet there are several similarities and overlapping ideas which will be identified in the last half of this chapter.

Since there is *no agreed-upon focus of change,* choosing a Christian style of counseling presents at least three alternatives. Does the counselor attempt to help people change their behavior, feelings, or thoughts? You may ask, why not try to change all three? This is a good question, well worth exploring, but don't expect much help from the current literature. A word of encouragement is probably needed by now. Don't fret about these issues to the point of giving up the search for a biblical view of counseling. My point in raising these issues is merely to indicate the need for development in a very young field—Christian counseling. I encourage you to keep your mind open to the options, avoiding premature closure and conclusions.

A fifth step to choosing a style of counseling is to understand the discussion on the *integration of spiritual and secular perspectives* on counseling. There are basically three positions you should be aware of as you read various Christian authors. Position ''A'' is represented by those Christians who believe there is no such thing as a unique Christian counseling style. Position ''B'' is represented by those who believe that a biblical approach to counseling is the only legitimate Christian approach. And position ''C'' is represented by those who believe that an integration between secular and Christian approaches is necessary and desirable and possible.

Your choice of a style of Christian counseling will largely reflect which of the three positions makes the most sense. You can't afford to ignore the issue of the relationship of the secular to the sacred. It is the classic Christian struggle of learning how to live *in* the world without being *of* the world. Position A basically *ignores* the relationship of Christ to culture. Position B *segregates* Christ from culture. And position C *integrates* Christ with culture when it is biblically indicated and acceptable. This third position is the most demanding spiritually and intellectually. It requires the greatest amount of thoughtful consideration.

A sixth step to choosing a Christian style of counseling is essential to the issue of the sacred-secular relationship. It is the question of *biblical authority*. Does the Bible provide us with all we need to know about counseling? Is the Bible the *only* source of knowledge which Christians can rely on in developing a style, technique, or focus of counseling? Position A argues that the Bible is of little or no help to us on the issue of counseling. Position B argues that Bible is the *only* source of information we should draw from. Position C argues that one's style of counseling can be constructively informed from both biblical and nonbiblical sources.

When choosing a style of counseling, one needs to involve oneself in the process of *thinking beyond theology and psychology*. To take this seventh step, one must be open to learning from secular sources and unashamedly reexamining and testing human knowledge for its truthfulness. On the other side, there is the danger that we may uncritically accept an approach to counseling largely because it sounds theologically and biblically correct. We must remember that no one has a corner on Christian counseling theory and practice.

At face value, these issues may leave the reader overwhelmed. While the issues present a challenge, they are resolvable. One way to resolve these issues is to begin by having a clear understanding of

1) the integration process
2) the biblical usage and meaning of counseling

3) common denominators in counseling theory and practice.

THE INTEGRATION PROCESS

At the heart of the question "How does one choose a Christian style of counseling" is the issue of Christ's relationship to culture. I have suggested three basic positions one may take. Position A *ignores* the distinction between Christ and culture. Position B *rejects* culture as having anything to teach us. And Positon C *integrates* Christ and culture. (See Niebuhr, 1951), for a general discussion of the Christ-and-culture issue.)[1]

Position C seems to hold the most promise for developing a credible Christian counseling style. It is open to learning from both theology and psychology. It is receptive to the dynamic interplay of the theological and psychological perspectives, which sharpen each other and contribute to the development of Christian counseling theory and practice.

When one chooses the integration position, Scripture is valued as the *ultimate* source of truth about man and about the basis of development of Christian faith and practice. The Bible is believed to be wholly true. Scripture is recognized for being *absolutely* true but not *exhaustively* true. That is, the integrationist does not believe or expect that Scripture is the only source of information on counseling. He does believe that Scripture is the most accurate and reliable truth about God and salvation. But he does not look to Scripture to teach him all there is to know about those subjects that the Bible was not intended to instruct.

A basic assumption of the integrationist position is, "Everything in Scripture is true, but not everything true is in Scripture." If you believe this, then position A (ignore Christ) and position B (ignore culture) are not possible for you to accept.

What then is integration? It is a *position* which begins with the acceptance of both biblical and extrabiblical sources of knowledge about counseling. It accepts a relationship between God's special revelation (Christ and Scripture) and God's natural revelation (culture and nature). Revelation and research are valued as being capable of informing and enriching man's knowledge of himself and the helping process.

But more than a position, integration is a *process* of discovering God's truth beyond the scriptural and scientific data. I conceive of integration as the conscious bringing together of the component aspects of psychology and theology without violating their individual autonomy or identity and without ignoring conflict, paradox, and mystery. Integration recognizes a reality larger than either theology alone or psychology alone. Therefore, it is not baptizing psychology with scriptural texts, yet it is more than merely lining up psychology and theology to see their points of correlation and convergence. This integration process will be demonstrated after a discussion of the biblical usage and meaning of counseling.

THE BIBLICAL USAGE AND
MEANING OF COUNSELING

The idea of counseling—listening and responding in such a way as to bring about change in another person—is a relatively modern procedure and process. Strictly speaking, the twentieth-century concept of counseling does not seem to have a biblical parallel. Biblically, the word "counseling" is never used. When the word "counsel" is used, it is limited to giving or taking advice. In the Old Testament, the words commonly translated "counsel" mean to deliberate, resolve, advise, guide, plan, consult. (See Proverbs 11:14; 15:22; 2

Chronicles 25:16; Isaiah 1:26; Exodus 18:19.) In the New Testament, the word "counselor" is used three times (*boulutees*—Mark 15:43; Luke 23:50; *sumboulos*—Romans 11:34) and is descriptive of a person's employment as an advisor.

Since a word study of both Old and New testaments indicates that present-day counseling is more a contemporary process than a historical biblical method, we need to be careful in labeling any counseling method as biblical. To describe a counseling approach as biblical, we need to go beyond the biblical usage and meaning of the words translated "counsel" and to utilize the whole counsel of God.

There are those Christians who do limit "biblical" counseling to a directive, confrontive approach.[2] Another author claims, "I simply attempt to speak the truth and face the facts."[3] These authors basically believe the Christ-and-culture positon B described above.

Included in this group, but more on the fringe of the Christ-and-culture position B, is Crabb, who describes his "biblical" counseling as evangelism, encouragement, exhortation, and enlightenment.[4] As an aid to choosing a Christian style of counseling I have described this posture as "prophetic" counseling.

On the other side of the coin is another school of Christian thought regarding counseling that I describe as "priestly" counseling. Representative of this group are Hulme, May, Lake, Clinebell, Hiltner, Tournier, Narramore, and Collins.[5] These authors are more or less in the Christ-and-culture position C.

The similarities of these two approaches include the claim to be inherently Christian and biblical. However, the claim to be biblical is their major difference also. "Biblical" counseling can be used in two distinct ways. In the prophetic sense, biblical counseling is a very narrow range of counselor behaviors (advice-giving, exhorting) limited by the usage and meaning of "counsel" and "counselor" in Scripture. In the priestly sense, biblical counseling is a broad range of counselor behaviors (listening, supporting, insight-producing, processing) informed by the whole of Scripture.

These two Christian approaches to counseling come to Scripture expecting distinctive information. Prophetic counseling comes to the Bible looking for methodology and illustration that provide a norm—rules, regulations, and techniques that are divinely inspired. To these Christians, the Bible is the *only* or *primary* source of information and instruction on counseling.

Priestly counseling comes to Scripture examining the relationship between a style of counseling and biblical teaching. Priestly counseling does not expect Scripture to teach all there is to know about counseling. Yet this Christian approach to counseling is committed to biblical instruction and the Lordship of Christ in all areas of one's life and practice. The Bible is accepted as the *ultimate* rule for faith and practice that also allows for humanly discovered and constructed ideas about counseling. Other sources of information are seen to be necessary and legitimate for the development of a Christian counseling approach.

CHRISTIAN COUNSELING APPROACHES

Prophetic	Priestly
convicting	comforting
confronting	confessional
preaching	interviewing
lecturing	listening
thinking for	thinking with
talking to	talking with
proclaiming truth	comforting the
disturbing the	disturbed
comfortable	

Therefore, the Christian counselor has two basic styles of counseling from which to choose. In addition to being identified with Christ-and-culture positions B or C, they can be characterized by these methods.

As one chooses a Christian style of counseling, he or she learns that the Bible plays a crucial role but is probably not the *only* source to be considered. The truth of the matter is this: anyone writing about counseling from a Christian viewpoint since the turn of the century is doing so as a result of counseling becoming increasingly popular and acceptable, and not because the Bible clearly teaches counseling. That is, Christians are reactive and responsive to the mass appeal to counseling and have been driven back to their Bibles and theology to cope with this new phenomenon. This is of course a desirable response, but it should be recognized that the impetus for present-day counseling comes more from the modern cultural invention of counseling philosophy and practice than from Scripture.

AN INTEGRATED BIBLICAL MODEL OF COUNSELING

The following model attempts to integrate the whole counsel of God in its development of a Christian style of counseling. That is, it is a conceptual framework which utilizes the whole of Scripture rather than relying on a single passage or a single biblical word. It is a model which recognizes that Christian counseling can be biblical in both a prophetic and a priestly sense.

Any Christian approach to counseling must begin with Christ, because it is Christ who is central in anything described as Christian (Colossians 2:4). Christian counseling begins with Christ because He is the integrating and sustaining dimension. Therefore, I describe this model as Jesus' style of counseling. When one considers the biblical and secular use of the word "counseling," it is more accurate to label this paradigm as Jesus' style of relating.

We can imitate Jesus' approach to people, but there are some limitations. We need to remember that Jesus was more than a man. As we imitate Christ we do so with the limitations of being only human beings. While we have God's Spirit living in us we do not have the depth of perception, height of power, breadth of understanding, or length of patience. We are not God, and therefore we should not expect to relate as well as Jesus related. Whatever His techniques of counseling, He possessed something quite unique—God-power, God-perspective, God-understanding, and God-patience.

Another limitation in our attempts to imitate Jesus' style of relating is to define Jesus' style rigidly and dogmatically. The danger here is one of making Scripture teach an exclusive counseling approach. That is, if we interpret Scripture as teaching a single normative view of counseling, we make the Bible say more than it was intended to teach. This violates a basic rule of biblical interpretation—look for biblical principles and guidelines, then apply these principles in our relationships to people. Scripture teaches more "what's" than "how to's"! For example, Scripture says "love your neighbor" and "honor your parents," but it gives few explicit instructions in how to implement these principles. God often leaves application to the Christian and his or her community.

My argument is underscored well by Waylon Ward: "The principles, or absolutes, are given in Scripture, but the process of applying these absolutes is not detailed. There is no one scriptural method of counseling; there are only scriptural absolutes that must be recognized and honored whatever method is used . . . [with] certain freedoms in application and methods. . . ."[6]

JESUS' STYLE OF RELATING

The prophetic and priestly counseling approaches in Christian thought are largely at polar extremes. After studying Jesus' style of relating, I do not see these dichotomous and exclusive positions to be biblical, necessary, or desirable. My argument is that Jesus incorporated both of these divergent approaches creatively and sensitively, adapting His style to the needs of the person He was encountering.

As a way of describing Jesus' style of relating, I have utilized the sociological concept of "role"—the expected behavior of a person holding a specific social status (position). I began my exploration of the question "What is Jesus' style of relating?" by searching the Gospels to observe what approaches Jesus made to people. What I found is this: Jesus' style of relating to people was varied. He did not use one role exclusively. He was selectively a Prophet and a Priest. At times Jesus was confronting, as in His treatment of the scribes and pharisees, while at other times He was comforting, as in His response to the woman taken in adultery.[7]

Reviewing Jesus' dealings with people, I found an interesting relationship between the role Jesus chose to play and His style of relating. For example, when Jesus took the role of prophet, He preached, taught, confronted, and called for repentance. When He took the role of priest, He listened, forgave, mediated, and called for confession. When He assumed the role of king, He paraded, ruled, and called for the establishment of the kingdom. When He chose the role of lamb, He sacrificed, accepted ridicule and rejection, and called sinners to be healed by His stripes and bruises. When He submitted to the role of servant, He washed feet, served food, gave of Himself, and called for humility. When He assumed the role of shepherd, He fed his flock, nurtured, protected, and called the lost to be found.

TABLE 1
Jesus' Role Repertoire

Status	Role
Prophet	Preaches, teaches, confronts, calls for repentance.
Priest	Listens, forgives, mediates, calls for confession.
King	Parades, rules, calls for establishment of kingdom.
Lamb	Sacrifices, accepts ridicule and rejection, calls sinners to be healed.
Servant	Serves food, nurtures, washes feet, cares for, gives self, calls for humility.
Shepherd	Nurtures, protects, calls lost to be found.

Jesus' techniques of relating to people were as varied as His status. He taught from Scripture, listened, drew pictures, asked questions, and told stories from which He asked His listeners to draw their own conclusions. As we take the whole counsel of God into consideration, we begin to see that Jesus was not limited to one style of relating.

Therefore, Jesus' style of relating suggests that a dichotomous view of Christian counseling is unacceptable. I am suggesting that a biblical view of counseling is continuous —that is, integrative. Instead of prophet and priest being separate and opposite positions, they are related and connected. Table 1 is a chart which attempts to visualize the relationship between Jesus' statuses and roles. While some of the roles are more characteristic of one status than another, it was the same Person who was playing different roles and statuses.

As one reviews Jesus' use of roles, it becomes obvious that role and technique are intimately related to status, but that role and technique are not exclusively limited to one status. My original formulation described only two statuses with their corresponding roles. In Table 2, building on Jesus' role repertoire pictured in Table 1, I have added a third descriptive status—pastoral. It was necessary to add the pastoral status to more accurately reflect Jesus' style of relating. In many ways the pastoral status and role incorporates the servant role.

TABLE 2
Jesus' Style of Relating

Counseling: A Continuous View*
Statuses: Prophetic, Pastoral, Priestly
R O L E S   Critic, preacher, teacher, interpreter, mediator, confronter, convictor, corrector, confessor, admonisher, advocate, sustainer, supporter, lecturer, advisor, burden-bearer, listener, reprover, warner, helper, consoler, pardoner.

*Illustrative but not exhaustive

As we learn to imitate Jesus' style of relating, it is crucial that we remember that His techniques flowed from who He was. He was not merely playing a role, but was really who He acted to be. His roles were an authentic expression of who Jesus was personally and spiritually. Thus, the distinction between technique and style of relating is unimportant when one acts who he or she is in a genuine, congruent expression of oneself.

"As we look at the technique of Jesus we find that it is a model for all of us. It is important to remember, however, that technique alone is not effective. Who the counselee was and who Jesus was were really the most important considerations. When Jesus counseled or ministered to others it was not just an appointment when someone came in for a few minutes and then left. Jesus worked with people through a process. He spent time helping them with their life's difficulties, helping them work through their problems in an in-depth manner. He did not see people with just a problem. He saw them with their potentials and their hopes as well.''*8

Therefore, Jesus' style of relating suggests several perspectives.

1. A biblical counseling model based on Jesus' style of relating demands a counselor to *be* as much as to *do*. *How* one relates is intimately connected to *who* one is. Ideally, the range of counselor responses (roles) is a reflection of one's true person as much as it is of one's training. The Christian counselor who is imitating Jesus must not merely act out the helping roles but must actually possess the attitudes and feelings of that role.

2. A biblical counseling model based on Jesus' style of relating demands that our repertoire of counseling roles and redemptive responses includes all three role models— prophet, pastor, and priest—if it is to be claimed as a biblical style of counseling. One can recognize the differences between roles, but one must appreciate their mutual importance. In Scripture, each role is related to another role and is an integral part of the larger role network identified as the body of Christ (see Romans chapter 12 and 1 Corinthians chapter 12). The Christian body is like our personal living bodies, which have parts that must rely on and support each other in order for a healthy body to grow and maintain itself. The New Testament describes these roles as gifts necessary for

---

*Used by permission of Christian Marriage Enrichment. See footnotes 7 and 8.

the development of each person in the Christian community. I conclude that Jesus' style of relating utilized the repertoire of roles now found in the church.

Whoever named the journal of the National Association of Christians in Social Work *Paraclete* understands my argument. The cognate verb of this Greek word is often translated "to exhort," but as John Carter[9] observes, "the concept is broad enough to support a variety of therapeutic techniques from crisis intervention to depth therapy, and it is a gift given to the church which is clearly different from the gift of the prophet or teacher." Another student[10] notes that "this gift of the Spirit describes many forms of relating, ranging from the paregoric (consolatory) and encouraging, to the hortatory and paraenetic (admonitory)."

3. There are many interventive roles from which the counselor chooses if one's model of counseling is to be described as biblical. Jesus' roles were not mutually exclusive, but they did have relative importance based on both who and why He was relating to a person. Jesus demonstrated role flexibility and variability. He was able to relate to people where they were. He did not have to choose between the prophetic, pastoral, or priestly roles. Many times He used all three redemptive roles in one conversation, as with the woman at the well.

The Christian counselor can be both directive and nondirective. He does not need to chose a directive approach which is dogmatic to the point of not being able to listen to where and why people hurt. He can be a listener without excluding teaching. The Christian counselor may be prophetic, but not at the expense of the hurting person's need for a priest. He may reprove, correct, and instruct, but, like prophets in Scripture, he must at times be the bringer of a message of consolation and pardon (1 Corinthians 14:3).

Granted that the Scriptures teach role variability in redemptive relationships, some counselors will have difficulty in achieving role flexibility, largely for three reasons. First, the counselor may be inadequately socialized into other therapeutic intervention models. Some may find that their training was rather one-sided, and will therefore need to expose themselves to other points of view and approaches through reading, teaching, and supervision. This problem is rather easy to overcome through more education and retraining.

The second possible reason for not being able to achieve role flexibility is the rigidness of the counselor's personality. That is, a counselor may not have personally grown through education and training. If one's identity, self-concept, and ego ideal are exclusively invested in one of the role models, then there will be a tendency to maintain that one particular role at all costs. Personality growth and integration are necessary if role integration is to be a possibility.

Third, a person may not achieve role flexibility because of the nature of one's spiritual gifts and calling. Here the problem takes two forms. One's spiritual gifts may be restricted or limited. Or perhaps God has called a person to a special task. In either of these situations, a person should not try to counsel when the needs of the person indicate exercise of different spiritual gifts. The person with one primary role needs to learn to ask for help from other members of the body of Christ when he or she cannot relate redemptively. This calls for a great deal of spiritual discernment.

4. A biblical counseling model based on Jesus' style of relating utilizes the scriptural insights and solutions to the problem, yet is willing to first listen and understand the client. The Christian counselor brings his or her knowledge and experience to the one needing help, but offers his or her expertize only after carefully grasping the nature of the problem and needs of the counselee.

Because contemporary prophets can only gather their information from the person seeking help, they are *empathetically* more confrontive than the biblical prophets, who received privileged information from God. This means that the Christian counselor is involved in exploring before explaining, listening before lecturing, and empathizing before exhorting and enlightening. Like the biblical prophets, today's Christian counselor brings a message from God to people when that is needed. The messsage always relates to where people are and what they are doing. Thus, we need to learn from the person who is being counseled. The biblical priest and his contemporary counterpart bring a message of forgiveness from God and send a message to God of confession from the sinner. Like the biblical priests, therapists must remember that only listening is never enough. Forgiveness and pardon follow confession and repentance. Many times, directives for restitution will also be part of the priestly counselor's role.

5. Using authority without being authoritarian is characteristic of biblical counseling. Jesus related with the confidence that He knew *who* He was and *what* He was saying. He and His message were experienced as authoritative by His audiences. His presentation of Himself and His message was obviously different from that of the scribes and pharisees. Integrity characterized all of Jesus' being and doing.

Authority is used for the client, but never for the counselor. Counseling authority cannot be legitimately used by the counselor to conceal his or her own feelings of insecurity, inadequacy, or inferiority. Some people are attracted to the counseling status as a way of being "somebody." Other people are attracted to the counseling role as a way of avoiding authority. Both are defensive postures which hinder effective therapeutic intervention.

6. Related to the need for authority is the need to be right. A biblical counseling model acepts the Christian values and biblical principles held by the helper without demanding that the helpee accept, recognize, or submit to the counselor's rightness. Often at the root of the counselor's

need to be right is the need for affirmation of his or her worth and dignity. To be right then means that one is "O.K.," if not actually superior. As a way of countering this tendency, it is helpful to remember that truth and rightness remain truth and rightness regardless of another person's acceptance of them. Most of the biblical prophets were not heard or responded to positively. Nevertheless, that is not evidence that their mission, message, method, or person were faulty. It is probably true that most people can be *led* to the truth more easily than *given* the truth. While counselors may know the truth, that truth cannot change the counselee's behaviors, attitudes, or feelings until it becomes his or her own truth. That is, the client must hear the truth and understand it before it will effectively bring change.

7. Sensitivity to the person's readiness to accept help characterizes the Christian counselor. Timing one's confrontations, interpretations, and suggestions is a crucial issue demonstrated by Jesus. He shared ideas, advice, and solutions without demanding that His audience hear these before they were ready. (Consider, for example the rich young ruler and Nicodemus.) The prophetic-style counselor is often a person who expects that he or she can change people by saying the right words regardless of his or her own personal preparation and readiness. As one minister confessed, "When I entered the ministry, I held the rather firm conviction that the Bible possessed all the answers to every human need and problem. I was under the impression that all a counselor had to do was come up with the right Bible verse for the problem, and presto, the problem would be solved. I soon learned in the crucible of everyday ministry that problems are not solved that easily, nor feelings changed that simply." He goes on to claim, "this does not imply that I lost confidence in the authority of the Scriptures to deal with human needs. It does imply that I lost a great deal of confidence in the approach and method I was using. I saw that it was ineffective and too

simplistic."[11]

8. Jesus teaches us also that sin and guilt are concerns equally important to all counseling roles. One can believe in sin and the importance of the consciousness of sin without necessarily playing the role of prophet. Many times clients are painfully aware of their sinfulness and wrongdoing. They are looking for someone who can help them deal with their guilt and the negative consequences of their behavior. They come to the counselor craving for the intervention of someone whom they can trust to help them out of seemingly impossible feelings and circumstances. These clients come not because they need to be confronted with their sin but because they need to confront their sin through confession and repentance. This is the very fundamental difference between the prophetic counselor proclaiming truth previously unheard or rejected and the priestly counselor affirming truth the hurting person finds difficult to face. Yet, whenever confrontation is necessary, it is more than speaking the truth. To the Christian counselor, confronting is speaking the truth in love (Ephesians 4:15), ". . . always with grace, seasoned with salt" (Colossians 4:6).

9. When one needs to be prophetic, God's Word will be expressed as convicting rather than condemning. The "paraclete," whether Jesus, the Holy Spirit, or a fellow Christian, plays the role of convictor. Therefore, the client will experience acceptance along with reproof and correction. Particularly for our Christian counselees we can proclaim, "There is therefore now no condemnation for those who are in Christ Jesus" (Romans 8:1). It is imperative to remember, however, that while the truth is freeing (John 8:32), at first it often creates considerable discomfort. Also, I have found that when the client experiences condemnation, its source is often self-inflicted, or the work of Satan, or the result of family and friends who are trying to help the Holy Spirit with His role. The spirit convicts; people and Satan condemn (see John

16:8). When a person is hurting, whether feeling convicted or condemned, it is at these times that the counselor must be able to be a priest more than a prophet.

10. We learn from Jesus' style of relating that the role of counselor-priest is to mediate between the divine and the human. He is a human representative to God. In counseling, this priestly mediatorial function takes on the added dimension of assisting the Christian client to be his or her own priest, to develop his or her own priesthood abilities. We do want the client to be decreasingly dependent on the therapist and increasingly dependent on God to work out one's own salvation. Hulme urges that the counselor "never violates the priestly prerogatives" of his clients to be their own priest.[12] While the counselor may mediate for the client, this is not to be the end of the therapeutic exchange. The counseling relationship should be a means to an end—the means to help clients do their own mediating, to develop their own confessional-prayerful relationship with God. "As the priestly function of the counselee becomes blocked, the [counselor's] task is not to jump in and mediate for him, but to [help him] remove the block so that he may resume his own mediatorship."[13]

CONCLUSION

1. I have suggested a model for choosing a style of Christian counseling which integrates two diverse approaches — priestly and prophetic. This model expands the repertoire of interventive roles and avoids two important pitfalls in counseling. The pitfall for the nondirective priest-counselor is the temptation never to speak the words of comfort, forgiveness, and healing. The pitfall for the directive prophetic-counselor is the temptation never to listen, to jump to conclusions, to speak the words of God before the person is ready to hear them. Bonhoeffer makes an important sugges-

tion to both the prophetic and priestly counselor: "We should listen with the ears of God that we may speak the words of God."[14]

2. In addition, I have suggested that biblical counseling is broader than most authors recognize. Biblical counseling is more than a prophetic or priestly approach; it is the thoughtful, prayerful utilization of the whole range of counseling statuses and roles. In fact, it goes beyond the Bible and Christian theology by recognizing God's common grace through creative human research and thought. It is an affirmation that Christ's creative work is to be legitimately continued by His creation, human beings. It is an affirmation that human creativity and culture are good when they are brought into subjection to Christ and produced to the honor and glory of God (Colossians 3:16,17).

3. This model of counseling has the potential for reconciling the differences between Christian counseling approaches by utilizing a frame of reference that is large enough to contain the polar extremes. Also, I have not attacked specific Christian counseling approaches because I believe that most of them are not so much wrong as they are partial and incomplete, and they exaggerate selected methodology and principles.

4. Jesus' style of relating suggests a wide range of redemptive approaches to helping people. The focus of this chapter has been more on the various roles which can be played by Christian counselors and on their presuppositional view of Christ, culture, and Scripture than on counseling technique per se. Counseling from a Christian perspective assumes that Christ and culture are distinguishable (separate) but not necessarily divorced (contradictory). It recognizes that love, wisdom, kindness, and listening are virtues of Christian relating and are common denominators between the prophetic and priestly counseling approaches.

That is, Jesus' style of relating suggests that the principles of counseling are more importantly executed in spirit than in method. Jesus' style of relating is based more on who Jesus is than on what Jesus says or does. Whatever role Jesus plays — prophet, priest, pastor, king, savior—He is Christ. Whatever Jesus' approach to hurting, sinful people, He is Christ. Whatever role or approach we use in counseling, let us depend on "Christ in us" (Colossians 1:27) as we counsel.

Therefore, let us recognize that methodology is not supreme or sufficient in Christian counseling. What is important? You and I as the helper. What are we like? How well do we relate? Truax and Carkhuff[15] taught us that approach is not the most important ingredient in counseling. What is? The personal characteristics of the counselor, such as accurate empathy, nonpossessive warmth, genuiness, congruence.

While the importance of relationship may not be equally recognized in directive (prophetic) and nondirective (priestly) techniques, it seems that relationship is a common denominator in these divergent counseling approaches. Patterson, summarizing divergent counseling theories, concludes that the counseling relationship is "characterized not so much by what techniques the therapist uses as by what he is; not so much by what he does as by the way he does it."[16]

5. As we select from the mosaic which is called Christian counseling, we need to recognize that the differences among counseling methods are often more complementary than conflicting. These differences represent different theoretical tenets, different words to express concepts and terms, and different mechanics to implement the various strategies. However, when considered in broad perspective, these differences are almost inconsequential. Perhaps the real difference lies in the counselor—he or she understands methods better than others, and because of this personal style and emotional comfort level, he or she can apply some methods better than others can.[17] However, the real difference in Christian counseling is Christ. All other differences are

relatively unimportant when we possess the mind of Jesus (Philippians 2:1-5).

FOOTNOTES

1. H.R. Niebuhr, *Christ and Culture* (New York: Harper & Row, 1951).
2. See J. Adams, *Competent to Counsel* (Nutley, NJ: Presbyterian & Reformed, 1974); *Christian Counselor's Manual* (Grand Rapids: Baker, 1973); and C. Solomon, *Counseling with the Mind of Christ* (Old Tappan, NJ: Revell, 1977).
3. E. Jabay, *Search for Identity* (Grand Rapids: Zondervan, 1967), p. 44.
4. L. Crabb, "Moving the Couch into the Church" in *Christianity Today,* Sept. 22, 1978, pp. 17-19.
5. W. E. Hulme, *Counseling and Theology* (Philadelphia: Muhlenberg, 1956); R. May, *The Art of Counseling* (New York: Abington, 1939); F. Lake, *Clinical Theology* (Londong: Darton, Longman, Todd, 1966); J.H. Clinebell, *Basic Types of Pastoral Counseling* (Nashville: Abingdon, 1966); S. Hiltner, *Clinical Pastoral Training* (New York: Abingdon, 1949); P. Tournier, *The Healing of Persons* (New York: Harper & Row, 1965); B. Narramore, *Guilt and Freedom* (Santa Ana: Vision House, 1974); G. Collins, *Effective Counseling* Carol Stream, II: Creation House, 1972).
6. W. Ward, *The Bible in Counseling* (Chicago: Moody, 1977).
7. For assistance in reviewing Jesus' style of helping others, see H.N. Wright, *Training Christians to Counsel* (Denver: CME, 1977), pp. 24-35.
8. Ibid., p. 26.
9. J. Carter, "Adams' Theory of Nouthetic Counseling" in *Journal of Psychology and Theology,* 1975, 3(3), pp. 143-55.
10. J. Ulrich, *the Practice of the Gift of Exhortaton According to the New Testament.* Unpublished master's thesis, Wheaton College, 1976.
11. T. McDill, *Peer Counseling in the Local Church.* Unpublished doctoral dissertation, Bethel Seminary, 1975.

12. Hulme, *Counseling and Theology,* pp. 120-21.
13. Ibid., p. 130.
14. Bonhoeffer, *Life Together* (New York: Harper, 1954), p. 99.
15. C.B. Truax and R.P. Carkhuff, *Toward Effective Counseling and Psychotherapy: Training and Practice* (Chicago: Aldine, 1967).
16. C.H. Patterson, *Theories of Counseling and Psychotherapy* (New York: Harper & Row, 1973), p. 536.
17. E. Peoples, *Readings in Correctional Casework and Counseling* (Pacific Palisades, CA: Goodyear, 1975), p. 372.

3

TOURNIER'S DIALOGUE COUNSELING

Gary R. Collins

For many lay persons the words "Paul Tournier" and "Christian counseling" are almost synonymous. Born at the turn of the century, Tournier trained to become a medical doctor but discovered that many of his patients had problems which were more personal, psychological, and spiritual than they were physical. Untrained in psychiatry or psychology, Tournier nevertheless learned to listen, and in 1940 he wrote the first of his eighteen books—books which have been translated into eleven languages and read by thousands of people all over the world.

Tournier was one of the first persons to be contacted about this present volume, but when asked to write a chapter on his own approach to counseling he responded in a way which is both typical and reflective of his humble manner.

"Ah! Dear friend," he wrote; "you well know that I do not have the soul of a professor, that I do not know how to teach, that I have no system, no doctrine, no method, no original approach, no discipline, no school. I seek only to understand those who want to work with me and to help them approach God and find His grace. I am not capable of doing what you ask, but I am very much touched to know that you have thought of me and I thank you very much for your letter. It is I who lack the instructional capabilities necessary for collaborating with you."

It is unthinkable that a volume on Christian approaches to

counseling should not include a significant section dealing with the work of Tournier. Since Tournier himself did not choose to write in this book, the editor has summarized the counseling views of Tournier in the present chapter.

This material is adapted from chapter 5 of *The Christian Psychology of Paul Tournier,* written by Gary R. Collins, copyright 1973 by Baker Book House (Grand Rapids, Michigan). Used by permission.

Dr. Viktor Frankl, the well-known psychiatrist from Vienna and founder of logotherapy, is reported to have once described his relationship with Freud and Adler. The description sounded something like a psychiatric totem pole, with Freud holding up Adler and Adler in turn supporting Frankl. Frankl felt that he could see farthest into the unknown, but only because he was supported by the solid (although less far-reaching) observations and conclusions of the two older masters from Vienna.

In another part of Europe—in Geneva, Switzerland—I once described Frankl's totem pole to Dr. Paul Tournier and went on to suggest that there are probably many people who have a better view of themselves and others because they stand on the intellectual and practical insights of Tournier himself. The old doctor from Geneva leaned forward in his chair and quickly rejected my suggestion. "People don't stand on my shoulders or on the shoulders of any man," he protested. "Together we stand on God. We are all upheld by Him."

Perhaps there can be no better description of the life philosophy of Paul Tournier. Sincerely interested in other people and genuinely humble in spite of worldwide fame, Tournier is first and foremost a committed follower of Jesus

Christ. "Now I am at the sunset of life," he said in a recent speech, "and as I look back it seems that my whole life has been an adventure led by God. The high point of this adventure has been dialogue—dialogue with God and with my fellowmen."[1]

This dialogue and interest in both God and other men did not come easily. Shortly after his birth on May 12, 1898, Tournier became an orphan who grew up as a lonely and unhappy child. His father had been a pastor, but the young Paul Tournier found little comfort in religion. At the age of eleven or twelve he visited a church and "heard a passionately evangelical sermon very unlike the staid services" to which he was accustomed. Too shy to respond to the altar call, he nevertheless "gave my heart to Jesus," but this did not have much of a practical influence on his religion or on his interpersonal relationships during the teenage years which followed.

However, largely through the efforts of an interested high-school teacher, Tournier began to come out of his shell and to interact with others on an intellectual level. He became a lively debater, an active participant in social work, and, according to his own accounts, somewhat of an agitator in the church. When he was twenty-five, Tournier graduated from the University of Geneva Medical School, was married, and settled down to practice medicine as a general practitioner.

During these early adult years Tournier interacted with other people in an impersonal and cold, intellectual way. He was aloof from his patients, abstract when he gave speeches, and unable to discuss personal matters, even with his wife. In addition, Paul Tournier was searching, perhaps for the meaning of life, which Frankl (and even Tournier himself) wrote about in later years.

A turning point came in 1932, when Tournier met some Christians who introduced him to the practice of daily meditation and encouraged him to talk with others about his personal feelings and frustrations. Following this advice, Tournier soon noticed a change in his own life. He was drawing closer to God, learning to share real feelings with his wife, building closer rapport with his two young sons, and becoming more compassionate with his patients. He asked forgiveness from people whom he had previously criticized, and before long even his medical colleagues noticed that Tournier was becoming a more warm and concerned person and less of a cold intellectual.

In the years which followed, Tournier continued his daily meditations with God (a practice he still follows) and slowly moved into two new careers—those of counseling and writing. He never had a formal course in psychology or psychiatry, but his sincere personal concern and perceptivity did much to mold him into an effective writer and sensitive counselor.

It is difficult to uncover the reasons for Tournier's success as a counselor. He has been asked to outline his techniques, but he claims that this is not possible. "I just try to help people," he once commented; and for him this undoubtedly is more important than trying to write a counseling do-it-yourself book. Instead of outlining a method, he prefers to tell the "real-life stories" of people whose lives have been changed. Instead of trying to teach or instruct, Tournier would rather share from his experiences. Analyzing and summarizing his techniques is a task that he would prefer to leave for others.

This will be our task in the pages of this chapter. We will attempt to discover what Tournier does when he counsels with people, and we will consider some of his views of psychotherapy. Before we get to the matter of treatment, however, it might be helpful if we look at Tournier's thinking on the nature and causes of neurosis. This is a subject which is discussed most clearly in his analysis of what Tournier calls strong and weak reactions.

THE STRONG AND THE WEAK

Tournier once received a visit from an eminent Englishman who was an intellectual and political leader in his country. The man radiated self-confidence and impressed other people with his capabilities and lack of fear. "I have just spent a wonderful week," the visitor exclaimed as he sat down in Tournier's office. "In order to get to know myself better I have tried to make a list of all the people, things, and ideas that make me afraid." It had been a fruitful exercise, for the man had filled several notebooks with his lists of fears.

The visit made a great impression on Tournier. In his daily work he had seen innumerable people who were ashamed to admit their fears, but here was a man who acknowledged quite openly that he was fearful. Tournier recognized that there were some fears in his own life, and he soon reached the conclusion that all men are afraid. Some people hide their fears, and others admit them, but everyone is afraid of something. We fear being trampled underfoot. We are afraid that our inner weaknesses or our secret faults will be discovered. We are afraid of other people, of ourselves, and even of God. So common is fear, Tournier concluded, that it can be considered a normal, universal, and healthy part of human nature.[2]

Everyone experiences fear, but people react to this emotion in different ways. Tournier illustrates this with the example of two schoolboys, each of whom goes for an examination after having studied only half of what he is supposed to know. Both boys are afraid of failing. The one is so concerned about his lack of knowledge that he panics during the examination, gets flustered, and fails to answer clearly even when questioned about the material he has studied.

The other student is spurred on by his fear. He answers enthusiastically and clearly when questioned about what he knows, and he cleverly turns the other questions on to topics with which is more familiar. One boy turned his 50 percent of knowledge into nothing, and the other stretched his 50 percent into 100 percent. One boy showed weakness in the face of fear, while the other showed strength. What distinguished the boys was not their fear; both were afraid (like all people are afraid), but one showed a weak reaction, while the other showed a reaction which was strong.

Weak reactions. People whose lives are characterized by weak reactions often appear in the offices of psychological counselors. Weak persons feel insecure, unhappy, and defeated. Life for them seems to be a series of failures which lead to the expectation that they will bungle everything they try. Crushed by criticism and a recurring lack of success, these people often give up in despair. They have little self-confidence, are hypersensitive, have great feelings of inferiority or worthlessness, and tend to be self-critical. Frequently they look dejected, and often they suffer from a variety of physical and mental illnesses.[3]

When a person feels weak, he or she tends either to do nothing or to hide the defeat by running away. Let us consider first the behavior of those who do nothing. Tournier calls this the "strike reaction," in which frustrated people, like frustrated laborers, refuse to carry on with the work of life. The lazy person, for example, is on strike; and so is the individual who wastes a lot of time or tends to be very forgetful. Some people escape from the hurly-burly of life by developing an incapacitating psychosomatic illness. Others become excessively pious and excuse themselves from involvement with the world. Frigidity in women and impotence in men, Tournier suggests, are sexual strikes which enable people to demonstrate the unexpressed and sometimes unconscious grievances that they feel toward their mates. Bad writing and a sloppy appearance are strikes against the social demands of others. But the most common "do-nothing" reaction, the first symptom complained of by neurotics, and the characteristic which Tournier calls "the weak reaction par excellence," is fatigue.

There are four overlapping causes of fatigue: overwork, excessive zeal or nervous activity, rebellion, and inaction accompanied by inner conflict. Genuine overwork is the rarest cause. More common is the zealous person who is trying to keep busy so that he won't have to think about his failures; the rebellious individual who is expending great energy opposing the injustices of life; and the inactive person who is being wearied by an inner battle between his fear, conflicts, and insecurities. At times we all find that we are too tired to keep pressing on with our responsibilities. It is then, Tournier suggests, that we should ask ourselves if God is trying to teach us something through our fatigue.[4]

While some people react to their feelings of weakness by doing nothing, others run away. In his first book, Tournier identified ten common flight reactions.[5] When faced with the frustrations of life, people may withdraw into a world of dreams or fantasy; turn all of their attentions to the good old days gone by (this is a flight into the past); escape by constantly making plans for the days ahead (flight into the future); unconsciously develop an accident proneness (since an accident could provide a good excuse for escaping from life's other problems); develop a psychosomatic illness; become slaves to tranquilizing drugs which calm them down; use stimulants to buoy them up; develop addictions to such vices as gambling or alcoholism; become excessively busy in overwork; or withdraw into the nonrealities of some religion. One could extend the list of flight reactions almost indefinitely. Each of the psychological defense mechanisms, for example, can help people escape, and so can the tendency of weak people to simply cut themselves off from social contacts or to go through life whistling like kettles in an attempt to conceal their inner tension.

These various attempts to avoid or conceal the problem of

inner weakness are only partially successful. Very frequently, the person gets trapped in one of the vicious circles which Tournier had seen so often and about which he writes in several of his books. Consider, for example, the weak person who tries to hide his weakness. The harder he tries, the greater is his tension and anxiety. As he gets more and more anxious, the more he is likely to fail and to show the very weakness which he is trying to hide. When this weakness becomes apparent to himself and others, he tries even harder to cover it up, and the vicious circle repeats itself. The same sort of thing happens when people feel guilty. They do something wrong, and this creates guilt. The existence of this guilt makes them angry and inclined to do further wrong, which in turn creates more guilt. Tournier believes that most neurotics experience these vicious circles in some form, so the counselor is faced with the difficult task of helping the person to break the cycle.

Strong reactions. Like the schoolboy who confidently bluffed his way through the examination, some people create an appearance of assurance and aggressiveness in order to conceal their real fears. In contrast to the weak reactions which immobilize a person, the strong reactions stimulate and motivate one to push ahead, even if this can only be done by overpowering others. The strong seem to be always successful and basking in one accomplishment after another. These people can be very charming, loquacious, and self-assured. Sometimes they are witty or humorous, but they also show a tendency to be critical, stubborn, vain, superficial, cynical, and aggressive, especially when they sense that their strong facade is in danger of cracking, thereby revealing the weaknesses underneath.[6]

The strong are more successful in life, but this does not mean that they are more stable than the weak. Both the strong and the weak are fearful. Both the strong and the weak feel an inner insecurity, and both long to be reassured. The weak person is more willing to admit his inner needs, but, apart from a few mature men (such as Tournier's English friend), few strong people can acknowledge that they are really weak and insecure like everyone else.

It should not be assumed that Tournier divides all people into two distinct and separate categories of the strong and the weak. These are extreme positions, and most of us are somewhere in between. In our daily lives we show a mixture of strong and weak reactions. Those people who show an overabundance of one or the other are really unstable and in need of psychological help.

The psychiatrists who give this help have noticed that neurotic people can be classified into diagnostic categories. These categories have such names as paranoia, hypochondriasis, obsessive-compulsive reactions, depressions, or sexual deviations. Tournier discusses each of these in his writings, but he would probably agree that they are each forms of the basic strong and weak reactions.

Whatever the diagnostic label, Tournier has noticed that there are four characteristics which appear in almost all neurotics.[7] First, there is anxiety. Sometimes it hides behind a mask of bravado and sometimes it is clearly visible, but it is always there. Second, there is sterility. The neurotic may dream of accomplishing a great many things, but the dreams never really materialize, and life remains sterile and nonproductive. Third, the neurotic is self-defeating. He or she tries hard to succeed, but one's actions almost always bring ruin and defeat instead. Finally, the neurotic is gripped by an unconscious inner conflict. There is failure to recognize real weaknesses, and one struggles to be strong. For some people this struggle comes out in the form of hostility or physical illness. For others the symptoms are more subtle and difficult to understand. But understanding is one of the goals of the therapist. By getting behind the social facade and trying to glimpse the struggle underneath, the counselor can better help the patient to live a life that is more satisfying and productive.

THE CAUSES OF NEUROSIS

When a person has a physical illness, the doctor is greatly interested in the symptoms, because these can tell why the patient is sick. Sometimes the physician tries to eliminate the symptoms, but he is much more concerned with treating the underlying causes of the disease. Aspirin might temporarily relieve the headache of a patient with a brain tumor, for example, but a more extreme treatment is needed if the cure is to be permanent.

In the opinion of a medical man like Tournier, we do not really help people until we can get beneath the surface symptoms and uncover the hidden causes of behavior. In psychology this is very difficult because the causes are often hard to find. Even when the counselor does discover facts about a problem, he or she frequently finds that the facts don't fit together logically. They seem unrelated to each other.

In the pages of his books, Tournier states many facts about the causes of neurosis. He describes some causes which are physical, some which are psychological, and many which are spiritual. Presumably any number of these, acting alone or combined with others, could bring about neurotic behavior.

Consider, for example, how a weak constitution, a faulty inheritance, or a physical disability can lower a person's ability to resist the psychological pressures of life. As the psychoanalysts have shown, the emotional shocks of early childhood are even more important. Broken homes, parental dissension, a lack of trust or love, mistreatment, overprotection or rejection by the parents, constant criticism, frequent failure, or a feeling that one is not loved—each can create problems in later life.

Often these experiences bring emotions which gnaw at an individual and lead to further psychological difficulties. Feelings of inferiority, guilt, fear, despair, doubt, shame, or rebellion give rise to psychological troubles and even to certain organic diseases. The same thing can happen when people try to hide their problems by pretending that they don't exist, when there is dishonesty about one's true feelings, or when a person avoids any discussion of his inner conflicts and worrisome problems.

Important as all these causes are, they cannot fully explain neurosis because they say nothing about the spiritual reasons for man's problems. Carl Jung firmly believed that there was a religious element in all neurosis, and Tournier would agree, but Tournier goes even further and states that the ultimate cause of all personal problems is sin.[8] The religious formalism of the church also can do great psychological harm, sometimes even causing an "ecclesiogenic" or church-produced neurosis. In addition, our inability fo find meaning and purpose in life can also lead to great psychological and spiritual anguish. But we must first consider the sin in the heart of people if we really hope to free them from their psychological problems.

THE TREATMENT OF NEUROSIS

Several years ago, a professor on the faculty at the University of Marseilles gave a lecture entitled "Surgery of the Person." The surgeon must be technically skillful, the lecturer stated, but this is only part of his work. He is dealing not just with kidney stones and diseased gallbladders, but with real people. It is important, therefore, that he take a personal interest in his patients and try to develop a warm relationship with each one.

Tournier once referred to the professor's speech with obvious approval. Here was a man who advocated both technical competence and personal concern—the two characteristics that form the basis for the "medicine of the person." Tournier has repeatedly emphasized that all of medical practice should reflect these two influences, and it is hardly surprising that he suggests the same thing for counseling.

To help people with their problems, Tournier believes that the counselor must be technically capable and deeply interested in people. The technical skills come from science. They can be taught in university courses or described in books. But this is not true for the personal interest. That is something which the counselor must develop "through his heart and his faith" rather than through intellect. Although he never states this specifically, Tournier seems to feel that a personal faith is what creates the personal interest and warmth. If we want to help people with their problems, we must apply both the technical skills of a man or woman of science and the spiritual concern of a man or woman of God.

The importance of technique. Tournier has great respect for the techniques that have been discovered by scientific psychiatry and psychology. He sees value in the work of Freud, Adler, Jung, Frankl, or Rogers, and he believes that every method can help, so long as the therapist has a positive attitude toward his patient. Tournier would never side with the people who hurl criticisms and sarcastic remarks at those who use a technique different from their own. Instead of denouncing the failure of others and boasting of our own success, he suggests that we should try to discover what we can from one another.

This eclectic position characterizes the methodology that Tournier describes in his books. He states that therapy should be nondirective, but at times he is most directive in telling the patient what is wrong. Like Freud and Jung, Tournier sees value in dream interpretation, but he also believes that the counselor should sometimes talk about his or her own personal struggles and problems. Listening is very important in Tournier's therapy, but he is not opposed to sharing his own values and insights when this seems appropriate, or to administering a psychological test.

Like most counselors, Tournier believes that we should not argue with the patient, or criticize, judge, condemn, preach, or direct. The counselor should not give a lot of advice but should help the patient to make his or her own decisions. Intellectual discussions should be avoided, since these and similar techniques are often used unconsciously by the patient to swing the discussion away from a painful consideration of his or her own problems and weaknesses.

Dialogue. For Tournier, the essence of all therapy is dialogue. As the patient tells about his or her problems, life history, and secrets, the therapist listens and tries to understand. A warm relationship builds up, and there is a sharing of mutual concerns and problems. This dialogue is not easy, because interaction with others leads us to discover things about ourselves that we would prefer not to see. Sometimes there are tears or long periods of awkward silence, but these are often needed if there is to be real progress.

The counselor personality. More important than all of the methods, however, is the personality of the counselor. Tournier began his work as a therapist at a time when European psychiatry was very concerned about technique. Freud was still alive and the various analytic shools were at the height of their influence. It was a time when the emphasis was more on what the counselor does than on what the counselor is. Scientific research would later demonstrate that the therapist's characteristics and attitudes are more important than what he says or how he acts, but Tournier reached that conclusion independently and stated it clearly at the beginning of his counseling career.

What are the characteristics of a good counselor? Tournier has dropped hints at various places throughout his writings, and by picking these up we can compile a description. The effective therapist must be patient, sincerely concerned about others, willing to listen, and wanting to understand. He or she expresses confidence, love, hope, acceptance, and support even when the patient is floundering or seems to be going in the wrong direction. The counselor should have an understanding of counseling technique, but this must be supplemented by self-insight and a good understanding of the difficulties in his or her own life. Tournier does not believe that we can help others until we find solutions to our own problems.

The counselor who has found these personal solutions and developed these psychological characteristics is likely to be effective whether or not he or she is a Christian. Throughout his career Tournier has met many people who believe that the Christian therapist is somehow more capable than the nonbelieving therapist. This is a conclusion which Tournier does not accept. Too often, he writes, people think that the Christian doctor will pray with his patient and somehow wave a magic wand which the secular therapist does not possess. Frequently, though, the so-called Christian psychotherapy is nothing more than preaching at the patient. This, of course, can sometimes do more harm than good. Tournier believes that all healing comes from God, who may choose to work through a believer but who also works through atheists.

In spite of this, Tournier's books list a number of spiritual characteristics that would be good for the therapist to possess. The counselor should be obedient to the Creator, humble, a man or woman of prayer, and one who has a good knowledge of the Bible. He or she must be a believer who is willing to honestly confess one's faults or weaknesses to God, to others, and at times to one's patients. This is the kind of counselor who commits one's work to God and even believes that there can be divine guidance in the choice of those scientific techniques that are used in therapy.

The goals of counseling. In addition to technical knowledge and a personal concern for others, the counselor should have some idea of what he or she hopes to accomplish in therapy. Does one, for example, want to teach the patient how to get along better with others or how to control emotions? Are we trying to relieve the patient's suffering, or give a new meaning to life? Many therapists would be able to make a clear statement of what they are trying to accomplish with their patients—but not Tournier. "When people tell me about their problems," he once commented, "I really don't know what to do." So he listens with sincere interest and tries to stimulate a dialogue with the patient. As he describes this procedure, one almost expects him to say that he hasn't the remotest idea why anyone gets better. Whether or not he feels this way, it is clear that Tournier does not worry about making lists of goals for himself and his patients to reach during counseling.

If one reads through his case histories, however, it appears that Tournier does have some counseling goals. We will consider four of these. First, Tournier wants to help people break out of the vicious circles in which so many people are caught. In his consulting room, a lady one day confessed that she was trapped in "that most vicious of circles," the lie. Whenever she told a lie she had to tell another to cover the first. Things had become so bad, this woman reported, that she had even begun lying to herself. The only way that one can break such a circle, Tournier had written, is with a deep religious experience. We must depend on God to pull us out of our attempts at self-justification. This is what the woman had done, and Tournier, who had a burning desire to strengthen her decision, told about a conversation that he had had with one of his colleagues. Regretfully, in an attempt to make the story more appealing, Tournier altered one or two of the details. The next morning he began to think about what he had done. In trying to help a patient to be truthful, he had lied. When she returned to his office, he confessed and asked her forgiveness. It was a painful request, but it built a real communion between the doctor and his patient. It also demonstrated again what Tournier has emphasized repeatedly in his writings: confession is a powerful therapeutic device. It liberates people from a whole host of problems and it can do much to crush vicious circles.

The second goal is what Tournier calls "the expansion of the field of consciousness." Tournier believes that much of our behavior is motivated by unconscious influences. When the person has greater knowledge and insight into these previously hidden forces, he or she has better self-understanding and greater self-control. As he or she sees the faults, weaknesses, and even the sins that are in one's life, the patient can confess these wrongdoings and set one's life in order. It is not easy or even possible for a person who is unassisted to bring what is unconscious into conscious awareness. We need help with this, and we also need support and encouragement to face and do something about the painful truths that we are discovering about ourselves. Through dream analysis, observation of the person's behavior, careful listening, and sincere dialogue, the counselor can help the patient to expand his or her conscious understanding of the forces that influence life.

Closely connected to this is the third goal of therapy: acceptance. One Christmas Day Tournier visited a friend who was dying in a hospital room. "There's something I don't understand," the patient said with difficulty, but he was too weak to finish the sentence. Clearly the man was sincerely troubled by his problem, but it would have been useless to begin a discussion at that point. Leaning over the bed, Tournier whispered that the most important thing in the world is not to understand but to accept. These words had a visible effect on the patient. "It's true," he responded shortly before his death; "I do accept everything."

In Tournier's experience, acceptance is the first step toward conquering our problems and weaknesses. We must learn to accept the fact that we are alive. We must accept our physical appearance, age, sex, marital status, parents, children, job, or mate. Sometimes we must accept the fact that suffering exists or that we are sick and in need of treatment. This does not mean that we must take pleasure in the things we accept. The grieving widow, for example, is not happy about her husband's death; but she must accept it with the help of God before she can adjust to her widowhood. Very often such acceptance is preceded by rebellion, and this is something which the counselor must accept. It is not by preaching that we help others, but by understanding how difficult it is for them to accept their lot. It is also helpful if we can confess that we would probably rebel too if we were in the patient's circumstances.

Another of Tournier's goals is what he calls soul healing. This means bringing an individual into personal contact with Christ. In a sense this is not really a part of psychotherapy, since discussions about morals or the meaning of life, sin, faith, or one's attitude to God are really beyond the realm of scientific psychology. Regretfully, many doctors fail to recognize when they have moved beyond the limits of psychology. They encourage patients to develop values and moral practices which are based not on science but on the therapist's own philosophy of life and views of theology. In contrast, Tournier openly acknowledges that he has Christian convictions that go beyond his psychological techniques. He believes that a person is only partially helped if we consider his or her physical and psychological needs but ignore the spiritual part of life. Tournier does not exhort his patients to become Christians, but he prays for them and seeks to guide them to a place where they will approach God, listen to His voice, and commit themselves to obey His will.

The therapist's tasks. Tournier once wrote an article in

which he identified four basic tasks of the psychotherapist.[9] In each of these, the counselor shows concern for both the psychological difficulties of the patient and the spiritual struggles. The first therapeutic task is to encourage catharsis —the free expression of one's feeling and problems. Sometimes as the patient unburdens and talks about psychological troubles, there is also a discussion of sin and moral failures. The second task is to be alert to transference. This is the personal attachment that the patient often feels for the therapist. This attachment can be unhealthy, as Freud warned, but it can also be a healthy channel through which there is psychological and spiritual growth. Guiding the patient into increased self-knowledge is the third task. As we have seen already, this can enable one to get control over psychological impulses and it can show the patient his or her sins and need for a Savior. Finally, the therapist exercises what Tournier calls a "philosophical function." This involves guiding the patient to consideration of theological questions for which technical psychotherapy has no answer. This is true soul healing.

TOURNIER AS A COUNSELOR

To this point we have seen what Tournier thinks about neurosis and we have considered some of his views on how troubled people can best be helped. But what does Tournier do in his own counseling? What are the techniques that he has found to be most successful in his own interviews with people?[10]

Tournier wants to engage patients in a dialogue. Although the intellectual discussion of a problem is important in psychotherapy, he believes that this is not enough. If true change is to occur there must also be a deep personal rapport of "spiritual communion" between the therapist and patient. At the beginning of the interview there may be small talk, nervous laughter, or attempts to change the subject. But in successful therapy these eventually give way to a trusting, person-to-person bond between two individuals. The counselor and patient stop viewing each other as impersonal strangers and instead start to see each other as human beings in need. To use Martin Buber's terms, there is a change from an "I-It" relationship to an "I-Thou" bond.

To build this bond, Tournier often prepares for his interviews by prayer and meditation, and he sometimes encourages patients to do the same. By spending time quietly before God, the counselor gets the inner strength that he or she needs, and is more willing to depend on God, who alone can help the patient. As a result there is a fresh liberation from the self-centered human characteristics that might interfere with effective counseling.

When the patient arrives and begins to talk about a problem, Tournier listens intensely to what is being said. He tries to understand the patient's difficulties, without asking a lot of questions or trying prematurely to find solutions. Tournier is willing to give as much time to this listening as is necessary, and he is surprised when people comment on his patience. "It is not patience," he replies, "but an absorbing interest in people."

As the counseling progresses, Tournier tries to give acceptance and support. Everybody is weak, he believes, and we all need something or someone on whom we can lean. The counselor who is not troubled already has a number of these supports, but the patient does not. He or she needs someone who will firmly but gently hold him or her up until one can find one's own supports and eventually experience the limitless support which comes from God.

As the patient begins to feel more comfortable in the counseling situation, he or she is sometimes helped to self-examination and self-understanding. As we have seen, Tournier believes that insight and recognition of our own psychological makeup can free us from many problems; but we can never get this insight on our own. We might sincerely try to understand ourselves, but our efforts are certain to fail. In counseling, therefore, Tournier enters into a dialogue with his patients because he believes that this is the only way that an individual can gain a valid self-picture.

When patients see themselves more clearly, they are likely to find things they don't like. It is important that they express their emotions and honestly confess both sins and weaknesses. People are reluctant to do this, but Tournier has found that they can be helped if the counselor, in all sincerity, is willing to tell about some of his or her own problems, sins, or spiritual struggles. Thus Tournier does not sit lording it over his patients as an impersonal judge. He treats them as brothers or sisters who, like himself, are weak souls in need of forgiveness and the healing powers of God.

It does not follow from this, however, that Tournier preaches to his patients or turns every counseling session into a worship service. He does not try to hide his Christian convictions, since that would be dishonest. He sometimes prays with patients, talks with them about God, and encourages them to meditate as he does. This can all be part of soul healing. But there are other patients with whom Tournier never mentions spiritual issues. He feels that by one's witness and life it is possible to bring another person to God even when we don't talk about soul healing at all.

Like every good counselor, Tournier adapts his method to fit the needs of the patient. Sometimes he asks a former patient to help with counseling. Sometimes he refers a person to a minister, priest, or psychiatrist for further help. On occasion Tournier becomes very directive in giving advice, or even engages in the biblical practice of laying on hands while praying for recovery.

Tournier is honest enough to admit that his counseling efforts don't always succeed. Sometimes a patient does not respond to treatment, shows a loss of faith, or even commits suicide. These failures are a great disappointment to a sensitive man like Tournier, but over the years he has tried to learn from them and to use them as stepping-stones to greater counseling effectiveness.

TOURNIER AS A WRITER AND LECTURER

Undoubtedly, Tournier has helped many people through his work as a counselor, but he is best-known as a writer. Any consideration of his methodology would be incomplete, therefore, if we overlooked his skill in helping people with his literature.

For Tournier, it is more important to give insights into behavior and to share experiences than to write in a systematic fashion. Writing is a way to converse with readers, even as counseling is a dialogue with patients. We don't talk with a lot of headings and subheadings in our speech, so why should we worry a great deal about systematically organizing what is written? Tournier prefers to write like the impressionists painted—with little glimpses of life that can only make real sense when they are seen in the perspective of the whole.

Why are Tournier's books so well-received by so many people in spite of their rambling style and lack of organization? Undoubtedly his conversational manner, his avoidance of technical terminology, his honest sharing of personal experiences, and his frequent references to real people all contribute to the popularity of what he has written. Perhaps there is also another reason.

Tournier once described the writings of his countryman Jean Jacques Rousseau. "He did not only put the ideas and theories . . . into his writings," Tournier wrote, "but laid bare his very self. That is what gave his books their seductive power. . . . He gave himself in person as he saw himself. His readers sensed this; and it explains the enthusiastic devotion which the people showed toward Rousseau." There could be no better description of Tournier's own work.

In a recent letter Tournier commented about the "very American" habit of giving and receiving help through the use of cassette tapes. This "does not correspond to my personal mentality," he wrote. "I am a man of intimacy. To speak, I must talk to someone or to several people, but to individuals and not to an abstract 'case,' and especially, I must listen before speaking."

Clearly, Tournier believes that his work is most effective when he can relate to people on a one-to-one basis. His counseling is mostly with individuals, and he has never attempted group therapy, although he acknowledges its value. As a writer Tournier tries to keep the individual reader in mind, and this same policy extends to his public lectures. Standing before an audience, he forgets the anonymous mass and instead selects three or four people to whom he can direct his remarks in a personal way. This, he has concluded, enables him to teach persons in individual dialogue instead of lecturing to impersonal masses of unknown people.

CONCLUSION

Tournier has been criticized on occasion for going beyond the borders of medicine and for practicing psychotherapy even though he has never been trained as a counselor. Some have accused him of being too naive, too religious, or too simple in his understanding of human behavior. Tournier himself describes his counseling as the work of an amateur who has "terrible gaps" in his knowledge and who wanders innocently, but joyfully, into the domains of psychology, philosophy, and theology.

Apparently Tournier likes to be seen as an amateur. For him this means someone who thoroughly enjoys what he is doing and takes his work seriously. It also seems to mean someone who at times is more sincere, more spontaneous, and more sympathetic than the professional. Consider, for example, the biblical parable of the Good Samaritan. The professionals left the injured man at the side of the road. It was only later that the Samaritan did what he could as an amateur doctor.

In reading Tournier's descriptions of himself, one gets the impression that he also uses the "amateur" label as a shield to protect himself from criticism. He has noted that amateurs can make a lot of mistakes which would be be unpardonable in a professional. But can Tournier really be called an amateur therapist after he has spent most of his professional life doing this kind of work? Can a man who has written almost twenty books still be considered an amateur author? Even if we grant his nonprofessional status, does a man like Tournier really need to defend himself against criticism?

To be an amateur is not necessarily to be ignorant or unskilled. This is demonstrated whenever the Olympic games are held. Professionals are excluded, but the amateurs who do compete are every bit as capable—and sometimes even more so—than the full-time athletes who temporarily sit in the stands. Tournier has no need to excuse himself as an unqualified amateur. His humility, his lack of training as a professional counselor, his casual writing style, and his refusal to use a lot of psychiatric terms might distract critics into thinking that he is incompetent or superficial. On the contrary, careful study of a book like *The Strong and the Weak* shows that he is a man of rare insight who possesses great skill as a counselor and a penetrating ability to understand the causes of human behavior.

Tournier accepts what he can from the writings of such highly respected counselors as Jung or Rogers, but he refuses to be bound by any one technique. He works solely with individuals and mostly engages in supportive counseling because he feels that this best suits his temperament. But he does not criticize those who prefer some other method. He is happy to tell about his successes but is honest enough to admit that he sometimes fails in spite of his best efforts. He strives to use the best of psychological techniques, but when spiritual needs are apparent he goes with his patient into the realm of the supernatural and leaves scientific methods behind.

As we have seen, Tournier believes that people must be helped with spiritual problems as well as with psychological and physical difficulties. The counselor, therefore, must not only be technically skillful, but should also be spiritually mature—a man or woman who is humble before God and obedient to the Holy Spirit's leading.

In his first book Tournier wrote that

> One of the tasks of the doctor is to help his patients to see what is God's will for them and to show them how to win the victories of obedience. But no one can lead others along this path without traveling it himself. Medicine has made tremendous progress. It will go on doing so. The world does not need a new medicine; it needs doctors who know how to pray and obey God in their own lives. In such hands, medicine, with all its modern resources, will bring forth its fruit in abundance.[11]

In reading these lines, one wonders if "medicine" could be replaced by the word "counseling." Tournier probably would have no objection to such an alteration, for what he says about his own field of medicine can doubtless apply to all of the professions, especially those concerned with mental health.

As much as Tournier emphasizes (and demonstrates) these spiritual characteristics, he does not claim that they are necessary. Instead, he believes that God often works through nonbelieving and even antireligious therapists to help patients with spiritual and other problems. Tournier has pointed out that there are many illustrations in the Bible to show that God uses nonbelievers to accomplish His divine purposes, and it is certainly possible that this may happen in counseling.

But there are many patients whose secular therapists have led them into spiritual confusion. Tournier suggests that one counselor is as effective as another, providing there is goodwill toward the patient. But if this is so, why does Tournier place such emphasis on the need for spiritual maturity in a counselor? We can certainly appreciate his desire to show that Christians are not magicians whose counseling success is automatically better than that of nonbelievers. It may be, however, that Tournier's tolerance for non-Christians has prevented him from seeing that the true follower of Christ may, after all, bring some unique therapeutic qualities to the counseling relationship. This is especially so when the counselor must help his patient to deal with sin, which Tournier believes to be the basic cause of all neuroses.

In retirement, Tournier was no longer active as a counselor or prolific writer. However, he had done much to pave the way for other Christian counselors, and, in spite of his denials, many *do* stand on Tournier's shoulders and *can* see further into the unknown because of the insights that are revealed in this counselor's work.

FOOTNOTES

1. J. Rilliet, "Apprendre a Vieiller" in *Tribune de Geneve,* January 26, 1972, p. 39.
2. P. Tournier, *The Strong and the Weak* (Philadelphia: Westminster, 1963), pp. 91, 21, 80.
3. Ibid., pp. 22-23, 28-29, 37, 97-128.
4. Ibid., pp. 101-7. See also Paul Tournier, ed., *Fatigue in Modern Society* (Richmond: John Knox Press, 1965), pp. 5-36.
5. P. Tournier, *The Healing of Persons* (New York: Harper & Row, 1965).
6. P. Tournier, *The Strong and the Weak.* Op. cit., pp. 109-13.
7. P. Tournier, *The Whole Person in a Broken World* (New York: Harper & Row, 1964), pp. 8-11.
8. P. Tournier, *The Healing of Persons.* Op. cit., pp. 189, 211.
9. P. Tournier, "The Frontier Between Psychotherapy and Soul Healing" in *Journal of Psychotherapy As a Religious Process,* January, 1954.
10. The material for this section of the chapter is based on my interviews with Dr. Tournier and on the facts about his own techniques that are revealed in his books. After writing the present section, however, I discussed it with Dr. Tournier in detail and made some minor changes in accordance with his suggestions. I now feel that this is an accurate picture of what he does as a counselor.
11. P. Tournier, *The Healing of Persons.* Op. cit., p. 269.

4

GROWTH
COUNSELING

Howard Clinebell

During the past decade, perhaps no voice in counseling has had a greater impact on seminary students than the voice of Howard Clinebell. His *Basic Types of Pastoral Counseling* has been used in innumerable classrooms and by students and professors who hold a wide range of theological views.

Clinebell's writing has not been limited to pastoral counseling. *The Intimate Marriage,* coauthored with his wife, Charlotte H. Clinebell, is widely recognized as one of the best books on marriage enrichment; *Understanding and Counseling the Alcoholic: Through Religion and Psychology* is a masterful treatment of pastoral counseling and alcoholism; and a book entitled *The Mental Health Ministry of the Local Church* is a practical and creative treatment of how the church's ministry can stimulate wholeness in the congregation.

In his correspondence with the editor, Clinebell wrote that his approach to counseling which has developed during the past years is what he now calls Growth Counseling. He describes this approach in the present chapter. Although the author says little about his counseling techniques, he does use a variety of methods drawn from contemporary approaches to counseling. Growth counseling, he writes, is "a natural for pastors and a very liberating model . . . of the church as a caring community devoted to helping people develop 'life in its fullness' (John 10:10)."

This chapter was prepared especially for this volume. A fuller description of the principal methods and theology of growth counseling is available in Clinebell's recently published book, *Growth Counseling: Hope-Centered Methods for Actualizing Human 'Wholeness* (Nashville: Abingdon, 1979).

Howard Clinebell is Professor of Pastoral Counseling at the School of Theology at Claremont, California. He received the B.A. degree from De Pauw University and a B.D. from Garrett Biblical Institute. Following study at Columbia University and Union Theological Seminary, he received a Ph.D. degree in Psychology of Religion. He has a Certificate in Applied Psychiatry for the Ministry from the William A. White Institute of Psychiatry in New York City. Before coming to his present position, he was a parish pastor for ten years on Long Island.

Growth Counseling (GC) is an approach to helping which has two goals. First, GC attempts to liberate the counselee's fullest potentialities at each stage of life, and second, this approach seeks to create a person-enhancing society in which every person will have the opportunity to use his or her potentialities.

GC is both a way of seeing people and a way of helping them. It looks at people in terms of their present strengths and possibilities, as well as their past failures or present problems and "pathology." GC holds that viewing people in terms of their strengths and what they can become helps them to accept themselves and move toward developing their potential. Seeing people (ourselves and others) through the glasses of growth is one of the best ways in which we can help others. *

---

*The "growth glasses" are bifocal—the bottom lens sees the pain and problems, while the top and larger lens sees their God-given resources and strengths.

GC sees people—"normal" as well as "abnormal"—as possessing a wealth of unlived life or latent potentialities. Each person and every relationship has a gold mine of latent possibilities. Most "normal" people do not use more than 25 percent of their potential. The task of education and counseling is the same: to help people to identify and realize their potentialities at each stage of their life journey.

GC sees people as having a persistent but often-blocked need to grow and to fulfill their hidden potentialities. All effective counseling and education uses this urge to grow. The effectiveness of a teacher or a counselor depends on her or his ability to awaken, stimulate, or liberate the growth drive in individuals and relationships.

GC assumes that a close complementary relationship exists between education and counseling. Education mainly stresses growth and nurture; counseling (a form of depth reeducation) attempts to repair the capacity to grow and learn. These are two interdependent sides of the same process.

GC uses short-term methods to reduce or remove the blocks that prevent people from growing. These blocks, which may have come from traumatic crises or experiences of emotional deprivation in early life, must be removed so that continuing growth is possible.

A network of growth groups in the life of an institution such as the church can prevent the need for counseling, in many cases, by allowing persons to use more of their inner strengths and potentialities. Such a network can also double the effectiveness of counseling by providing small communities of mutual growth in which the progress made in counseling can be sustained and shared with others. In the church, *pastoral care*—the nurturing of persons throughout the life cycle—is central. *Pastoral counseling* is a secondary task which involves repairing broken relationships and removing blocks to growth.

GC sees the *will to relate* to be a basic human drive or need, for it is only in relationships that people become or remain human. Only in relationships can people satisfy their deep psychospiritual needs or hungers, and only as these needs are met can potentializing flourish. Therefore, GC sees the quality of one's interpersonal network or support system as being the crucial variable in facilitating or blocking growth. In order to maximize one's growth, a person must have at least one depth relationship in which the "growth formula" can be experienced.

The basic principle for facilitating growth is expressed most concisely in the following formula:

GROWTH = CARING + CONFRONTATON
OR
GROWTH = LOVE + HONESTY

This means that growth will occur in any relationship to the extent that people experience *love* which does not have to be earned (because it is there in the relationship) and honest *confrontation* with reality. This confrontation concerns both the destructive parts of reality, which we have been ignoring, and the constructive parts, which involve an awareness of our unused potentialities.

GC focuses primarily on the *present* and the *future*. It views the past in the context of the present and the future. The power of the future to pull a person forward is at least as great as the power of the past to push him or her in a given direction. The "living past"—that part of the past that still lives in the present—is not really past. It is a present influence which currently affects people, relationships, and institutions.

GC sees personal, relational, and institutional change as three interdependent dimensions of one process of creative change. Each level of change needs to be supported and nurtured by the other two. Counseling and therapy approaches that focus on all three levels at the same time are the most likely to liberate human potentialities. Liberation of the individual and his or her close relationships cannot be separated from the process of liberating our institutions (including many churches), our society, and even our relationship with the ecological environment from the multitude of crippling growth-blocking forces and influences.

GROWTH COUNSELING AND THE INDIVIDUAL

GC sees crises as turning points in one's life and as potential growth opportunities. GC aims at helping people use both the accidental and the normal developmental crises as occasions for growth. It seeks to do this by surrounding the person by a context of caring and by helping a person to act constructively in order to find meaning in the event and to reach out to others by using the pain of the crisis as a bridge to relate to the pain of others going through similar crises.

GC regards spiritual growth as the integrating core of all human growth, since spiritual growth involves that which is most uniquely human in human beings—awareness, decision, freedom, meaning, commitment, and the quality of one's spiritual life and relation to God. Facilitating spiritual growth is an essential aspect of all counseling and therapy, whether done by a secular or by a religious counselor. This is the area of special training and expertise for those who are trained both theologically and in counseling theories and methods. Theologically trained growth counselors have a special and needed contribution which they can make to the secular counselors who lack this training. The minister is, essentially and centrally, a *spiritual* growth facilitator. It is her or his opportunity to guide secular professionals in this area and to serve as a spiritual growth trainer of lay people helpers.

GC, in contrast to many traditional psychotherapeutic approaches, holds that our deepest growth need is to develop our spiritual selves. Thus, the "spiritual" does not come from other, more basic psychological drives. The spiritual is central and essential in understanding what is most human about human beings and in liberating the inner potential of persons. The goal of spiritual growth counseling is to free people so they can experience the transforming reality of spirit in the here and now.

GROWTH COUNSELING AND SOCIAL CHANGE

GC views the goal of social change as that of liberating our organizations, laws, institutions, and social structures to nurture rather than negate the full growth of persons, to facilitate rather than frustrate human becoming. One goal of individual and relationship counseling is to free persons and relationships so that they become change agents to help institutions experience creative change.

Empowering people to work to eliminate the racism, sexism, and economic injustices of our society, which blocks the full growth of persons on a massive scale, is an essential goal of sound Christian counseling. The growth approach to ministry can help a pastor and his or her people liberate the rich potential of a church to be a better human wholeness center—a garden for nurturing spiritual, whole-person growth. Churches have enormous undiscovered possibilities for increasing their effectiveness as people-development, relationship-enrichment, training-for-outreach centers. Most schools also have significant wasted potentiality for helping persons learn to enjoy using their minds more fully. Counseling agencies also have a wealth of unused possibilities to be better people-development centers. These possibilities are largely buried under "treatment" procedures which are derived from the pathology model (the opposite of the growth model), which has dominated most counseling and psychotherapy theory and practice since Freud. The *church* as a spiritual growth center, the *school* as a place of lifelong intellectual adventure and continuing learning of skills for living, and the *counseling agency* as a place of positive prevention and training (rather than only a place of repair work)—these are images for institutional renewal in the light of the growth perspective. GC views growth as a lifelong process. To make possible this process is the exciting opportunity confronting our people-centered institutions.

GC uses growth or nurture groups as its central methodology. In such groups people can relate to each other with the caring and openness that stimulates maximum mutual growth. These groups should be attractive to "normal" people and should be widely available in our churches, schools, and social agencies. Marriage-and-family-enrichment groups, grief-growth groups, creative-singlehood groups, spiritual-discovery groups, and growth-action groups are examples of such growth groups in local churches.

GC sees the basic helping and growth resource that is needed in our society as being *people helping people,* giving each other mutual support and caring. This resource can be developed by helping lay persons discover their capacity to use their own pain and growth to help others deal growthfully with their own pain. A major role of professionals such as clergy, teachers, counselors, etc. is to help lay persons develop their inner capacity for helping and for facilitating growth in others. This involves training nonprofessionals to become an essential part of the network of growth that is sorely needed in our depersonalized, lonely, ethically confused world. A major need in professional education and continuing training is for abundant opportunities for those in the helping profession to continue their own personal growth. To help others grow, we must be growing persons ourselves. We can't give away what we don't have ourselves. The "lay renaissance" in churches and the widespread use of trained volunteer and paraprofessionals in mental health centers are two examples

of the nonhierarchical egalitarianism that is basic to the
growth approach.

THEOLOGICAL-BIBLICAL FOUNDATIONS AND
ASSUMPTIONS OF GROWTH COUNSELING

The growth approach to people has many historical roots in
the Hebrew-Christian tradition. Here are some elements of a
theological-biblical foundation for GC:

1. *The rich potential in human beings is a gift of the
Creator.* The concept of the *Imago Dei* (Genesis 1:27) can be
understood as a ringing affirmation of the tremendous potentialities that are within persons—a capacity for godlikeness
which is most evident in our uniquely human characteristics
—self-awareness, creativity, conscience, valuing, freedom,
decision, intentionality, compassion, caring, transcendence.
John Calvin declares, in his commentary on Genesis, that the
creation of human beings in the divine image is "a
remarkable instance of divine goodness which can never be
sufficiently proclaimed."[1] Von Rad's observation that in the
anthropology of the Old Testament, this concept applies to
the whole of human beings and not just their minds, is
significant and in harmony with the whole-person emphasis
of the growth approach.[2] Since God is the source of all
growth, we cannot and need not manipulate ourselves or
others to grow. Our task is to facilitate openness to receive
and develop fully the gift of growth.

2. *The growth motif appears repeatedly in the biblical
record.* For example, consider the image of the "tree planted
by streams of water" in the description of a good man (or
woman) in Psalm 1:3, or the emphasis of Jesus on
childlikeness as a prerequisite for entering the kingdom of
God (Luke 18:16,17). Openness and rapid growth are key
characteristics of children. The emphasis on "giving up
childish ways" (1 Corinthians 13:11) is a recognition of the

necessity to grow in one's attitudes, responses, and personality.

3. *There is an awareness in the Bible that somehow, mysteriously, the fulfillment of our potentialities is supported and undergirded by the universe.* It is as though the gravitational pull of the spiritual universe is on the side of potentializing of the rich possibilities that are in all human beings. The paraphrase of Romans 8:19 by J.B. Phillips declares: "The whole creation is on tiptoe to see the wonderful sight of the sons [also the daughters] of God coming into their own."

4. *The biblical record is also acutely aware of the deep resistances to growth and self-actualization in human beings and in history.* Concepts such as the fall of man, of corporate sinfulness, and of Jesus weeping over Jerusalem because it knew not the things that make for peace—all of these point to the powerful tendency in us humans to block our own fulfillment, individually and collectively. To be a viable method of ministry, GC must have an adequate understanding of sin, evil, and pathology.

5. *The goal of growth and of growth approaches to people is defined by the biblical record as shalom, meaning whole, sound, or healthy (as well as peace).* Such wholeness flourishes in relationships. In a community which develops a shalom quality of relationships, there are abundant opportunities for the free and full development of persons.[3] In the Fourth Gospel, Jesus' purpose in coming is described as being so that persons could find "life in all its fullness" (John 10:10 NEB). This is another way of stating the goal of growth approaches in working with people.

6. *There is an awareness in the biblical record that, though growth is a gift of God, it requires struggle, pain, and risk to receive the gift.* Images of dying and rising again and of the strait (narrow) gate and narrow way (Matthew 7:14) are examples of this awareness. The realization that, before one

can experience rebirth (Romans 6:5-11) something must die in the person, is deep in the biblical understanding of growth. Before one can be resurrected to new levels of aliveness and awareness, one's old defenses must die. Before a marriage can experience a rebirth of communication and sensuality, the partners must risk lowering their defenses against getting hurt in close relationships. The potential for continuing growth is a gift, but to receive it requires full, intentional participation by the individual. Thus growth is both a gift and an achievement.

7. *The process by which the "new being" is coming is a process of growth.* The new level of consciousness, caring, and justice (the kingdom of God), which is the societal goal of Christian growth, is coming like a mustard seed (Matthew 13:31), like leaven in a lump of bread dough (Matthew 13:33), like talents that are invested so that they increase (Matthew 25:14-30), and like the results of sowing seeds in a variety of places (Matthew 13:18-23). The process of growth by which this new being will be actualized is a process in which each of us is invited to participate as a Christian. Growth into the new being is a gift of God; it is, in an ultimate sense, a mystery in which we are invited to participate.

8. *The growth formula, expressed in the language of the New Testament, consists of "speaking the truth in love"* (Ephesians 4:15). Theologically, the formula can be stated in terms of the integral relatedness and interdependence of grace and judgment.

9. *The normative style of relating, as exemplified by Jesus, is characterized by seeing people through the growth perspective.* The Synoptic Gospels show that Jesus elicited extraordinary responses from very ordinary people. For example, he saw in a weak fisherman, Simon Bar-Jona, a potential for great strength and character. Jesus facilitated Simon's awareness of his potential by giving him a new name meaning

"rock" (Matthew 16:18). By seeing and affirming his potential, Jesus helped him become Peter, a dynamic leader in the
early church.

Jesus' way of relating to women is an equally dramatic example of the power of the way one sees others, to influence
the way they respond and grow. His ability to see women as
whole human beings, and not merely as the property of men
or functionaries limited to cultural stereotypes—e.g., the
Mary and Martha story (Luke 10:38-42)—sheds light on the
response which Jesus got from His women disciples. Jesus em-
bodied the growth formula in His way of relating to people.
He communicated this by His words and actions. For example, He expressed both the grace and acceptance of God
("Arise and walk; your sins are forgiven—Mark 2:1-12) and
the confrontation with the need to behave in constructive
ways ("Go and sin no more"—John 8:11). Jesus as the living
Christ is the liberator of full human becoming.

10. *The recognition that growth is facilitated by investing
oneself in others is implicit in the biblical words, "He who
saves his life shall lose it. . . "* (Matthew 16:25).

The philosophy of the human potentials movement can be
enriched, informed, and corrected (when it falls into superficial optimism) by the biblical insights about the nature of
being human and of growing.

KEY CONCEPTS IN GROWTH COUNSELING

Potentializing. This key working idea in GC was discussed
above—i.e., that persons have tremendous untapped
creativity, intelligence, and capacity for socially useful and
personally fulfilling lives; that this potential can be
developed, and that the proper task of institutions such as
churches, schools, and agencies is to facilitate this development. Health is much more than the *absence* of gross
pathology. It is the *presence and full use* of one's poten-

tialities in each life stage and circumstance.

Hope. GC views hope as the essential and indispensable motivation for creative change. GC therefore uses procedures which are designed to awaken realistic hope. Hope is awakened in persons when they begin to recognize and use their power to develop their own futures. When faith (or trust) and love are at a low ebb, hope initiates the process of potentializing which leads to the enhancing of trust and love.

Intentionality. GC uses the principle of intentionality as a central working concept. Intentionality means discovering and developing one's options choicefully. It involves the awareness that one has more freedom to choose than one is usually aware of in the midst of the need to choose. The opposite of an intentional lifestyle is drifting or playing the game of "victim" (of the past, of one's unconscious, of one's social situations, etc.). While recognizing the many areas in which one's life situation is "given," the ability to choose one's attitude toward these givens and to rearrange them in some more creative pattern is always there to be used. GC challenges persons to make and implement plans for a better future, even if that future is brief or their options seem very limited.

GC views constructive action, including constructive thinking, as the way to express intentionality. Action that is both responsible and responsive to others is the way in which the future is opened up and the way a person or a relationship grows. By using one's present options and abilities, however limited these may be, one's options and abilities grow, as do self-esteem and sense of inner strength and cope-ability.

Growth pursued for its own sake becomes a cul-de-sac. The way to keep growing is to give your growth away. Thus, every growth group should also be a training-for-action and an outreach group. This is the bridge between personal and spiritual growth on the one hand, and social action for community change on the other hand.

Blocked potentializing. GC views human sin—both individual and collective—as a continuing reality, which is best
understood and changed when seen as blocked potentializing. GC does not ignore the messy, destructive, trapped side
of human life. It seeks to confront these realities and to cope
with them. The enormous destructiveness of humankind,
and the ingenuity of humans in devising new ways to hurt
themselves and each other, are best understood as subversions
or distortions of the enormous creativity that is present potentially in persons. The fact that so much of this potentiality is
never realized, and dies with the person, represents a tragic
waste of God-given talents. It is also a major cause of the mass
destructiveness of human beings throughout history. Viewing
the negative side of human life in the context of realistic hope
for change and growth is the best way to bring about libera-
tions from evil. If we see this evil as inherent and inevitable,
then we tend to slip into a sense of hopelessness, resignation,
and powerlessness. If it is inherent, then a person has no
power except to surrender or wait to be rescued by science or
by God. This passivity hinders our constructive coping with
the reality of interpersonal and corporate evil. An active, intentional response to sin and evil liberates us to experience
the growth which comes from God.

GC seeks to facilitate growth in the six basic dimensions of
human experience—in one's mind, in one's body, in one's
relationship with others, in nature, in institutions, and in
God. Growth is often risky and painful, but it is also
challenging and satisfying.

THE INTERRELATIONSHIP BETWEEN
CULTURE AND PERSONALITY

If the growth approach is to become more than just a
system designed to help individuals and close relationships

grow, it must devise a conceptual bridge that effectively relates the larger sociocultural factors with personality factors. It must show how personality needs and sociocultural dynamics interact and influence each other. GC rejects both the view that personality formation is entirely a matter of sociocultural influences and the view (which Freud held) that sociocultural configurations are simply the extension of intrapsychic dynamics. It is certainly true that personality is shaped by culture. But it is equally true that there are certain basic needs in human beings which tend to influence and shape the development of culture, including its social institutions.

Abraham Maslow's thought provides some of the key insights which undergird GC.[4] Maslow's formulation about basic needs is a useful tool in this effort to integrate psychological and sociocultural factors. He held that there are five levels of needs, and that these needs constitute basic human motivations.[5] These are: 1) *physiological needs*—e.g., hunger, thirst, sex; 2) *safety needs*—for an orderly, consistent, reliable, and safe world; 3) *love-and-belonging needs*—for warm, accepting relationships; 4) *self-esteem needs*—for mastery, competence, adequacy, confidence, status, recognition; 5) *self-actualization needs*—to develop one's fullest talents, capabilities, and potentialities. In this hierarchy of needs, lower needs take precedence over higher needs; most people concentrate their energies on the lowest level of need which has not been satisfied.

To Maslow's hierarchy I would add another kind of needs which influences the way the other needs are perceived, defined, and satisfied on each of the five levels—*spiritual needs*. There are profound human needs for meaning and purpose in all of us for what Erich Fromm calls "a framework of orientation and an object of devotion."[6] Many people in our society meet their spiritual needs by participating in organized religions. The way in which people express their religious needs is influenced by the level of the hierarchy of needs on which their cultural situation causes them to focus most of their energies. For example, in a cultural where interpersonal insecurity is high, religious beliefs and practices tend to focus on giving people transcendent or supernatural sources of safety. To a considerable extent, the quality of a person's spiritual life influences how he or she chooses to satisfy other basic needs.

AN ENERGIZING VISION FOR OUR TIMES

Potentializing—the development of the capacities of human beings for becoming more than they are—is an idea whose time has come. Our period of history gives this concept enormous attractiveness and utility. The flowering of growth centers and movements, the emergence of growth-centered therapies (of which GC is only one), and the widespread interest in consciousness enhancement are indications of this fact. The liberation movements, in both the developing and developed countries, are other expressions of the powerful striving for opportunities to develop one's full potentials and the opposition to all the structures of oppression that block this potentializing. The liberation from political, economic, and psychological colonialism, for which peoples in developing countries are struggling, is another expression of this energizing vision.

Duane S. Elgin, a social policy analyst at the Stanford Research Institute, believes that a new frontier has opened in America—that a new challenge has dawned to replace the challenges of the settling of the West and the challenge of industrialization and technology (the first and second frontiers). The new frontier is one of individual growth and creative social change. The challenge of this new frontier is "realizing our human collective potential." He regards the inward-turning that is widespread in America as not mainly escapism from society's problems, but as one phase of a new stage in human development and consciousness.[7]

If potentializing is an emerging striving in our world, with planet-wide expressions, then social institutions will be viable and relevant to the hurts and hopes of people in the decades ahead to the degree that they become facilitators of human growth and wholeness. Inner growth, including spiritual growth and commitment to the development of the humanizing ethical values necessary for our survival on a livable planet, are two interdependent dimensions of growth.

It may be that we are on the threshold of a *human growth renaissance*, a new stage in the human journey, a new dimension of consciousness, relationships, ethical commitments, and community.

The growth approaches to counseling and therapy offer practical ways to participate in the unfolding of human possibilities and in the actualizing of the vision of life in its fullness for persons everywhere.[8]

FOOTNOTES

1.   John Calvin, *Commentaries on the First Book of Moses Called Genesis*, Vol. 1, translated by John King (Grand Rapids: Wm. B. Eerdmans, 1948), p. 96.

2.   Gerhard von Rad, *Genesis, A Commentary* (Philadelphia: Westminster Press, 1961), p. 56.

3.   Douglas J. Harris, *The Biblical Concept of Peace, Shalom* (Grand Rapids: Baker, 1970).

4.   Abraham Maslow, *Toward a Psychology of Being* (New York: D. Van Nostrand, 1968).

5.   Abraham Maslow, *Motivation and Personality* (New York: Harper & Row, 1954).

6.   Erich Fromm, *Psychoanalysis and Religion* (New Haven: Yale University Press, 1950), p. 21.

7.   D.S. Elgin, "What Waits Across America's New Frontier?" in *Los Angeles Times*, December 19, 1974.

8. The following resources, all by Howard Clinebell, provide futher information on Growth Counseling: *Growth Counseling: New Tools for Clergy and Laity* (15 do-it-yourself cassette courses with *User's Guides,* Abingdon Press, 1973). Part I, "Enriching Marriage and Family Life"; Part II, "Coping Constructively with Crisis"; *Growth Counseling for Marriage Enrichment: Pre-Marriage and the Early Years* (Fortress Press, 1975); *Growth Groups: Marriage and Family Enrichment, Creative Singlehood, Human Liberation, Youth Work, Social Change* (Abingdon Press, 1977); *Growth Counseling For Mid-Year Couples* (Fortress Press, 1977); *Growth Counseling: Hope-Centered Methods for Actualizing Human Wholeness* (Abingdon, 1979); *Contemporary Growth Therapies: Resources for Actualizing Human Wholeness* (Abingdon, 1980).

5

TRANSACTIONAL ANALYSIS

H. Newton Malony

Of the recent secular approaches to counseling, transactional analysis (TA) has been one of the most widely proclaimed and accepted. Conceived by Eric Berne, and made popular by Thomas Harris (in his best-selling book *I'm OK—You're OK)*, TA has been used by Christian and non-Christian counselors alike.

H. Newton Malony is one of several Christians who have seen the possibilities of using TA in conjunction with the teachings of Christianity. He currently is writing a book on this subject, although the present chapter was prepared especially for this volume.

In addition to his work as a practicing clinical psychologist, H. Newton Malony is Associate Professor of Psychology in the Graduate School of Psychology at Fuller Theological Seminary, Pasadena, California. He holds a bachelor's degree from Birmingham Southern College, an M. Div. from Yale Divinity School, and an M.A. and Ph.D. from George Peabody College. He has edited or coauthored several books, including *Current Perspectives on the Psychology of Religion.*

"Get well first—we can talk about it later."

—Eric Berne

"I thought that if I did good secular counseling in a church building—it would somehow come out Christian."

—Benjamin Jones

Look again at the above quotes. The first is from Eric Berne, the founder of Transactional Analysis (TA). The second is from an unknown counselor. They illustrate, on the one hand, one of the more important aspects of TA, and, on the other hand, one of the dangers Christians incur whenever they use secular counseling techniques.

While many Christian counselors are attracted by Berne's emphasis on "non-nonsense healing" they would be wise not to put off talking about TA until later. Otherwise they might fall into the trap of the counselor noted above. He assumed that secular counseling in a church building would come out Christian. It won't.

The motto for Christian counselors might best be "the earlier the better" when it comes to talking about TA or any other secular approach. For it is at the level of assumptions and methods that compatibility or conflict with the Christian faith occurs. Just counseling in a church building or saying a prayer at the end of the session is not enough.

Thus, this chapter is written to Christian counselors who would like to think through TA before adapting or rejecting it as their approach. While I am committed to its use and convinced of its utility, I am fully aware of its limitations. TA would have to be reconsidered in some important ways before it could be termed a "Christian" approach to counseling.

This chapter will include separate sections on the assumptions, the theory, and the techniques of Transactional

Analysis. It is written with the knowledge that TA has become very popular in the recent past. Most persons know something about it. *I'm OK—You're OK*[1] and *Games People Play*[2] have been read by many. Terms such as "Parent, Adult, and Child" are part of common talk. Thus an introduction to TA may not be necessary.

Yet a little knowledge can be a dangerous thing, as has often been said. Persons may think they know more about TA than they do. Much reading is advisable for more serious counselors.

Most important for the present, I hope that those who read the rest of this chapter will acquire skill in evaluating what they know or read about TA. Thus it may become possible to determine whether TA can be of value to Christian counselors.

THE ASSUMPTIONS OF TRANSACTIONAL ANALYSIS

There are a number of underlying assumptions in TA that Christian counselors would do well to consider. While the TA attitude toward religion has fluctuated between disdain[3] and appreciation,[4] the issues of faith or heresy go much deeper. Whether TA quotes the Bible or mentions the church, it (like all other themes of conseling) is always making basic assumptions about the nature of reality. These assumptions are basically religious. They declare which things are of ultimate worth or authoritatively true. Whether these assumptions are Christian or not remains to be seen.

Life Position. For example, take the TA presumptions about Life Position. Thomas Harris suggested that the basic attitudes toward life were four in number. They are as follows:

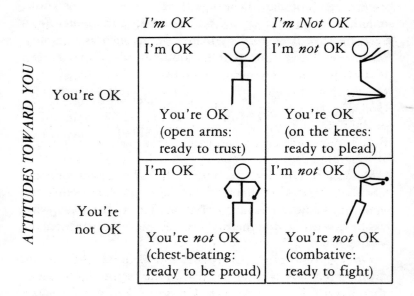

ATTITUDES TOWARD MYSELF

These basic attitudes toward life are assumed to lie behind all human behavior. They are like four different diving boards on which people stand before they jump into the water. They are called Life Positions because each of them represents a stance toward the world.

The foundation of all TA is that we are born with a trusting (I'm OK—You're OK) attitude but lose it in the process of living. We somehow move over into one of the other three positions and become either proud or frightened or combative. To get well is to return to our beginning position of trust. To affirm our own and others' OK-ness is the only way we can live freely and fully. This is the basic assumption of TA therapy.

However, we must ask "Is it really true that we are all OK?" An attitude is one thing. Reality is another. TA asserts that the world is a good and trustworthy place. This cannot be proved, but it can be assumed.

Now Christian faith goes beyond TA at this point. It both agrees and disagrees with the assumption of "OK-ness." It affirms the TA presumption that this is God's good earth and that all persons are created in innocence. But note the difference. For Christians, the earth is good because it belongs to God. He created it and stands behind it. It is not good in and of itself, as TA assumes. Christian faith goes beyond TA to affirm a Maker of heaven and earth. This gives validity to the affirmation "I'm OK—You're OK." It could be said "I'm OK—You're OK because God's OK." TA agrees with the Christian doctrine of creation but does not acknowledge it.

Again, Christian faith differs from TA in describing what happens when a person reaffirms OK-ness as a step on the way to health and wholeness.

On the one hand, Christians would agree that an individual rediscovers what was true in the beginning (namely, that I *was* OK and you *were* OK at birth). Yet Christians would not agree that the other positions of fear, pride, and combativeness were only misperceptions. They, too, are real. The issue is not wrong attitudes or incorrect perceptions, but sin. In fact, the Christian faith assumes that the most correct statement of reality is "I'm not OK—You're not OK"; "All have sinned and come short of the glory of God" (Romans 3:23).

What happens from a Christian point of view when persons affirm their OK-ness? Not a change of attitude, as TA suggests, but a recognition that sin has occurred and that only God can make it right. No effort or insight can return persons to the "I'm OK, you're OK" position. The Christian gospel (cf. Romans 8) proclaims that God in Christ has done this for us. He has forgiven our sin and restored us to a position of OK-ness. Therefore, the Christian corrective to TA is as follows:

"I'm not OK—You're not OK, but that's OK." This is redemption. And again, as in the doctrine of creation, the Christian places faith in God rather than in the world.

Scripts and Games. So it is with several of the other TA assumptions. Take, for instance, the concepts of "scripts and games."

Scripts are those lifelong dramas in which people live life at less than its best—i.e., without joy or fulfillment. This happens when the "Adult" within the personality is weak and life is lived in accordance with an adapted or rebellious "Child ego state." Persons exist in tyranny or turmoil because they decide early in life to sacrifice autonomy and to give power to the critical "Parent" in themselves. Their Child lives in terror of not pleasing or of being caught. TA suggests that scripts can be broken when the Adult is energized and when the Free Child/Nurturing Parent ego states are given power. The person decides no longer to live life in accordance with the wishes or expectations of others.

This is where games come in. Each script contains a number of games. These games are the self-destructive ways of acting which perpetuate unfulfilled lives. All games have at their root "not-OK" child feelings. In fact, games are played, according to TA, to confirm the presumption that one is not worthy of intimacy, or power, or freedom. All games end with "See, I told you so. I'm no good. Nobody loves me." Games can only be ended by changing this assumption.

Once again, I believe that the Christian faith both agrees with, yet goes beyond, this TA analysis. On the one hand, the description of games and scripts could easily be affirmed by Christian counselors, especially since TA does not project blame for the human condition onto the environment or to other persons. Instead, it lays responsibility squarely at the doorstep of the individual. An early life decision was made by the game player and consequent script character. No one else can change the reality except the person himself or herself. A new decision based on trust and a desire to be free must be made. Insight alone will not cure.

Christianity would agree. Sin is original in the sense that it is more personal than racial. Problems come when individuals decide to imprison themselves in the wishes of others rather than in the design of God for their lives. Only personal conviction of this sin and a decision to be free will save persons from this dilemma.

At this point, however, the Christian faith parts company with TA. TA does not analyze the human condition with enough seriousness, and thus it lacks the power to transform person from scripts to freedom. It has a weak doctrine of sin and an inadequate doctrine of salvation. It fails to see that beneath games and scripts lies a universal tendency to live by one's own power rather than to the glory of God (for which persons were created).

Further, TA does not acknowledge that freedom is more the reception of a gift than the achievement of a state of mind. From the Christian perspective, even insight-filled, well-meaning persons remain too guilty or discouraged to change their own lives. Affirming their OK-ness will not work for long.

The only thing powerful enough to break games and scripts is the God who has made all things new through His Son, Jesus Christ (John 1:1-18). Only by faith in something God has done is freedom from the past and freedom for the future possible. This is a Christian corrective to TA assumptives.

TA, therefore, makes assumptions which can be utilized by Christian counselors if they keep in mind that TA is based on humanistic presuppositions which need correcting by the affirmation of the Christian faith. Only then do they become truly health-giving.

Stroking. Four final TA assumptions need mentioning,

each of which has Christian parallels. The first has to do with "stroking," which TA postulates to be the essence of life. People live for strokes. Strokes can be physical touches or visual recognitions. Life wtihout affirmation from others is death. The Christian faith would agree. Persons were created in fellowship and for fellowship (cf. Genesis 3). Even the Trinity exists as a model for what human fellowship is to be.

Transactions. If strokes are the essence of life, transactions between persons are the building blocks of time. It might be said that "Transactions are what we do while we're waiting to die." Life equals transactions. It is no accident that TA stands for *Transactional* Analysis. Personality for TA is not an inner quality but a way of life. History is taken seriously. Life has a sequence of events and certain crisis events. Time is important.

The Christian faith would agree. It is a historical faith grounded in the will of God for persons on this earth, and it involves the presence of a Person who came to this earth. It is transactional in the best sense of the word. It is to TA's credit that it, like Christianity, takes relationships so seriously.

Healing. An additional assumption integral to TA is that healing is possible and probable. The Berne quote with which this chapter began is testimony to this assumption: "Get well first! We can talk about it later." This confidence in the possibility of getting well is characteristic of most TA therapists. They are not content to sit back and listen passively to their clients for months on end. Instead, they are very active and confrontive. They believe in making progress. They think people can change. They expect results.

This optimism about health and wholeness is also characteristic of the Christian faith. But once more this apparent agreement with TA is grounded more in the acts of God than in the inherent power of persons. The Christian faith believes in healing because Christ has come and made all things new (Revelation 21:5). Christians live between the times—the time of His first coming and the time of His return. While the kingdom of God is yet to come there is a strong sense in which the kingdom is already present. Christians expect things to happen to persons. Change and healing are to be the norm in this new age, just as TA suggests.

Language. Finally, TA emphasizes the use of a language which everybody can understand. Such terms as Parent, Adult, Child, Games, and Scripts have become part of everyday language. And this is just what Eric Berne would have wanted. Although some have discounted the popular nature of TA terms, Berne would applaud this development. "Please—no jazz," Berne would say to TA therapists. "Don't use jargon; put your ideas in terms which everyone can understand. Language is for communication—not for increasing the status of the therapist."

Here once again, Christianity would agree. The faith belongs to everybody—not just to biblical scholars. This emphasis on the average person in both TA and Christianity reflects a concern for giving power to the individual. It affirms the privilege and responsibility of each person to work out her or his own way, in psychotherapy and in salvation. As Berne once said, "There is no Santa Claus; in the final analysis each person can and must do their own work." This is good TA and good biblical religion.

THE THEORY OF TRANSACTIONAL ANALYSIS

As has been suggested, TA is a theory based on the assumption that personality refers primarily to the way persons interact, or transact, with each other. This does not mean, however, that there is no personality inside individuals. Persons do indeed have a personality structure which lies beneath their transactions with others.

Most people are familiar with the TA personality structure. The three components of Parent, Adult, and Child (P-A-C) ego states are well-known. What is less well-known is that these are *not* simply new names for Freud's Super Ego, Ego, and Id. Although TA derives from psychoanalysis, the two sets of terms are not synonymous. While TA acknowledges the importance of unconscious forces (such as the Super Ego and Id) it assumes that conscious influences are far more important. Therefore P-A-C are conscious components of the Freudian term "ego." They are only minutely related to Freud's other two components.

TA theory suggests that underneath all interpersonal transactions are P-A-C ego states which have been formed out of personal experience with the important people in one's life. These ego states "intervert" with each other in a manner similar to the way persons interact with each other. In a complex and individualistic manner these conscious ego states permeate, block, or contaminate each other in preparation for transaction with other people. Ideally, the adult ego state determines the transaction and satisfies the desires of the child and parent in a way that is realistic and fulfilling. However, this rarely occurs in a pure sense.

Paralleling this basic structure are certain functional components through which the ego states are expressed. These differing formats are diagramed below.

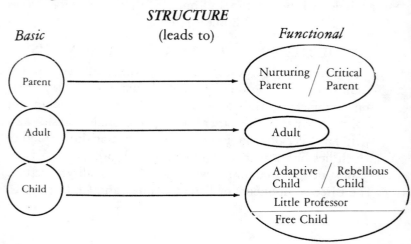

STRUCTURE

Basic   (leads to)   *Functional*

The Parent ego state of another person is experienced as critical or nurturing. Further, we experience the child ego state as adaptive, rebellious, wise, or free. It should be remembered that the basic structure underlies and leads to the functional structure.

TA theory moves from basic P-A-C structure to Life Scripts in successive steps. Basic leads to functional structure. Function leads to transactions. Transactions lead to programs or Games. These, in turn, lead to Scripts. The movement is from single to multiple interactions. The following diagram illustrates this:

Basic   (P)   Functional
Structure (A)→Structure ——→ Transactions→Games→Scripts
        (C)   (a group
                                                    of games)

At this level of description the Christian counselor can use and appropriate TA theory at face value. It is an ingenious and well-thought depiction of *how* persons interact with each other. It includes a fairly authentic analysis of the ways relationships become distorted. I feel that its assumptions that people exist for each other and that personality is the habitual way people get strokes are valid for almost all times and places.

TECHNIQUE IN TRANSACTIONAL ANALYSIS

There is no such thing as *the* TA technique. There are TA *emphases* which are characteristic of most TA therapists. The stress on healing as quickly as possible and the inclination of the therapist to be active and confrontive have already been mentioned.

There is a further tendency for TA therapists to be

teachers. They know that what most people learn in therapy is a language or a way of talking about their problems. TA therapists often spend time in therapy drawing diagrams and explaining terms. They want to share everything they know with the client. There is no hidden jargon which the therapist will use and pretend the client cannot understand. The therapist expects the client to learn the language and to use it in self-exploration. Often the reading of such books as *Born to Win*[5] are prescribed and discussed. Work between sessions is presumed. Although it is *redeciding* rather than *insight* that heals, the knowledge gained through study of TA terms and principles is assumed to provide the foundations on which change is based.

Several other facets of TA therapy need to be noted. The first is the importance of the therapeutic contract. No therapeutic work can occur unless the counselor and client are both clear about what change is desired. The TA therapist puts much effort into getting a contract before beginning to work. Aimless chatter, discussions of the past, or passive listening are foreign to TA. "What would you like to work on today?" is often the beginning sentence. It is assumed that change for the better comes with small steps. Ideally, each session should end with the client feeling that some change has occurred in terms of new knowledge, new feelings, or new skills. Therapy is hard work, and the client should know that a contract is agreed upon and effort is expected.

This leads to the basic approach of the therapist. The therapist offers three Ps—Permission, Potency, and Protection. If, as TA presumes, most problems stem from the tyranny of the Critical Parent over the Adaptive or Rebellious Child, then what most people need is permission to disobey their Critical Parent. The TA therapist becomes the Nurturing Parent for them and gives them that freedom. This is the beginning of change.

Then the TA therapist encourages the client to lean on him

or her. Dependency is nurtured. The therapist says, ''Rely on me—you can make it—I'll share my power with you.'' This is Potency; the therapist is not afraid to be strong, and assures the client that change is possible.

Finally, the therapist knows that change does not come easily. It is very frightening to stop doing what one has been doing, even if that was painful. The client feels threatened when habitual transactions are in jeopardy. At this point the therapist protects. ''Don't be afraid—you are all right,'' are words the therapist offers as the client struggles with new-found freedom.

Thus, Permission, Potency, and Protecton are three typical characteristics of TA therapists as they guide persons toward the goals of healing, freedom, and intimacy.

As with TA therapy, Christian counselors can appropriate TA technique without hesitation so long as they can find ways to incorporate into their basic assumptions the elements of Christian faith. If one presumes in counseling that all there is to rely on is the humanness of client and therapist coupled with a pollyannish affirmation of the goodness of the world—that is one thing. But if one uses the same techniques but assumes that both client and therapist exist in holy history under a God who has conquered death and sin through His Son, Jesus Christ, then that is another thing. It is to this latter stand that I pay allegiance, and I encourage all Christian TA counselors to do likewise.

In summary, this chapter has reconsidered TA assumptions, theory, and techniques in light of the Christian faith. I believe TA to be one of the more viable alternatives for Christian counselors, provided they do not use it naively without reinterpreting TA's optimistic humanism in light of the revelation of God in Christ.[6]

FOOTNOTES

1. T. Harris, *I'm OK—You're OK: A Practical Guide to Transactional Analysis* (New York: Harper & Row, 1969).
2. E. Berne, *Games People Play: The Psychology of Human Relationships* (New York: Grove Press, 1964).
3. Harris, op. cit.
4. M. James, *Born to Love: Transactional Analysis in the Church* (Reading, MA: Addison-Wesley, 1973); and James and L.M. Savary, *The Power at the Bottom of the Well: TA and Religious Experience* (New York: Harper & Row, 1974).
5. M. James and D. Jargeword, *Born to Win* (Reading, MA: Addison-Wesley, 1971).
6. For further information see the following publications by H. Newton Malony, which can be ordered as a mimeographed packet for $6.95 from S & N Distributors, 1315 Medford Road, Pasadena, CA 91107.

TA—Background; TA—Persons As They Are (Personality); TA—Persons As They Become (Psychopathology); TA—Persons As They Could Be (A Prescription); I'm Not OK—You're Not OK—But That's OK; TA—A Bibliography; TA—A Psychotherapist's Confession of Faith: Part I.

6

FAMILY COUNSELING

John A. Larsen

Traditionally, counseling has involved one counselor meeting with one counselee who has a problem and is in need of help. Within recent years, however, counseling has taken a much broader perspective. Groups of counselees often meet together with one, two, or sometimes several counselors. Counseling takes place in a variety of settings, and the goals of counseling are diverse.

One of the most interesting developments has been the growth of family counseling. One family member may "have the problem," but the counselor assumes that no problem stands alone, apart from the influences of a family. Rather than counseling exclusively with one person, therefore, the family counselor meets with the whole family and works with them together.

In this chapter, the author surveys the family counseling approaches, especially as these are based on something termed "systems theory." Systems theory is not easy to understand, perhaps, and neither is it a Christian theory. Nevertheless, it presents an approach which many Christian counselors have adopted.

This chapter was prepared especially for this book.

John A. Larsen is staff psychologist at Klingberg Child & Family Center in New Britain, Connecticut. A graduate of Bethel College in Minnesota (B.A.) and of Duke University (M.Div.), his Ph.D. is from Boston University, where his major field of study was pastoral psychology and counseling. He is a family man (he and his wife have two sons) in addition to being a family therapist.

Family counseling has come of age as a profession. Launched as a movement less than three decades ago, it now claims its own methods based upon an expanding theoretical and empirical base. All the characteristics of a profession are found in the field: degree and training programs, groups which set standards (such as the American Association of Marriage and Family Counselors), a code of professional ethics, licensure in some states, journals, and professional conferences. A majority of family counselors reject the notion that their field is a subspeciality of psychology, psychiatry, or social work. Rather, they claim a distinct professional identity apart from the major mental health disciplines.

Family counseling or therapy represents a radical departure from traditional approaches geared to helping individuals. The most obvious difference is the counselor's emphasis. In family work the target of intervention is a small social group, not an individual. In addition, the approaches, goals, and techniques of family treatment bear little resemblance to those used in individual counseling. Hence, not only is this a relatively new way of helping, but it also is dissimilar in most respects to the more familiar traditional approaches.

Christian counselors, including the clergy, are becoming more and more attracted to family-oriented methods of helping individuals in need of counseling. Though not inherently Christian, the assumptions and goals of family therapy are compatible with the Christian understanding of persons as social beings and with the high value asigned to the family by the church.[1] The church and family counselors both agree that the family fulfills vital personal and societal needs and that it is an institution worth preserving. In their own separate ways, both are working to strengthen this severely threatened social institution.

ASSUMPTIONS

Undergirding all counseling approaches are some basic assumptions which influence the counselor's thinking and actions in relation to counselees. In the discussion to follow, two sets of assumptions are considered—those pertaining to Christian counseling in general and those which specifically apply to family counseling.

In the author's view, two conditions are essential if counseling is to be designated as Christian. *First, the counselor must be identified personally with the Christian faith in such a way that his or her religious orientation can be described as "intrinsic."*[2] By this we mean that the counselor is Christian in attitude, thinking, and behavior. This is in contrast to the person who uses faith primarily as a means of satisfying self-centered needs and desires. The genuine Christian identity of the counselor is necessary, therefore, if counseling is to be considered Christian. But it does not follow that counseling is Christian simply because it is done by a believer.

Second, the events, transactions, and processes which occur in counseling actually or potentially must move the counselee toward that which is defined as good and valuable by Christian standards. In other words, the goals of counseling are directed toward Christian ideals, and the means of achieving these goals are consistent with Christian ethical behavior. No attempt is made here to distinguish between that which is ultimately worthwhile from what is of value for the present. In the Christian view both are considered valid and important ends toward which counseling may be directed.

Christian counseling is different from the related activities of evangelism and spiritual guidance. Evangelism aims at bringing the individual to a point of faith in Christ; the goal in spiritual guidance is to strengthen one's faith and commitment. Because faith is always central in evangelism and spiritual guidance, the content of these activities is uniformly and explicitly Christian.

The aim in Christian counseling, however, is to help people adapt to circumstances and to function more effectively as persons. Not confined to spiritual issues alone, Christian counseling is equally concerned about the social and emotional aspects of human experience. Because the emphasis shifts from one issue to another—depending on the location of the barriers which prevent healthy functioning—the content of counseling does not necessarily deal explicitly with Christian subject matter, as it does in evangelism and spiritual direction. Again, the Christian integrity of the process is ensured by the counselor's identity and by the treatment goals rather than by the content of counseling.

Family counseling is one emphasis among many which a Christian counselor might use in treatment. Specific to this approach are the following assumptions: *first, an individual's thinking, feeling, and actions are best understood when we are familiar with social contexts in which he or she operates.* Behavioral scientists have long recognized that social groups have a major influence on an individual's behavior. Probably all of us have noticed how our own behavior varies depending upon the social situation in which we find ourselves. For example, we tend to act in one way with our employer and in another way with our spouse. Few would dispute the claim that social context influences behavior.

Second, since individuals are strongly influenced by social groups, especially their families, counseling ordinarily is enhanced by considering and/or altering the person's family structure. Some problems, to be sure, are unrelated to kin.

However, in a majority of cases personal difficulties are embedded in the family context and are affected by this important social group. The family may create, encourage, and sustain problems in subtle, unknowing ways. On the other hand, it may support distressed family members and prevent further difficulties from developing. In either case, family participation in the counseling effort may be important, if not necessary, to therapeutic success.

A final assumption pertains to Christian counselees specifically. *While Christian families require special considerations in counseling,[3] they are vulnerable to the same problems and influences as those encountered by their nonreligious counterparts.* The Christian faith offers resources for making the most of the human predicament, but it exempts no one from universal human frailties. Hence the Christian family is susceptible to the full range of potential family problems, including scapegoating, marital conflict, and faulty communication.

THEORETICAL APPROACH

The emergence of various "schools" of family therapy is evidence of a growing diversity in the field. A sampling of approaches could include structural family therapy, strategic family therapy, Bowenian therapy, group family therapy, multiple family therapy, family network therapy, multiple-impact family therapy, and conjoint family therapy. Despite wide differences in technique, all of these schools share a common base in an approach known as "systems theory."[4] In describing this approach it will be necessary to use some technical terms before we discuss counseling methodology.

Family as a system. From a systems perspective, the family is seen as a social unit, otherwise known as a "system." This family system includes various individuals and subgroups (subsystems). A system can refer to the nuclear family alone, or it can involve the multigenerational extended family, depending on how inclusive one cares to be. Subsystems are made up of individuals, groups of two, or any combination of family members.

A family is organized in such a way that a change in one member or subsystem will result in compensatory changes in the others. When one member marries, for example, the whole system is changed. Thus the total system is influenced by what happens to the individuals within it. Similarly, a change in the larger group will affect individual members. Because the members are tied together emotionally, the family functions as a unit rather than as a group of unassociated individuals. This is the fundamental assertion in family systems theory.

System boundaries. Each social system is assumed to have boundaries. There are two important types in a family. First, there are the system boundaries which separate the family from the nonfamily. These boundaries are like the borders of a country. They mark the separation between the innner and outer environments. Second, there are subsystem boundaries which differentiate the system internally. They are like state or regional borders within a country. In the family they enable the various members and subsystems to execute their tasks, roles, and responsibilities without interference from other parts.

Social systems require clear boundaries for proper functioning, just as individuals need good self boundaries in order to manage well in life. According to Minuchin,[5] good boundaries are characterized by some degree of permeability. That is, they can be crossed as other people are consciously and voluntarily given access into the individual's personal "space." In contrast, some boundaries are either too diffuse or too rigid, and this can create confusion. The same is true in families. When boundaries are vague, members are overly involved with each other. Rigid boundaries, on the other hand, produce emotional distance between members.

Family therapists agree that a family gets along best when there are clear boundaries between generations. For example, a child should not intrude into the parents' marital relationship. This does not prevent access to parents, but marital issues are considered out-of-bounds to children. It is one thing to relate to one's parents; it is quite another thing for a child to take over the place of a spouse or to become a counselor to one's parents. At the same time, parents should avoid relating to their children as if everyone were equal. In a family, when generational differences are overlooked, this inevitably will lead to internal disruption and conflict.

System boundaries are important in determining who should be included in counseling. However, subsystem boundaries are of greater clinical importance, since family problems frequently stem from an extreme vagueness or rigidity of the internal boundaries.

Relationship between subsystems. In attempting to understand problems, we normally look for a prior cause of causes which have created the counselee's difficulties. Systems theory does not do this. It assumes that every person or subgroup in the system is contributing to the problem in some way, either knowingly or unknowingly. Thus the question of the first cause of a problem becomes irrelevant. The diagnostic challenge in family counseling is not to uncover the source of a problem but to determine the specific ways in which each member is relating and/or contributing to the presenting problem.

Consider, for example, the classic example of a "helpless" husband and a "controlling" wife. The more she controls, the more helpless he becomes; the more helpless he becomes, the more she controls. Both are caught up in a cycle in which each is reinforcing the very same behavior in the other that is being complained about. From a systems perspective, the behavior of each spouse to a great extent results from the other's behavior. Hence, an adequate understanding of the problem requires a consideration of the total interactional pattern of the marriage, and not just an understanding of one person's problem.

This rather recent clinical discovery of the circular causality in a system is similar to the ancient Hebraic notion of corporate responsibility.

Systemic balance. Families are organized in a relatively stable fashion. Jackson[6] used the term "homeostasis" to describe the stability maintained by families even in the face of high stress. All families, regardless of how healthy or unhealthy they may be, attempt to maintain a balance and stability. When potentially disruptive events crowd in on the family system, members do what they can to keep the family unit stable and together.

We can see this striving for balance when we look at the behaviors of family members. Sometimes there is a fixed and repetitive type of interaction used by the family in relation to certain issues. Because they are subtle and ordinarily denied by the family, these behaviors often are difficult to decipher, even by the trianed eye. But once they are identified, predictions about how the family will respond to a given event often can be made with a high degree of accuracy.

Another indication of the striving for balance is seen when one member of the family blocks the growth in another member. In this case, one family member's attempt to change is met by an overt or covert countermove by another. This serves to minimize the change and maintain family balance. This illustrates how a striving for stability is often preferred even when such stability prevents positive changes that could alleviate family stress.

Finally, a striving for balance is seen when one person in the family begins to develop symptoms as another begins to improve. Roles are changed or exchanged but the basic family structure is not altered. The family is no better off as a result of the "problem member's" improvement. Another family member has developed a problem, since in order to keep a stable balance the family apparently needs one member with symptoms.

Any threat to the family balance predictably will be met by a closing of the ranks to maintain the status quo. For example, a family that typically uses a victim or scapegoat to maintain its stability will, in the face of losing that target member, attempt to retain him or her. If the victim succeeds in breaking free from the role, another member will be selected to serve as a scapegoat. To change a family such as this, the perpetual victimizing cycle must be stopped and replaced with a more adaptive way of operating. Collusion among members to maintain their particular systemic balance is a strong influence which often hinders positive change in the dysfunctional family.

Triangles and triads. The triangle is used in family therapy to picture the interactions between three people. Originally proposed by Bowen[7] in the early 1960s, the concept of triangles has gained wide acceptance among family therapists. In fact, the central triangle—usually comprising a child and both parents—is often considered the cornerstone of family dysfunction.

Bowen repeatedly observed in his study of family processes that two-person relationships (also called "dyads") tend to be stable only so long as they remain calm and free from conflict. Unresolved differences in a dyad typically prompt one or both members to enlist the support of a third party in the family. When this maneuver successfully involves a third person, a triangle is formed.

To illustrate, let us consider a "distancing" husband who keeps his wife at arm's length, and a "pursuing" wife who tries to get as close as possible to her husband. Assume that these people fail to resolve their differences within their empty relationship. No longer able to contain their frustrations, the conflict spills across marital boundaries, and the children are exposed to their conflict. This may take such forms as fighting or belittling and criticizing one another in the presence of the children. There are subtle and unconscious attempts to enlist the aid of the children, although this can be as blatant as directly asking for a child's support against the other parent. One of the children, usually the most vulnerable, will eventually succumb and become emotionally "triangled" into the marital conflict. Far from resolving the problem, this diversionary maneuver by parents only enlarges it by involving a third person.

The rigid triad[8] is one of several types of triangles encountered in a family. In this the parents, who were originally in conflict, join together in a common concern for the triangled child, who is now showing signs of stress. Tension has shifted from the marital side of the triangle to the child, who is showing emotional and behavioral problems. The child thus provides a reason for the parents to come together, and by keeping the focus on this child, attention is diverted away from the parents' troubled relationship. In this case, the child's condition is the price paid for maintaining the delicate marital balance.

A closer look at triangles and their inner workings will shed light on their destructive potential. When two members of a triangle are in a state of conflict, it is better to be on the outside. The child, for example, does not want to be drawn into the marital problem, for by siding with one parent this alienates the other. Predictably, though, each spouse will attempt to involve the child in a coalition against the other. This puts the child in a highly stressful bind.

During periods of calm, two people in the triangle tend to be close while the third is "out." Feelings excluded, the outsider will seek to position himself or herself closer to one of the others so as not to be on the outside. This would not occur, of course, if the third person were not emotionally enmeshed with the other two. If this move succeeds, one of the previous "insiders" is pushed to the outside, thereby setting up another round of maneuvering.

The emotional forces within triangles result in ceaseless moves and countermoves which serve to shift tension from one place to another. Ironically, the tension which throws a two-person relationship off-balance is the same force that keeps the triangle stable. Tension is spread about and contained within the triangles, but the tension is not relieved, since the underlying problem has not been resolved. Hence triangles feed on conflict and provide a hospitable environment in which conflict is kept alive.

Triangles often span across generations,[9] and they can include persons from outside the family. Even God may be triangled into a conflict between a Christian couple. This occurs when couples refuse to deal with each other and instead turn to God in the hope that by so doing their differences will dissipate.

To summarize, a triangle is a defensive interpersonal involvement which serves to protect one or more of its highly vulnerable members. "Triangling" (pulling others into the triangle) is a defensive reaction which comes when there is painful interpersonal conflict. It results from an inability to resolve differences through negotiation and compromise. Triangling, a diversionary maneuver designed to escape conflict, is to be distinguished from responsible attempts to engage a third party to help solve a problem. Because of their defensive approach, triangles and triangling do not resolve family conflict. They perpetuate it.

FAMILY COUNSELING

The particular strategies and techniques used in family counseling depend primarily upon the nature of the problem

and the goals of treatment. Family situations presented in
counseling can, for the most part, be placed along a con-
tinum with two extremes. At one end are those cases in which
an external event (e.g., death of a friend) has temporarily
upset the balance of an intact, well-functioning family. The
problem here is acute, the people are healthy, and the
therapeutic aim is to restore the normal balance. Such situations usually can be helped by brief, directive, and supportive
therapeutic intervention in which defenses are shored up and
people are helped to cope.

At the other end of the spectrum are those situations in
which an external (e.g., arrest for shoplifting) or internal
(e.g., child abuse) event indicates that there are some chronic
systemic difficulties within the system. Individuals and subsystems within these families generally lack clear boundaries.
The therapeutic goal in such cases is to change the system
rather than to relieve symptoms.

A variety of methods may be used at different stages of
family therapy to bring about systemic change. Our discussion of strategies and techniques will be organized around the
stages of relationship—building, assessment, identification
of the homeostasis, goal-setting, and working for change.

Relationship-building. No part of counseling is more important than the beginning. From the outset, the counselor
must attempt to build a strong working relationship with all
family members by winning their trust and respect. This is
difficult to accomplish in a family where there is conflict and
where family members pressure the counselor to take sides.
Nevertheless, good credibility and rapport is needed with all
members if they are going to be challenged to risk a change.
The temptation to become overidentified with certain individuals, or, conversely, to see one person as the problem,
can be minimized by a solid grounding and strong commitment to a systems orientation.

Assessment. An understanding of the problem is necessary

if treatment is to be successful. Because most problems brought to counseling are presented as individual in nature, an early task is to determine whether the problem is, in fact, individual or if it is embedded in family dynamics. If it is family-related, the assessment must then consider the whole system.

A systemic assessment involves drawing a map (in your mind or on paper) of the family organizational scheme. The positions of people relative to one another, the boundaries separating them, and the bridges connecting them are all important considerations in arriving at an overall picture. The counselor looks for coalitions, triangles, and other combinations of people forming key subsystems. The marriage, for example, is carefully scrutinized. Often referred to as the ''executive'' subsystem, it is considered the axis around which other relationships in the family are formed.[10]

The condition of family boundaries is assessed by observing the interactions of members. A mother's overinvolvement with a child, for example, may suggest diffuse or vague boundaries; the absence of communication between a father and a child could indicate a rigid boundary between them. As a boundary-repair agent, the therapist must size up individual boundaries as well as those which differentiate grandparent, marital, parent, and sibling subsystems.

Assessment must also consider how the family members interact. Here the emphasis is on discovering how members relate to each other in fixed and repetitious ways. Are there triangles within the system? It may be discovered, for example, that a father disciplines his son; the son complains to the mother, who in turn approaches the father to plead for leniency. The father refuses to alter his position, and the parents become embroiled in a disagreement. The parents argue and the child gets off the hook. Families often develop fixed patterns of relating around the same controversial issues or critical events. When these are discussed, they trigger.

Such issues and events play a very important function in the family.

Communication must also be sized up. If it is breaking down at critical points, one must determine when, how, and between whom. The counselor must be alert to the possibility, however, that communication problems might result, not from structural difficulties within the family, but because people have never learned how to communicate. The basis of the problem will, of course, dictate what type of counseling is required.

Finally, the positive elements of the family's situation must also be identified. Though troubled families tend to minimize their strengths and overemphasize negatives, some strengths are present in every situation. Resources outside the family are also available in most cases, and these may be tapped to help reach the goals of treatment. The counselor must not only help the family to identify strengths and resources, but also to mobilize them.

Several diagrammatic tools are used at the assessment stage of therapy. In one of these, known as "sculpting,"[11] individuals are spatially positioned in the room according to their relationships at a given point in time or around a particular issue. Members assume postures and expressions capturing their feelings about being in their particular position in the family. For example, a father might be placed in the center of the family, standing on a chair with a frown on his face and pointing at the "problem" child. His position, elevation, expression, and posture signify his place in the family, his authority, his anger, and his focus on the child's misbehavior, respectively. The others are also arranged in ways that depict the interconnectedness of all family members. Besides being a good diagnostic aid, sculpting enables family members to see in an experiential way how they are related to one another. The behavior of the "problem member," for example, is more clearly understood as being related to family dynamics when he or she is placed in the family tableau.

After sculpting the family as it is, the same exercise can be applied to the family's ideal. Contrasting the two in this way provides a visual sense of the changes needed in the family. Hence, the goals of treatment become more concrete and clear to members after their actual and ideal families have been visualized through sculpting.

To summarize, a systemic assessment ordinarily is concerned with the family structure, family interactions, key issues and events, and strengths and resources. The principal diagnostic objective is to uncover the interaction and to determine the part played by each member in maintaining the family balance.

Identification of the family balance system. If a family enters therapy focusing on a single "problem member" (with the problem viewed as his or hers only), then the members must be helped to reformulate their view of the problem along systemic lines. This requires an educational process through which the family is shown how each member plays some part in either maintaining the current situation or allowing it to continue. Up to this point, the counselor has accommodated or gone with the movement of the family, but now a different perspective is introduced.

Anxiety inevitably is aroused at this juncture, since the counselor's approach is certain to challenge the family's defensive structure. A blunt, direct approach will trigger defensiveness, and the family might retreat from therapy. On the other hand, a soft, nonthreatening presentation will probably be ignored. One way of proceeding is to ask for accounts of specific recurring incidents involving the various family members. After listening carefully to details, the therapist returns the same vignettes along with an interpretation of the underlying family interactions. By looking at day-to-day encounters, the family becomes its own illustration of how all are caught up in the presenting problem. Usually this process must be repeated many times over before a systemic understanding replaces the family's long-held views of the problem.

Helping the members to understand how they function as a unit and to see that the "problem member" may serve an important part in maintaining family stability often requires confrontation. This goes beyond educating to challenging defenses. It can be a painful process because it cuts to the heart of the systemic problem. This intervention, like any confrontation, must be made with care and sensitivity as well as with a recognition of the risks involved.

Goal-setting. It is best if treatment goals can be negotiated after the family recognizes its harmful balance and when members agree that this system pattern needs to change. When systemic change is sought, goals are aimed at changing everyone involved. Hence, if one spouse works at not distancing, the other should work on not pursuing.

Goals determine the direction of treatment and are essential to a good therapeutic contract. Without a clear direction, the process will flounder, and both family and counselor will become lost in a succession of aimless encounters. The therapist should ensure that goals are based on what is best for all involved—that they serve the interests of the family and not simply the desires of any single member. Ordinarily this means that goals are negotiated for each person in the family.

Working for change. A shift occurs in the therapeutic process after the treatment goals have been agreed upon. Instead of exploring problem areas and discussing needed changes, family members now begin to actively work toward interpersonal change. In an emotional system like a family, change comes through action rather than through insight alone.

Structural changes may be brought about through a series of prescriptive "homework" tasks to be carried out during the week. A rigid triad, for example, might be broken through a series of assignments aimed at realigning the threesome along more natural lines. The parents could be directed to go out for dinner and the child instructed to invite a friend over for the same evening. The objectives here are to separate the overinvolved parent from the "helpless" child, strengthen the tenuous marital relationship, and compel the child to become involved with a peer.

When wisely used, structured exercises can be effective techniques for bringing about interpersonal change. Sculpting and role plays, for example, are different exercises which help family members gain new perspectives and develop empathy. They provide a structure in which the threat of the unknown is sufficiently reduced to enable individuals to try new modes of relating.

Verbal and/or written contracts between members can be used to govern various aspects of family life. Contracts spell out details of the new ways in which family members have agreed to act. The therapist, as a neutral third party, is in a good position to bring about the negotiation of contracts and to ensure that the agreements reached are fair and equitable.

The family counselor's techniques are geared toward creating a workable structure within the family. They are also aimed at developing mutually satisfying interactional patterns in place of destructive modes of relating. The assumption behind the use of these techniques is that if systems are modified, individual change will result.

LIMITATIONS

Any treatment approach is vulnerable to criticism, and family therapy is no exception. Three difficulties with this approach are apparent. First, because the family system is central, the individual can easily be overlooked. Second, a circular view of causality introduces considerable confusion concerning the question of individual responsibility. Third, a closed-system view of the family may discount the impact of society and the larger environment upon family functioning. The counselor must be conscious of these difficulties, all of which are significant in family therapy.

Logistical problems are also common in family work. Some families are so conflicted and fragmented that the cooperation and involvement of key persons cannot always be enlisted. The difficulty of maintaining good contact with each member deserves mentioning again, since this is a point where therapy often breaks down. The pressure on the counselor to take sides can be extreme, especially in a polarized family. These illustrate some of the difficulties involved in orchestrating a family through the often-tedious process of therapy.

CONCLUSION

Family therapy is a relatively short-term approach now being used in a variety of settings to deal with a wide array of problems. Though it is by no means a panacea for all the ills people encounter, in many cases it does offer an attractive alternative to traditional approaches which focus narrowly on the individual. The intervention opportunities in family work are multiplied many times over, as are the possibilities for change. Family therapy commends itself as an active approach for any counselor interested in helping individuals and families.

Christian therapists using a family orientation to treatment are in a unique position to aid their clients. As Christians they are in touch with the vast resources of the Christian faith. In family therapy they have a specialized technology for effecting positive family change. The healing traditions of Christianity and family therapy come together and enhance each other in treatment conducted by the Christian family therapist.

FOOTNOTES

1. S.R. Reiber, "Western Christian Conceptual Framework for Viewing the Family" in F.I. Nye and F.M. Berardo, eds., *Emerging Conceptual Frameworks in Family Analysis* (London: Macmillan, 1970).
2. G. Allport, *The Person in Psychology* (Boston: Beacon Press, 1968).
3. J.A. Larsen, "Dysfunction in the Evangelical Family: Treatment Considerations" in *The Family Coordinator* (in press).
4. V. Satir, J. Stachowiak, and H.A. Taschman, *Helping Families to Change* (New York: Jason Aronson, 1975).
5. S. Minuchin, *Families and Family Therapy* (Cambridge: Harvard University Press, 1974).
6. D.D. Jackson, "The Question of Family Homeostasis" in *The Psychiatric Quarterly Supplement*, 1957, *31*, 79-90.
7. M. Bowen, "Theory in the Practice of Psychotherapy" in P.J. Guerin, ed., *Family Therapy: Theory and Practice* (New York: Gardner Press, 1976).
8. Minuchin, op. cit.
9. J. Haley, "Toward a Theory of Pathological Systems" in G.H. Zuk and I. Boszormenyi-Nagy, eds., *Family Therapy and Disturbed Families* (Palo Alto, CA: Science and Behavior Books, 1967).
10. V. Satir, *Conjoint Family Therapy,* 2nd ed. (Palo Alto, CA: Science and Behavior Books, 1967).
11. F. Duhl, B. Duhl, and D. Kantor, "Learning, Space and Action in Family Therapy: A Primer of Sculpture" in D. Block, ed., *Techniques of Family Psychotherapy* (New York: Grune and Stratton, 1973).

7

SEXUAL COUNSELING

Curtis Wennerdahl

Some people have suggested that ours is a sex-saturated society. The relationship which God created and intended for procreation, mutual giving, tenderness, and enjoyment has become a perverse, self-centered, manipulative, hedonistic force which dominates much of our thinking. It is used to control other people and sell everything from underwear to kitchen cabinets. Unhealthy attitudes toward sex dominate the business, entertainment, academic, military, and government worlds. It is inevitable that such attitudes should seep into the churches and into the thinking and actions of believers.

Problems of sexual control, unrealistic expectations, and inability to perform sexually are among the issues discussed by Christian and non-Christian counselors alike. To date there are no uniquely Christian approaches to sexual counseling, but there are clear biblical teachings about sex—teachings which must guide our approach to people with sexual problems and insecurities.

In this practical chapter, the author begins with a recognition of the biblical basis for sexuality and goes on to discuss sex counseling within marriage. Some causes of sexual problems are considered, and several techniques of sexual counseling are discussed. The author argues that Christian counselors, including pastors, have a responsibility to counsel people with sexual problems and not to avoid this area, as may have been done in the past.

Curtis Wennerdahl has a B.A. from Rockford College, an M. Div. from Trinity Evangelical Divinity School, and a M.S.W. from the University of Illinois. He has completed the two-year certificate program in Family Therapy at the Family Institute of Chicago, and is a clinical member of the American Association of Marriage and Family Counselors. He has had workshop training in sexual functioning at the Reproductive Biology Foundation and at the Institute for Sex Research. He has a private practice of individual, marital, and family therapy in Grayslake, Illinois, and is a visiting Professor in Pastoral Counseling and Psychology at Trinity Evangelical Divinity School in Deerfield, Illinois.

Today the Christian counselor is called upon to be an expert in many areas. With the current proliferation of sexuality books, Christian counselors (especially pastors) are confronted with yet another specialized area of expertise. To what extent should a Christian counselor be involved in sex counseling? As with other priority decisions, the final answer will depend on many variables, including the counselor's skills or interests, and the needs of the church and nonchurch community.

For at least three reasons, it would be helpful if counselors could become acquainted with the current thinking in the field of human sexuality.

First, Christians are reading the many books and articles on sexuality. Frequently, ideas and assumptions from these writings are quoted in church group meetings. Whenever a counselor or church leader conducts these discussion groups, it can be advantageous for him or her to understand the materials and concepts which are being mentioned by the group members.

Second, as pastors and other Christian counselors continue to do marriage counseling, they will find that more couples are presenting sexual functioning as a problem in their relationship. Thus, it is becoming more difficult to avoid talking about sex both in marriage counseling and in premarital counseling. To be silent when even the Christian media have become more explicit is to run the risk of implying that sexual adjustment is not an important aspect of Christian marriage.

Third, in many areas more clinics are providing sex counseling. When considering referral, it is important for the counselor to know the specific treatment procedures and philosophies. This is especially essential when referring couples for sexual problems. Knowing the assumptions and techniques of a particular sex clinic will enable the counselor to make more-appropriate referrals.

SEXUAL COUNSELING IN BIBLICAL AND HISTORICAL PERSPECTIVE

In this chapter I will summarize some of the assumptions and techniques in the field today. This discussion will be limited to sexual functioning *within marriage.*

At the outset, I would like to make it clear that the Christian writings have been greatly influenced by secular researchers and writers, most of whom draw heavily from behavioristic and humanistic thought. As such, many of their ideas are not acceptable for the Christian. Sexuality and pleasure as ends in themselves are rejected. However, within God's plan for the permanence and the enhancement of marriage, many of the teachings in the current sexuality literature are very relevant for the Christian. As I have studied the secular works, I am continually impressed with the extent to which they are applicable to Christian sexuality and marriage. Most noteworthy is the work of William Masters and Virginia Johnson, of the Reproductive Biology Foundation in St.

Louis. Although most Christians would disagree with their laboratory methods of gathering data, many of their findings are very useful in counseling Christian couples.

For example, Masters and Johnson consider the quality of the relationship to be a prerequisite for optimal sexual functioning. In their counseling program, as summarized in *Human Sexual Inadequacy,* the "relationship is the patient."[1] Although technique is important, far more crucial is effective communication in the relationship. This is consistent with the biblical teaching about sexuality and marriage. The Bible says little about actual sexual technique, but there is much teaching about the roles, responsibilities, and the permanence of marriage.

Although the word "sex" is not in the Bible, God created and fully sanctions sexual expression for the enhancement of the marital relationship. The "marriage bed" is proclaimed to be "undefiled" (Hebrews 13:4). Even though there is a strong biblical emphasis on the procreative function of sex (Genesis 1:27), there are numerous references to the communicative and intimacy aspects of the sexual relationship. The word "know" is frequently used to represent sexual intercourse (Genesis 4:1; Matthew 1:25). There is no doubt that in Christian marriage the sexual relationship is declared by God to be normative, wholesome, and healthy.

In 1 Corinthians 7:3-5 there is a beautiful portrayal of mutuality in marital sexuality. Partners are told not to "defraud one another" (1 Corinthians 7:5). In the marriage bed there is no room for indiscriminate withholding. The use of sex as a vicious weapon is condemned. Rather, the scene here is one of total giving and sharing. Both the male and the female are clearly given this teaching. There is no double standard.

Far-reaching technological and sociological changes have influenced marriage today. More-sophisticated methods of birth control have enabled us to separate more efficiently the procreation from the other functions of sex. The communication and recreational aspects can be expressed without the fear of unwanted pregnancy. Longer life-expectancy and smaller family size have increased the period of time during which couples will not have the daily responsibility for children.

Overall, the family is no longer production-centered. Most theorists now think that members are expecting the family to fulfill deeper emotional needs. Roles such as education have been shifted to other societal institutions. As a result, the demand for marital intimacy, including sexual expression, has increased. In a way, sexual functioning was less problematic when it was more closely related to procreation. Even though the Bible teaches that sex has always had more than a biological function, it is important to remember that Christians also are influenced by the sociological and technological changes within society. As with others, perhaps Christians are expecting too much from the marital relationship. This view is espoused in a most helpful article by the late Sidney Jourard.[2] The suggestion is that marriage itself can become an idol. My intention is not to be overly pessimistic, but I am convinced that if we can be more realistic, fewer couples will seek divorce in their disillusionment with marriage.

Uncomfortable feelings, disappointments, unloving behavior, and unfulfilling sexual experiences are all possible at times in a Christian marriage. Given our sinful nature, a perfect relationship does not exist. However, as couples grow in their Christian experience, hopefully the negatives can be minimized. Knowing the limits of our humanness can help us avoid blaming the marriage per se for every bad feeling. The adjustments, including the highs and lows, would also be experienced with any other human being as a marital partner.

The enrichment of sexual functioning can help couples to feel closer and thus more completely to fulfill their "oneness in Christ'' (Ephesians 5:31). This does not imply that sex should become the all-encompassing goal. There is a need for balance and proper perspective. Sex is only one aspect of Christian marriage. The principle of moderation needs to be applied (Philippians 4:5).

Historically, in psychoanalytic thought, sexual problems have been viewed as symptoms of deeper personality conflicts. For example, a female who was not having an orgasm during intercourse may have been seen as immature and needing long-term psychotherapy to resolve her oedipal conflicts. Similarly, an impotent male would have been viewed as suffering from a castration complex, and would need to work on his conflictual feelings about his mother. In these instances, an important assumption was that the sexual problems were symptoms of underlying personality problems. In counseling, the content of the sex problem was generally not discussed. As the underlying problems would be resolved, it was thought that the sexual problems would automatically improve.

As the practice of marriage counseling matured in the 1950s, a sexual dysfunction was seen primarily as symptomatic of communication problems in the marital relationship. Usually, sex was not discussed. Again, it was thought that sexual functioning would naturally improve as the marital communication system changed. It was not necessary to talk about sex.

According to contemporary theory in the field of sex counseling, sometimes sex itself is the problem. Sexual dysfunctions are not necessarily symptoms of deeper emotional problems or faulty marital communication. Sexual adjustment is discussed openly in the sessions. Specific assignments related to sex are given to the couple. In most settings, all of these tasks are completed at home.

Sex counseling does have a unique focus. However, the differences from other approaches are sometimes more apparent than real. It is my opinion that, at its best, sex counseling draws heavily from all the previous personality and counseling theories.

THE REASONS FOR SEXUAL PROBLEMS

Sex counselors do take thorough individual histories. They do explore many relationship issues in a marriage in addition to sexual functioning; they do help couples improve communication skills; and they do attempt to understand the etiology of sex problems. Counselors also recognize that one contributing factor is the lack of adequate information about sexuality.

Inadequate information. In our society, even with its liberal attitudes, the discussion of sex, even between marital partners, has been taboo. (For Christians this is somewhat puzzling, considering the frankness of the *Song of Solomon.*) Due to this silence, information has been obscured. As in other contexts, when adequate information is missing, human beings tend to fill in their own details. Silence tends to foster misinterpretation. In a work situation, for example, inadequate communication from management regarding the rationale for policy changes characteristically leads to misinformation and suspicion. In sexual problems, both the lack of information and misinformation are considered to be contributing factors. Sometimes problems are alleviated when accurate information is given to a couple. No further help is needed. No other problems develop.

For example, Jim and Sue came to a counselor with the complaint that Jim was impotent. Marital tension and conflicts had ensued because of this, but no medical basis could be found. As the situation was explored, the counselor learned that Jim was unable to have an erection only immediately after they had had sexual intercourse. There is a simple biological explanation for this supposed problem. A male has a refractory period. This means that after a male has ejaculated, physiologically he is unable to ejaculate again for a specific period of time. Although the length of time varies, all men have a refractory period. This has nothing to do with a husband's love for his wife, as Jim and Sue had previously thought. Women do not have a refractory period. Not knowing about this biological difference between males and females, Jim and Sue had assumed that Jim did not love Sue as much as she loved him. As the counselor shared this biological information with them, they were visibly relieved. The conflict and tensions subsided as they realized that their situation was normal.

Another couple, Ed and Joan, reported that, from time to time, they were unable to reach simultaneous orgasm during intercourse. The counselor explained that, although this is very pleasurable when it does occur, it is quite unrealistic for a couple to work toward this as a necessary goal each time they have intercourse. Differences in physiological structure, as well as emotional factors, provide an explanation for why couples do not achieve a mutual orgasm each time they have intercourse. Ed and Joan were encouraged as the counselor gave them this information.

For Jim and Sue, as well as for Ed and Joan, there is no reason to believe that they had severe underlying personality or marital problems. The lack of accurate sex information was the problem itself. In our attachment of emotional meaning to sex, we have disconnected it from its biological components. This does not mean that sex is only biological and is to be expressed indiscriminately apart from God's standard for sexual conduct. But clearly, sex is a natural biological function. Accordingly, as Christians we need to be aware of the biological as well as the emotional and spiritual dimensions of sexual functioning.

Fear. In addition to the lack of accurate information, fear causes sexual problems. We are a performance-oriented society. Outward appearance and measurable productivity have become evidences for adequacy. Not surprisingly, such standards are used in sexual functioning. Television, advertising, and the printed media all tend to portray sex as a gymnastic event. This creates an evaluative atmosphere in which the participants keep score. "How am I doing?" becomes an obsessive thought. As we mentally compare ourselves to the present distorted societal image of sexuality, we are in danger of feeling inadequate. This mental process creates an inner fear. Since couples seldom feel comfortable sharing their mutual fears, these inner thoughts tend to become powerful and overwhelming. Such fears can cause sexual problems. Because sex is a natural function, the process of observing how one is doing can interfere with the spontaneity of its expression.

A sex counselor helps counselees to talk about their sexual fears. Talking alone will itself frequently improve sexual functioning. The counselor will point out that our societal images of sex are unrealistic and artificial. In many instances, secular man attempts to fill his spiritual vacuum by the indiscriminate practice of sex. Myths have developed partially because of our unwillingness to talk openly about sex. For the Christian, it is especially helpful to talk openly about God's plan for sexual expression.

As mentioned before, accurate information can lessen fears about sexuality. Very frequently, the male is embarrassed about the size of his penis. However, this fear is unwarranted. The elastic vagina adjusts to the size of the penis. In addition, although the size of the flaccid penis does vary among men, differences in the size of the erect penis are minimal. All of this is to allay the fears of males. Meaningful sexual expression is not related to the size of the penis. Accordingly, responsiveness is not dependent on the size of the female breast.

Marital conflicts. Sexual problems do not always improve

as information is given and fears are allayed. In such instances, the sexual problems may be more interwoven within a dysfunctional marital style. The marital relationship needs help. Although sex is discussed, much of the focus is on alleviating the marital conflicts. In most sex counseling, all aspects of the couple's relationship are assessed and discussed. This conveys to the couple that sex is only one aspect of marriage, and that all marital behavior can potentially influence sexual functioning.

For example, Rita felt used sexually by Ralph. As the counselor talked with Rita and Ralph, it was learned that Rita also felt used in some of their other marital roles. Ralph often made marital decisions in a unilateral fashion, seldom considering the wishes of Rita. He did not compliment her efforts. He expected her to do all of the housework because "it is her job." The phrase "I love you" usually was absent from his vocabulary. Rita had become angry and had felt used for some time, but she had never told Ralph about these feelings because she did not want to hurt him. Eventually she became unresponsive sexually because of her feeling of being used. The sexual problem was one aspect of a broader relationship problem. Counseling attempted to help this couple to see the need for changes in the whole relationship.

Doug and Wendy told the counselor that their sex life had become dull, mechanical, and boring. As the situation unfolded, it became apparent that this was an apt description of their lives generally. Previously they were growing, vibrant, and involved Christians. Spiritually, they had come to a standstill. Appropriate intervention could help them to enrich their lives spiritually as well as sexually. To treat this only as a sex problem would have been to miss other important factors.

When they come for counseling, couples like Doug and Wendy usually are convinced that their only problem is sexual. If sex was better, all other difficulties would disappear.

Although this may contain a grain of truth, it is important for the counselor to help the couples look at all of the dimensions of their relationship. However, the focus must be shifted carefully. It would be a mistake to simply tell them that sex is not the problem. A counselor needs to begin where the conselees are. In the process, all of the important dimensions unfold as each person feels the safety of the counseling atmosphere. As a result, the couple is able to look at the relationship in a more realistic manner. They are then able to see **the connectedness of all the aspects of their marital functioning.**

COUNSELING TECHNIQUES

A variety of techniques is used in sex counseling. They do not contain magical powers, but are simply human tools for helping a couple to improve their sexual relationship. Without the cooperation of both partners, they become inept, meaningless exercises. Further, the techniques are closely related to basic marriage-counseling skills.

As implied previously, a very basic goal is that of helping couples to discuss their sexual feelings in an open, accepting atmosphere. The barriers which are so characteristic for a couple who has had a history of sex problems can be let down. Such a setting enables them to express their needs in a clear manner. This is not done in a selfish, demanding tone, but in a cooperative spirit, with each party wanting the marriage to grow. Different sexual needs are now viewed as uniquenesses given by God. They are no longer evidences of personal inadequacies and reasons for battles.

Teaching communication skills. The teaching of communication skills is another technique used in sex counseling. Repeatedly, couples report that they do not understand each other.

The market today is flooded with communication materials, but there is one program which I have found extremely helpful.[3] Although not specifically biblical, the ideas are applicable to Christian marriage. The program is designed for groups of couples, but I use many of the concepts from *Alive and Aware* when working with couples individually. The focus is on teaching specific communication skills, rather than on dwelling on the negative past.

In successful sexual expression, communication is vital. Frequently, wives have not had permission to communicate their sexual needs. This is not in accord with the biblical view of marriage. I have frequently told Christian couples that, in order for a husband to fulfill his loving role, he must know all of his wife's needs. Mind-reading lends itself to misunderstanding. The female sexual response cycle is more variable. Stimulation which is pleasurable at one moment may become abrasive if continued. Contrary to cultural myth, men should not be expected to automatically know what women need sexually, nor can women be expected to know how to stimulate men. Ongoing communication is necessary.

History-taking. This is another important technique. In the book *Human Sexual Inadequacy* there is a thorough format for the historical exploration.[4] Especially important are the specific life events which have influenced the person. Even more crucial are the personal meanings which have been attached to these events. How a person feels about a traumatic experience, such as the death of a parent, is necessary information. For example, the impact may be more traumatic because of a fight just before a parent died.

The history-taking can be done orally or in writing, although the actual oral interview allows for a more accurate assessment of personal feelings about one's life events. Both the written and the oral formats provide helpful data, and therefore counselors use both methods with couples.

As I have administered sex histories, sometimes significant

changes have occurred even before other formal techniques have been employed. An explanation is that the mere asking of questions about sexual functioning enables couples to communicate more fully and to explore new possibilities for sexual expression. The counselor's comfort with sexuality is contagious.

In taking a thorough history, the counselor tries to identify the existing sexual value systems. All people have a sexual value system, which consists of their expectations about what is meant by a meaningful sexual experience. Counseling is done within the values that each spouse defines as important for sexual expression. Contrary to popular belief, most sex counselors do not attempt to radically change a couple's sexual values, behaviors, or beliefs.

After the process of history-taking, the couple is given feedback as to how the counselor sees the total picture of their situation. Personal family background, personality development, the present (and past) marital relationship, and sexual value systems all are explored in detail. As this feedback is given, the atmosphere is nonthreatening. For example, when looking at an individual's family background, I make the assumption that characteristically a person develops a unique style of relating in his family of origin. When a family has an unusual amount of tension, trauma, and conflict, the members adopt patterns of behavior in order to cope and to survive emotionally.

For example, Bill and Mary seek counseling with the complaint that Bill frequently withdraws both physically and emotionally. As the counselor looks at Bill's family background, he learns that his parents fought continuously. Bill would hide in his bedroom. He would read books and turn on the radio to block out his parents' loud voices. When he rode in the car with his arguing parents, he would mentally tune them out by thinking about something else. This defense mechanism probably helped him to survive emotionally in such a traumatic environment.

But now Bill is using the same tactic in his relationship with Mary. He withdraws physically, and frequently does not listen to her even when they are in the same room. In response to minor conflicts with Mary, he behaves as he did with his parents. Past feelings are triggered whenever Mary wants to negotiate with him. He fears that they will get into vicious battles similar to those of his parents. Appropriate intervention by the counselor will help Bill and Mary to see that, although his pattern of behavior was useful when he was growing up, it is not as appropriate in his marriage. It is possible for Mary and Bill to disagree without getting into destructive battles. Mary need not continue to blame Bill for his withdrawing. Bill need not feel embarrassed or guilty about what he has been doing. In the counseling sessions, they learn new skills for effective communication. Both are capable of meaningful changes.

Frequently, a couple will appear to be totally incompatible. In the process of the marital evaluation, the husband and wife (independent of each other) are asked to complete the following sentences:

"For me, the most important thing in a marriage is . . . ."
"What I really would like from my spouse is . . . ."
"In our marriage, I would like to be able to . . . ."

Couples who are convinced that they have conflicting needs often will learn from this exercise that, surprisingly, they have very similar wants for their marriage. Repeatedly, friendship, companionship, and communication are listed as crucial ingredients. The counselor identifies these commonalities as a strength in the relationship. Counseling will focus on the various alternative means for realizing their mutual goals. Both a husband and wife may consider spiritual growth to be an important dimension in a successful marriage. In all of their conflict, this similar belief has been blurred.

Forming a therapeutic plan. As the couple's situation is assessed in detail, a specific therapeutic plan is formulated. When there is no commitment to the marriage, sex counseling is usually not indicated. Here the first task would be to help them make a decision about the marriage. Also, a marriage which is enmeshed in severe destructive battles is not a good candidate for sexual intervention. The noise of the relationship needs to be lessened before they are ready for sex counseling techniques.

Sexual dysfunctions can be caused by physical illnesses, Thus, it is very important to have any possible physiological involvement ruled out prior to doing counseling. Because sex is a natural function, it is affected by other physiological processes in the body. Most clinics include a physical examination as an integral part of the counseling program. As in all other counseling situations, possible physical factors must always be evaluated.

Referral. I recommend that the counselor research carefully any counseling resource prior to referral. Some clinics require nudity in the office. For some, this is only a part of the physical examinations by medical personnel, but in other instances there is sexual stimulation by nonmedical counselors to demonstrate physiological processes. This is usually called a sexological examination. A counselor should not hesitate to ask detailed questions, so that he or she can assess a particular clinic program. Practices vary greatly, so one needs to exercise caution.

Sensate focus. In counseling, touch can be employed to help couples to express more-positive feelings. In our fast-paced world, we tend not to allow adequate time for the full range of expression during sex. By assigning touch exercises we give couples permission to take more time for touch rather than rapidly moving to intercourse. This assignment has been called *sensate focus.* Couples are encouraged to explore all parts of each others' bodies. At first, they are told not to touch the genital areas, and intercourse may be prohibited for a period of time. This takes off the pressure. Couples can then explore new dimensions of expression in a nondemanding atmosphere. The mistakes and hurts of the past are minimized. An impotent male no longer hears the demand to have an erection. (As stated before, the fear of not being able to get an erection can in itself cause impotency.) As with other techniques, touch exercises do not automatically change a marriage. A spirit of cooperation and an openness to change are needed. If not, it is possible for couples to use these exercises as additional weapons in their ongoing nonproductive battles.

Frequently in sexual counseling, couples are assigned specific homework tasks. Commonly, physical touch is used. In our society, touch remains an important means of communication, and in a time of crisis, touch becomes an especially meaningful expression of caring. Likewise, in a marriage that has been plagued with misunderstandings, touch can be an efficient method of communicating. In contrast to words, it is less apt to be misunderstood.

Gift exercises. For both marriage and sex counseling, I have developed a structured gift exercise. The husband and wife are instructed to give each other a gift each day for a specified period of time. Usually this is for seven days between appointments. The gift can be anything that they think their partner would like. It could be a tangible object, or something that they do for the other. This exercise has yielded many significant benefits. Because the counselor is making an assignment, there is a tendency for couples to become less defensive and give more freely to each other. This technique highlights the giving and receiving nature of the marital relationship. In the next counseling sessions, each is asked to recount the most meaningful gifts. New learnings and insights are encouraged. Often this exercise can rekindle the creativity and pleasuring which were experienced when they were dating. It also demonstrates that counseling is an active process needing their full participation.

Furthermore, during sex counseling couples are helped to enrich the overall quality of their lives. In sexuality, popular culture has overemphasized intercourse. Contemporary sex theorists stress that intercourse is only one aspect of sexuality. Couples are encouraged to develop several activities which draw them closer together. For Christian couples, sharing their spiritual growth can enhance feelings of intimacy. Going for a walk in the park or reading a book together can be meaningful. Although intercourse is an important expression, ideally a couple can identify many other ways to enrich their relationship.

In sex counseling, a safe atmosphere is created in which spouses can become vulnerable with each other. Strengths as well as weaknesses can be acknowledged. This opening up can in itself create closeness. If used discreetly, humor is very helpful. There is no intent to demean or make fun of the participants. However, humor can take the pressure off. Life sometimes becomes too serious.

Failures. Setbacks and making mistakes are an important part of sex counseling. Sometimes the counseling proceeds too smoothly in a superficial manner. In these situations, change often is short-lived. Couples should be prepared for the positive value of failure. Their characteristic, nonproductive styles of relating become very clear when they are not successful in completing the assigned tasks. New learning can readily take place at these times. Like all of Christian experience, significant growth frequently occurs during episodes of pain, frustration, and failure.

CONCLUSION

Hopefully, some of the ideas from the field of sexuality contained in this chapter can be incorporated into the Christian counselor's marriage-counseling ministry. Not all techniques are appropriate in every situation. God has enriched our relationships with uniqueness. Also, for many problems there are no easy human answers. Prayer, patience, and perspectives are needed.

Sexuality is only one dimension in God's plan for our lives. As with other social movements, it is tempting to see a supposed human solution to problems as the final, definitive answer. Such is mere folly. Better marital sexual adjustment is only a partial solution for marital problems today.[5]

FOOTNOTES

1. William Masters and Virginia Johnson, *Human Sexual Inadequacy* (Boston: Little, Brown & Co., 1970), pp. 2-3.
2. Sydney Jourard, "Marriage Is for Life" in *Journal of Marriage and Family Counseling,* July 1975, pp. 199-208.
3. Sherod Miller, Elam Nunnally, and Daniel Wackman, *Alive and Aware* (Minneapolis: Interpersonal Communication Programs, Inc., 1975).
4. William Masters and Virginia Johnson, op. cit., pp. 34-51.
5. For further information on sexual counseling see the following:
    Helen Singer Kaplan, *The New Sex Therapy* (New York: Brunner/Mazel Inc., 1974).
    Tim LaHaye and Beverly LaHaye, *The Act of Marriage* (Grand Rapids: Zondervan Publishing House, 1976).
    William Masters and Virginia Johnson, *Human Sexual Inadequacy* (Boston: Little, Brown & Co., 1970); *Human Sexual Response* (Boston: Little, Brown & Co., 1966); and *The Pleasure Bond* (Boston: Little, Brown & Co., 1970).
    Sherod Miller, Elam Nunnally, and Daniel Wackman, *Alive and Aware* (Minneapolis: Interpersonal Communication Programs, Inc., 1975).
    Ed Wheat and Gay Wheat, *Intended for Pleasure* (Old Tappan, NJ: Fleming H. Revell Company, 1977).

8

NOUTHETIC COUNSELING

Jay E. Adams

In his book *Competent to Counsel,* Jay Adams describes how he became involved in the field of counseling. As a pastor, with "virtually no knowledge" of how to counsel, Adams was frustrated in his attempts to help needy parishioners. With degrees in homiletics and speech, he had had no formal training in counseling, and his attempts to use Rogerian and Freudian principles proved disappointing. So he read as many books on counseling as he could find, enrolled in counseling courses, and spent a summer with O. Hobart Mowrer at the University of Illinois. Slowly, Adams began to develop his "nouthetic approach," an approach which was introduced in *Competent to Counsel* and has been developed in numerous books and pamphlets subsequently.

Among evangelicals, especially evangelical pastors, Adams is perhaps the best-known and most widely heeded teacher of Christian counselors. Nevertheless, his work is surrounded by controversy, and especially among those who disagree with his criticisms of contemporary psychology and psychiatry, who fail to share his views of Scripture, or who resist the somewhat combative style which characterized the writing in his earlier books.

The present chapter, which was prepared specifically for this volume, gives the reader a concise overview of nouthetic counseling, and makes reference to those books which outline the theory in more detail.

Jay E. Adams is Dean of the Institute of Pastoral Studies,

editor of *The Journal of Pastoral Practice,* and Visiting Professor of Practical Theology at Westminster Theological Seminary. He has the A.B. from Johns Hopkins University, the B.D. from Reformed Episcopal Seminary, the S.T.M. from Temple University School of Theology, and the Ph.D. (in speech) from the University of Missouri. He held a Post-Doctoral Eli Lilly Fellowship in psychology at the University of Illinois. He presently lives with his family near Macon, Georgia.

Nouthetic counseling was born out of desperation. Because both the referral method (''refer and defer to more professional help'') and the integration model (some Bible, some psychology, etc.) had proven unsatisfactory,[1] it became necessary to strike out on new paths. The new proved to be the old.

At length, the Scriptures of the Old and New Testaments were found to contain ''all things necessary for life and godliness'' (2 Peter 1:3), not only for normal everyday living but also for the change of attitudes, beliefs, values, and life patterns.[2] In other words, we discovered that counseling was not the business of a caste of self-styled and self-appointed professionals, but was the work of pastors (when practiced as a life calling) and the task of every Christian (in informal contexts).[3] While physicians have a valid work to do (in medically treating those whose abnormal behavioral patterns stem from organic causes like brain damage, brain tumors, ingestion of toxic substances, etc.) and psychologists rightly may study human functions experimentally, descriptively reporting these (I am thinking of such work as the studies done by the Harvard Sleep laboratories on the effects of sleep loss), neither physicians nor psychologists have biblical warrant, training, or standards provided by their training for doing counseling.

Counseling has as its object the task of changing the way in which people live their lives. It involves the alteration of values, attitudes, beliefs, behavior, and the like. Where can the proper standard for such change be found? Nouthetic counselors see the Bible as the one source.

From the Bible alone generations of Christians, living before Freud, were able to advise one another rightly, and Jesus Christ (using only the Old Testament) was able to become the world's perfect Counselor. God did not leave His people without adequate instruction for living and changing all those years before modern psychotherapy appeared. The Bible, with its messages of salvation and sanctification, has all that anyone needs to live in patterns that are pleasing to God and beneficial to one's neighbor. Indeed, the advent of psychotherapeutic counseling meant that unbelievers had determined to develop new and different ways to teach man to live and to handle his problems—ways that did not include salvation or sanctification; ways that ignored Jesus Christ. In thus wrongly entering the area of counseling in this way, psychotherapists of all sorts have (in effect) set themselves up competitively over against God and the Bible. That is why integration of *counseling psychology* (or psychiatry) and *biblical counseling* is impossible.[4]

Nouthetic counselors see the admitted chaos in the field of counseling (Zillborg says that the field is in "disarray," just as "at the beginning")[5] as the direct result of the failure to use the Bible, God's textbook, as the basis for counseling. There is no consensus in the field of counseling (unlike most others) because the one book that could have brought consensus has been set aside for human substitutes.

Over the years, since 1969, when Nouthetic Counseling was introduced, it has enjoyed a phenomenal acceptance among Bible-believing pastors and Christians. Literally thousands today are successfully engaged in doing Nouthetic Counseling. Training is offered at several centers in the U.S.A. (especially at the Christian Counseling and Educational Center, Laverock, Pennsylvania),[6] as well as in Bible colleges and theological seminaries. A laymen's course on tape as well as a program taught in the Washington, D.C., area by John Broger has been developed. Books on Nouthetic Counseling by now have been translated (or are being translated) into twelve languages, worldwide interest has been expressed (training centers for other countries are being planned), and lecture tours have been conducted on four continents (with invitations from a fifth). Recently I even had the opportunity to lecture about Nouthetic Counseling at the University of Vienna psychiatry clinic to a capacity audience. Austrian Christians claim that this was the first time that the gospel has been publicly presented there. Several master's theses and one doctoral dissertation have been written on Nouthetic Counseling. Interest in biblical counseling has grown immensely since its inception. God has blessed beyond all expectations.

Negative evaluations by those who hold other viewpoints (some of whom are writing other chapters in this book) increasingly show concern over the spread and acceptance of Nouthetic Counsleing. Yet the systems they offer instead are highly unsystematic and usually eclectic in nature. "How-to" material is significantly lacking. It is not the desire of Nouthetic counselors to argue and debate with them; rather their concern is to continue to help those who want to become better counselors. Already the influence of Nouthetic Counseling can be seen in the writings of some who have been opposed to it. Our hope is that at length many others will join forces to help us become even more biblical in our approach.

In 1977, the National Association of Nouthetic Counselors was formed. The purpose of this organization is to promote and upgrade biblical counseling by certifying counselors, counseling centers, and training centers.

THEORY

The Greek word *nouthesia,* frequently appearing in the Greek New Testament in counseling contexts,[7] is the term from which "Nouthetic" has been derived. There are three distinct but interrelated elements in the word *nouthesia:*[8]

1. *Change* is needed because the counselee is living in a manner that is inconsistent with biblical standards;

2. *Confrontation* of the counselee by verbal means (counsel) designed to bring about the desired change must be given; and

3. *Concern* for the counselee's welfare is uppermost. The confrontation and change flow from love. This love is familial.

Love, then, is the motivating factor in Nouthetic Counseling—love by the counselor that seeks to promote love for God and neighbor in the counselee.

All nonorganically caused problems[9] are considered to be hamartigenic (sin-caused). Sinful living (failure to express love toward God and one's neighbor, as such love is defined in the Scriptures) is at the heart of the counseling focus.

Even when a child has been tragically sinned against (and Nouthetic Counselors do not minimize the tremendous influence of parents and others, as some falsely claim), it is possible (and always necessary) for the counselor to discover the sinful patterns of response to such sin that the counselee developed (perhaps as a child). Others, though very influential, exert their influence only through such responses. A child, born a sinner (because of his sinful nature), will develop many such wrong habitual responses that may persist into adulthood and cause him much difficulty. But—and this is important—others cannot *cause* those patterns. Nor can they cause the ulcers, etc., that at length also may appear. Others are responsible for their sin against God and the counselee, but God also holds him responsible for his response to it. Jesus did not get an ulcer on the cross. Rather, He prayed for those who crucified Him. He assumed responsibility for His response to such sin and handled wrongdoing toward Himself righteously. He has required His disciples to do the same.[10]

Change occurs in Christians because Jesus Christ died for them, paying the penalty for their sin and freeing them from its power. He did not die to change their genes, to heal so-called "mental-illnesses,"[11] or to change the counselee's past. He did not come to heal our memories (there is absolutely nothing in the Bible about this), but to pardon our sin and change our relationship to God and our neighbors. Through biblical direction by the Holy Spirit's power He enables us to recognize and overcome sinful patterns so that more and more we may walk in God's new righteous ways instead. Biblical counselors, like all other counselors, are concerned with change. However, these alternative patterns of life are not merely tacked on or substituted for the old sinful ones; they issue from a changed heart (the inner life of the believer) that transforms outward behavior.

Because of this commitment to change at a level of depth (in the heart), Nouthetic Counselors consider evangelism an absolute necessity when attempting to help non-Christians. They are unwilling to offer unbelievers something less than the gospel[12] because

1. God has not authorized us to reform people outwardly;

2. To do so would misrepresent the true nature of His magnificent redemption in Christ; and

3. They see a danger in effecting outward change —counselees may rely upon it with false assurance that problems have been solved, when what has happened is that one outward set of ungodly responses has been exchanged for another.

Problem-oriented evangelism (or precounseling), however, must be adapted to each situation as (indeed) all evangelism must. Minimal initial help (never offered as counseling, but rather clearly distinguished from it) may be given

1. to clear the way of encumbrances for a presentation of the gospel to the unbelieving counselee;

2. to raise hope when there was none or when it has been lost.

But in all that he does in precounseling, the counselor makes it plain that this is preliminary to the real counseling that can really solve the counselee's problems. At some point he will explain that such solutions are the right and privilege of those who become members of God's family. Regeneration, then, is *the* prerequisite for change at a level of depth.[13]

Counseling proceeds on the basis of the four-step biblical process for change outlined in 2 Timothy 3:16.[14] The Christian counselor:

1. Confronts the believing counselee with God's requirements for faith and life found in the Bible ("teaching");

2. Uses pertinent Scripture portions (with exposition in context—not as if handing out a prescription) to bring about acknowledgment and confession of sin ("conviction");

3. Helps the counselee to get out of his predicament through forgiveness, leading to a change

of relationship with God and others ("correction"); and

4. Shows him the alternative biblical lifestyles that please God and helps him to develop these in place of those patterns previously adopted ("training in righteousness").

The Scriptures are used as the basis for all counseling. This is what makes Nouthetic Counseling unique. "Why do you use the Scriptures as the textbook for counseling when you don't use them as the textbook for engineering, medicine, or a hundred other disciplines?" is a question frequently asked. The answer is simple: the Bible was not intended to be a textbook for engineering, medicine, etc., but it *was* intended to be the textbook for helping people come to love God and their neighbors. It is *the* textbook for living in this world, and, preeminently, for learning all that is necessary to change from a sinful to a righteous way of life. All that is needed to form values, beliefs, attitudes, and behavioral styles is in the Scriptures. Indeed, no other book can do so, and all other books that attempt to do so thereby become competitive.

In the training of biblical counselors, the Bible again is the guide. The discipleship method is used. In John 8:26, 28, 31, 38; 5:19,20,30; 3:32 there is a theological base for the method. Jesus Christ entered into a Father/Son discipleship relationship that becomes the model for Christian training. He tells us that He learned by seeing and hearing. In contrast to the Greek "academic" model (derived from the academy), which emphasized hearing alone (and spawned the textbook/lecture method), the biblical method is fuller and stresses teaching by both verbal instruction and observation. The whole man is taught in an integrated manner by the whole man. Truth is integrated into life.[15] In order to teach counseling this way, Nouthetic Counselors have established centers in which counseling is taught not only by lecture, reading, and discussion, but also by role-play, case study, seminars, and participant observation in actual counseling sessions. Content and skills are taught in an integrated way.

One of the principal concerns of Christian counselors is to introduce God into every counseling problem and every counseling session—not in some peripheral way, but at the center of all that is said and done. Pleasing Him—not relief from the problem—must be uppermost. Every counselee is called upon to "seek first God's empire and His righteousness." He is shown that what has happened has not happened apart from God (even a sparrow that falls does so only in His providence). Quite to the contrary, God is deeply involved in it all, working for His honor and the welfare of all His children (two things that always go together). Counselees do not always see this readily, but when presented in depth and accepted as the working basis for all else, everything changes. For more on this, see "Counseling and the Sovereignty of God" in *Lectures on Counseling.*[16]

This stance toward one's problems, along with the many details that grow out of it, leads to Christian hope[17]—an essential ingredient in all effective counseling. For more about hope, see *The Christian Counselor's Manual.*[18]

Recently views aimed at countering the idea that Christians can change in their own strength (this idea often is called "depending upon the arm of flesh") have begun to stress that the Christian's only responsibility in solving his problems is to assume no responsibility for doing so. The more he "lets go and lets God" the better. The intention behind this is good, but the alternative offered is erroneous and dangerous. Galatians 2:20 is often misinterpreted to mean that the believer must let Christ (instead of the believer) live His life through him in such a way that he is quite passive. Actually, the verse says that the believer is responsible for living his life. It is the Christian—not the Holy Spirit (Christ in us)—who does the believing and the obeying. The true biblical teaching combines human responsibility with divine power. Changes (sanctification) must be made by the Holy Spirit's power (not ours) and at His direction, but by His power *enabling the counselee to accomplish them.* [19] If Christians had no responsibility to do anything other than to get out of God's way (as it is often put) most of the New Testament wouldn't have been written. First Corinthians, for instance, could have been reduced to about a page's length. The details of the responsibilities for change that are set forth in such depth would have been unnecessary. No, the Holy Spirit does not do *instead of us* what He *requires of us* and instructs and empowers us to do.

METHODOLOGY

Nouthetic methodology is not borrowed from other systems. A distinction is made between "means" and "methods" (which are means committed to achieving the ends of a particular sort of talk designed to accomplish one or more of the goals of a system). All sorts of means may be used by Nouthetic Counselors in developing biblical methods, but methods must always grow out of and be designed to effect those ends that are set forth by God in His Word.

This means that Christians cannot be eclectic in their use of methodology, but are obligated to do the hard work of understanding problems biblically, addressing biblical answers to them, *and doing so by means that are consistent with biblical presuppositions and principles.*

Among the numerous counseling methods that have been developed from biblical sources are these:

1. Attempting to have all involved parties present in the counseling session (cf. *Competent to Counsel);* [20]

2. Allowing no slander or gossip in counseling

sessions about persons not present (cf. *Competent to Counsel; The Big Umbrella*);

3. Sorting out each counselee's personal responsibility before God and his neighbor in the problem (cf. *Competent to Counsel*);

4. Analyzing and defining problems in scriptural (not medical, psychological, or euphemistic) language (language has sign value; labels are signposts: "sickness" points to a physician for help, "sin" points to Jesus Christ. Cf. *The Use of the Scriptures in Counseling*); [21]

5. Laying out biblical plans of action founded on adequate data gathering (cf. *The Christian Counselor's Manual*);

6. Emphasizing the two-factored nature of sanctifying change ("from" and "unto"; the put off/put on dynamic) that is in accord with the basic change that has already occurred "in Christ" (cf. *The Christian Counselor's Manual*);

7. Working within the framework of the church by its care and discipline, with its full authority and employing all its resources (cf. *Your Place in the Counseling Revolution;*[22] *Shepherding God's Flock, Vol. 2);*[23]

8. Expecting change following every session, and planning and prescribing for it (cf. *The Christian Counselor's Manual*);

9. Focusing upon the period (usually a week) between sessions as the time when change principally occurs in ordinary life situations (cf. *The Christian Counselor's Manual*);

10. Teaching counselees the biblical dynamic of

the change that occurred, how to avoid future failure, and what to do (without running back to a counselor) to get out of it should they happen to fall into it (cf. *The Christian Counselor's Manual*).

LIMITATIONS

While much has been achieved, much more needs to be. Nouthetic Counseling is in its infancy. And even though all sorts of problems from depression to marriage difficulties have been solved biblically, more scriptural teaching, more sophisticated methodology, etc. are yet needed.

There are—of course—no limitations to what God can do. Other than those limitations that we impose upon the counseling sessions by our failure to understand fully or apply adequately what He has revealed in the Scriptures, there is no limitation in a biblical system of counseling that deals with sin. The umlimited power of the cross is at the disposal of every counselor who seeks to change the life of his counselee.

CONCLUSION

Biblical counseling is a growing movement. It is of no importance for a counselor to call himself a *Nouthetic* counselor (I have used the term merely for convenience). But it is of the utmost importance for him to use the Bible and the Bible alone as the basis for his counseling. Biblical counselors know that they simply cannot talk about man (or about changing man) without wading knee-deep into theology. It is important, then, for a Christian counselor to have a background in the Scriptures—in exegesis (the interpretation of Scripture), in theology (the systematization of scriptural teaching), and in practical theology (the application of Scripture to life in preaching and counseling). In short, Christian counseling is one important aspect of the ministry of the Word.

FOOTNOTES

1. Jay Adams, *Competent to Counsel* (Grand Rapids: Baker, 1973), Chapter 1.
2. Cf. 2 Timothy 3:15-17. See expositions of this passage in Jay Adams, *Competent to Counsel* (Nutley, NJ: Presbyterian and Reformed, 1970); and Jay Adams, *The Christian Counselor's Manual* (Nutley, NJ: Presbyterian and Reformed, 1973).
3. Cf. relevant arguments in Jay Adams, *Competent to Counsel, The Christian Counselor's Manual,* and *Lectures on Counseling* (Nutley, NJ: Presbyterian and Reformed, 1977).
4. For more on this see "The Sovereignty of God and Counseling" in *What About Nouthetic Counseling?* (Nutley, NJ: Presbyterian and Reformed, 1976).
5. Cf. Jay Adams, *Competent to Counsel,* p. 1. Zillborg is both right and wrong. The field *is* in disarray, but the problem is worse than at the beginning.
6. Inquiries should be sent to Dr. John Bettler, director of CCEF, 1790 E. Willow Grove Ave., Laverock, PA 19118.
7. *Parakaleo* also speaks about counseling, but less frequently in counseling contexts, and in John's writings has the idea of "counselor-at-law."
8. It was because no English word combines all three that the Greek term was brought over into English.
9. Nouthetic counselors work closely with physicians to help determine what behavior is caused by organic factors.
10. Cf. *How to Overcome Evil,* a book that deals with this portion of Scripture (Nutley, NJ: Presbyterian and Reformed, 1978).
11. For more on this euphemistic and misleading term, see "Is Society Sick?" in *The Big Umbrella* (Nutley, NJ: Presbyterian and Reformed, 1973).
12. 1 Corinthians 2 sets forth the two points of the gospel: 1) Christ's substitutionary and penal death for sinners; 2) His bodily resurrection from the dead.
13. That is why Nouthetic Counselors look on all other counseling as shallow and inadequate.
14. I have discussed this in a number of books in detail, especially *The Christian Counselor's Manual, Competent to Counsel,* and *Lectures on Counseling.*
    For more on this see comments on "example," "imitation," and "modeling" in *Competent to Counsel* and other books.

16. Op. cit.
17. This is never a "hope-so" hope, but a confident expectation based upon the unfailing promises of God in the Bible.
18. Op. cit.
19. I plan to say more about this in a forthcoming book on the theology of counseling.
20. In this section the references in parentheses all refer to books listed earlier in these footnotes, unless indicated below.
21. Jay Adams, *The Use of the Scriptures in Counseling* (Grand Rapids: Baker, 1975).
22. Jay Adams, *Your Place in the Counseling Revolution* (Nutley, NJ: Presbyterian and Reformed, 1975).
23. Jay Adams, *Pastoral Counseling: Shepherding God's Flock, Vol. 2* (Grand Rapids: Baker, 1975).

9

BIBLICAL COUNSELING

Lawrence J. Crabb, Jr.

In one sense, many of the chapters in this book could be titled "biblical counseling," but this is a term which Dr. Crabb uses consistently to describe his work. His "Institute of Biblical Counseling," established several years ago in Florida, seeks to "provide local churches with adequate resources to meet their own counseling needs (and to minister to their community) by training mature Christians from each church in biblical counseling.

The author believes that biblical counseling involves three emphases. First, *encouragement,* which often comes from a community of believers, and which provides loving support for people who are struggling to meet the crises and demands of life. *Exhortation* involves "pointing out specific biblical solutions to the problems of life." Thirdly, *enlightenment* involves helping people to see and understand how wrong ideas about themselves, about life in general, and about God can result in ineffective patterns of living.

Lawrence J. Crabb, Jr., is a graduate of Ursinus College and holds an M.A. and Ph.D. in Clinical Psychology from the University of Illinois. Currently he is in private practice in Boca Raton, Florida, is a popular speaker at conferences and seminars, and is Director of the Institute of Biblical Counseling. He is author of *Basic Principles of Biblical Counseling* and *Effective Biblical Counseling.*

A woman recently told me, "I'm at the point of wondering if God really is active in our lives today. I've tried so hard to follow His way, but I'm not the new creature which the Bible says I should be. What's wrong?"

Christians have long proclaimed with joyful certainty that "Christ is the answer." Our churches are full of people who smilingly testify to each other that "Jesus changed my life" and then, in the privacy of their closet, they wrestle with unfulfilled longings and painful emotions.

As our culture has become more open about acknowledging personal hurt, we have become more aware that the Christian life as taught from the pulpit and practiced in the pew often does not each down into the fabric of life. Many people who claim to have sincerely "tried Christianity" are not finding the answers they need to maintain an even keel in life.

In their disillusionment with Christianity, some have outrightly opted for a humanistic approach to life: live for whatever maximizes *my* pleasure and minimizes *my* pain. Others have retained the Christian vocabulary and externals (church attendance and other "Christian" activities) but have turned to the humanistic solution of self-gratification to dull their discontent. Some continue to cling to the hope that Christ really is the answer despite inward aching and unmet longings.

The choice for many seems to be: give up Christ and get happy or hold on to Christ and stay miserable. Fear and guilt bind some to their Christian profession. Stubborn, well-entrenched conviction holds others. And an attitude of "Lord, to whom else shall we go" keeps still others faithfully within the evangelical boundaries of belief and behavior.

In response to the perplexing situation of an unabundant Christian life, a new breed of helper has appeared. He or she is called a "Christian psychologist" or "Christian counselor." He or she helps people to retain true biblical beliefs and at the same time to resolve hang-ups, neurotic symptoms, empty feelings, temper outbursts, unhappiness, lethargy, and the entire host of nonmedically caused human problems.

In the last two decades, the field has burgeoned to the point where we now have almost as many different "Christian" counseling approaches at we have secular approaches. Christianized versions of T.A., gestalt therapy, rational-emotive therapy, psychoanalysis, and behavior modification compete for the allegiance of evangelicals. For some, confusion has given way to clarity in Bill Gothard's "Systematic Theology of Practical Christian Living." Others have warmly responded to the nouthetic counselors' insistence that their approach is truly biblical.

In this brief chapter, I want to add my voice to the din, hoping that the result will not be further confusion but rather a move toward clarifying an approach to counseling which is narrow enough to be accurately called biblical and broad enough to transcend psychological denominationalism.

INTEGRATION OF PSYCHOLOGY AND CHRISTIANITY

The first step in developing a biblical psychology which touches people where they live seems to be arriving at a broad position on the thorny and far-from-resolved problem of integrating psychology and Christianity. The problem facing evangelicals who are wrestling with integration is simple enough to describe. There is a body of revealed truth in propositional form to which all true evangelicals are committed. This is the inerrant, inspired Word of God. There is another vast literature consisting of the diverse, sometimes-contradictory theories and observations which we can simply call secular psychology. Let each be symbolized by a circle. The circle of revealed truth revolves around the Person and work of Jesus Christ. Secular psychology is built upon the very different presupposition of humanism, a doctrine which fervently insists that mankind is central in the universe and that his or her individual welfare is supreme. The question facing the integrationist is "What is the relationship between the two circles?"

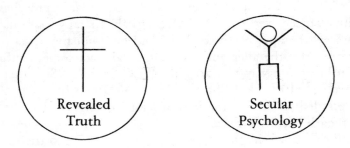

Evangelicals have generally followed one of four positions. Some regard the two fields as SEPARATE BUT EQUAL. If you have the flu, see a physician. If you want to design a building, talk with an architect. If you suffer from psychological disorder, consult a psychologist or psychiatrist. The most critical issue in selecting a professional to help you is competence, not religious beliefs. If your problems are spiritual, however, check with your pastor. This position can be sketched like this.

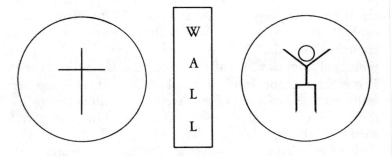

A second group tends to snatch a few relevant concepts from Scripture, mix them with helpful ideas from psychology, and serve up a tasty blend called Christian psychotherapy. The problem with this approach, which I call the TOSSED SALAD model, is that concepts with antagonistic presuppositions do not get along well over a period of time. A definite tension exists, which can be resolved either by discarding all but one set of presuppositions or by adopting a Hegelian view, in which truth exists as the interplay between opposite positions. The latter solution, which has crept into much of our thinking, is spiritual suicide. Rather than concerning ourselves with final truth based on Scripture, we use whatever procedure seems right to us according to the pragmatic criterion "Does it work?" We assume that truth represents that synthesis of all competing ideas which best seems to fit the current situation. The absolutes of Scripture become flexible limits which can bend to accommodate our understanding of what appears most workable.

A biblical approach to knowledge, however, is firmly rooted in the logical law of antithesis (if A is true, non-A is false), which absolutely refuses to accept concepts which are in any way inconsistent with each other regardless of their apparent value. When we treat this law casually, the authority of Scripture is lost and man's wisdom becomes supreme. There is a way that seems right to a man, but Scripture teaches that the long-term consequence of following that way is spiritual death. We must not only insist upon the authority of Scripture but we must also go to great lengths to be sure that all of our concepts come under that authority. At the very least, that means that integrationists will need to be as familiar with Scripture as they are with psychology and that whenever the findings of psychological research contradict Scripture, these findings will be discarded.

We might sketch the TOSSED SALAD model in this way.

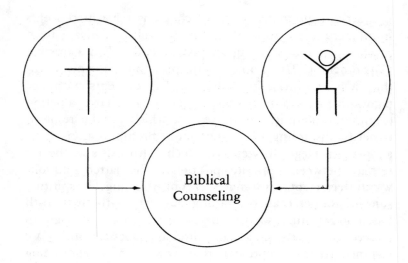

A third group has neatly solved the problem of integrating two disciplines by eliminating one of them. Because they insist that secular psychology, with its humanistic stain, has nothing to offer, I call them NOTHING BUTTERISTS. Nothing But the Word, Nothing But the Lord, Nothing But Faith. This approach can be easily sketched.

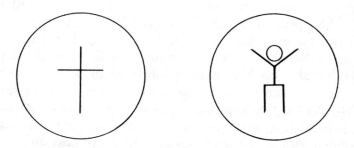

Many of our current popularizers of Christian psychology, especially those from the pastoral community, would fall into this category. I take issue with my Nothing Butterist colleagues on at least two grounds. First is their insistence that psychology has nothing to offer. In contrast, I think that much truth has been discovered which in no way violates the truth which God has propositionally revealed. Second, for some reason, Nothing Butterists seem to reduce counseling to a simplistic model of "identify sin and command change." A certain gentle sensitivity to emotional pain is often lost in their unwarranted assumption that all problems can be solved by straightforward behavior change.

I subscribe to a fourth view of integration which I call SPOILING THE EGYPTIANS. This is based on the historical account of the Israelites' departure from Egypt centuries ago. Leave Egypt (psychology) in the strength of a redeeming God, absolutely depend upon His infinite resources, refuse any compromise with His commands, but gladly accept whatever help which God provokes the Egyptians to offer. Let me sketch the model this way.

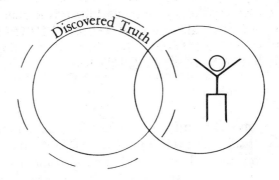

Secular psychology often stumbles onto a biblical concept, then develops it through research. Christians are free to profit from the thinking of secular psychologists but must carefully screen and reject the concepts which depend upon humanistic presuppositions and contradict Scripture. Whatever involves no departure from the character and Word of God is quite acceptable as sustenance on our difficult journey to the Promised Land. As I sketch my model, you'll notice that I have spoiled a number of Egyptians, who although they are regrettably still in Egypt, have helped me in my pursuit of a biblical psychology.

ASSUMPTIONS AND THEORY

After choosing a position on integration, the next step in developing a biblical model is to define the limits of what can be considered biblical, or put another way, to clearly articulate the presuppositionary base upon which one intends to build. We need to agree on a few clear essentials. One conservative theologian has stated that the central presupposition of Christianity is Jesus Christ as the second Person of the sovereign triune God as presented in the Bible, His infallible Word. He adds that this presupposition is ". . . the central truth of the entire system of truth and reality in the universe, the truth so integrated with all other truth as to sustain it and be revealed in it." Everyone who accepts this belief and is fervently committed to working within its broad boundaries can rightly be called evangelical. Those who reject or question this position should not, in my judgment, call themselves evangelical.

I begin my model with the irreducible fact that an infinite personal God really exists. He is infinite, but I am finite. I am therefore a contingent being. He is personal and I too am personal, made in His image. So I am a dependent personal being. As a personal being, I have certain personal needs which must be met if I am to truly live as a person. As a contingent being, these needs must be met outside of myself. What are these personal needs? Paul stated that his purpose in life was Christ: to honor Him, please Him, serve Him. Frankl insists that our lives require a meaning beyond ourselves. I am suggesting that our first personal need is *significance,* the compelling necessity to see our lives as fitting into and moving toward a logically and personally meaningful goal.

The second essential ingredient required for effective personal living is *security,* the experience of being loved unconditionally by someone whole. Glasser stresses the need to be caringly involved with at least one other person. Rogers builds his entire approach to counseling around this need for genuine, unconditional, nonpossessive acceptance. Paul basked in the thrilling knowledge of a personal God who loved him and gave Himself for him. I am proposing, without taking further time to defend it, that as a personal being I basically need *significance* and *security* if I am to be truly whole.

Let me underline what I am saying. We really do need significance and security. Without these ingredients we cannot live a full life. With them, we can enjoy a deep richness which provides a central strength regardless of our circumstances. I am a personal being who can function with a sense of wholeness in any set of circumstances if my needs are met (Philippians 4:11-13).

As a contingent being, I require a source of meaning and love outside of myself. No finite point can serve as its own framework for integration. The finite depends for its existence and character on its infinite context. I am finite. So I turn to the infinite. If that something infinite is impersonal, then I am in trouble. Undesigned impersonality can provide nothing but 1) random direction which is logically meaningless and 2) brute impersonal matter which is incapable of love. If there is no personal God, or if I fail to make Him the context of my life, then I can have neither significance nor security. However, if the infinite is personal, then there is meaning available in infinite design and direction. I become a truly significant being in a meaningfully ordered universe, a being who actually can shape the course of history by my choices. I can also enter into a relationship with a personal

God. We are two persons who can care for each other. There is therefore love available through involvement with the infinite Person. Christians believe that Christ is the only valid source of significance (a life full of meaning) and of security (a persevering love which accepts me at my worst).

But our entire race has been separated from God by sin. Apart from God we are left to our own resources to meet our needs. And so we develop alternative strategies for finding significance and security, strategies which sooner or later will not work. They must fail—if not now, then in hell forever. *It is my thinking that the core of all psychopathology is the desperate but sinful attempt to meet needs apart from God, an attempt based on the satanically inspired belief that it can be done.* All of us have been programmed by Satan through a false world system to believe that in order to be significant and secure, we need _____. How we have learned to finish that sentence is the basic problem. We believe a lie and we organize our lives around it. Adler calls this a guiding fiction. Perhaps we believe that our personal worth (our significance or our security) depends upon financial success, flawless behavior, great achievement, consistent praise, the absence of all criticism, a loving spouse, a closely knit family, etc.

We are not only personal beings who need significance and security. We are also *rational beings* who evaluate our world in accordance with our basic beliefs. Since the fall of mankind, we have become foolish rational beings who naturally evaluate our lives from a perspective which says "I can and I must make it in life without God."

We are also *volitional beings* who choose to respond to life's events according to our evaluations of them. If we believe we need a spouse's love to be secure, we will evaluate a husband's or wife's rejection as threatening and will engage in sinful, selfish behavior designed to change our spouse to meet our needs. If we succeed we will *feel* good. If we do not succeed, we will *feel* bad (frustrated, angry, scared, etc.). As *emotional beings,* we experience emotional consequences when we reach or fail to reach goals which we believe we need.

Whenever a problem arises which we unconsciously believe is a threat to our significance or security, we consciously *evaluate* that event as terrible and consequently *feel* personally threatened. We may try another behavioral approach to overcoming this obstacle to our significance and security, and if we are successful, we feel much better. But the real problem has not been solved. We are still depending on something other than God and what He chooses to provide to meet our needs.

Our modern thinking on marriage offers a classic example of depending upon something or someone other than God to meet our deepest needs. So many books teaching women how to be Christian wives are really textbooks on how to more effectively manipulate husbands. The message seems to be, "You need your husband to love you or you can never be secure; here are a few feminine tricks to seduce your husband into meeting your needs." Now I have not the slightest objections when my wife follows every bit of the advice offered in these books. I love it. But I am concerned that a central problem is remaining untouched: spouses are regularly turning to each other to meet their personal needs. I call this a tick-on-a-dog relationship. The problem with most such marriages is that there are two ticks and no dog.

If we cannot manipulate our environment to better provide for our needs, the natural response is to retreat into a position of safety. "If my husband cuts me down, I will establish a distance between us so that his cuts won't hurt so much." Now what is the problem here? With her conscious mind, this woman evaluates the event of her husband's criticism as terrible. This evaluation is the visible evidence of a deeply programmed belief that she needs her husband's love if she is to exist as a secure, worthwhile person. To rebuke her withdrawal and, in the name of Scripture, to command submissive acceptance of her husband is to suggest that she put her personal neck on the chopping block. Before she will be able to willingly and rationally move toward her husband, she will have to change her mind about what she requires to be secure.

Let me sketch my theory of mental health and psychopathology.

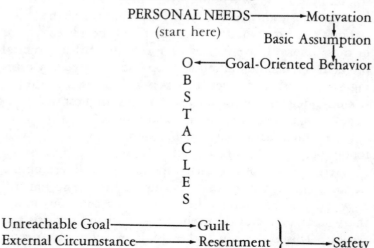

MENTAL HEALTH

Vague sense of Emptiness→PERSONAL NEEDS→Motivation
(start here)

Temporary Satisfaction   Basic Assumption

Goal ←————————————— Goal-Oriented Behavior

MENTAL PROBLEMS

PERSONAL NEEDS————→Motivation
(start here)   Basic Assumption

O ←——Goal-Oriented Behavior
B
S
T
A
C
L
E
S

Unreachable Goal————→Guilt
External Circumstance————→Resentment }————→Safety
Fear of Failure————→Anxiety

I have personal needs for significance and security. I am motivated to meet my needs, so I learn a basic assumption which tells me what goal I must reach in order to become significant and secure. I then engage in behavior designed to reach that goal. If my behavior is effective and I reach the goal, I feel good. But, because nothing apart from Christ truly satisfies, I soon sense a vague discontent and go back through the cycle again. I believe that most people today whom we would *not* call neurotic function in the way that this sketch of mental health suggests.

If, however, I encounter an obstacle en route to meeting my goal, I become frustrated. Behavior therapists, reality therapists, nouthetic counselors, and others emphasize changing your behavior from inappropriate to appropriate, or from irresponsible to responsible, or from sinful to biblical. But the real problem is not the behavior. The person is headed toward a wrong goal determined by a false idea about what constitutes significance and security.

If the obstacle derives from an unreachable goal (for example, "I need to be perfect in order to beloved"), the person will likely come down hard on himself for failing to reach the necessary goal and will feel guilty. If the obstacle is an environmental circumstance (for example, "I need to win the promotion to be significant, but the boss gave it to someone else"), the likely consequence is resentment against whatever the client perceives as blocking his path to the goal. A third possible obstacle is a fear of failure (for example, "I need to have a man love me but I'm afraid to get married; my husband might reject me.") In this case, the predictable psychological reaction is anxiety. Miller and Dollard's classic conflict approach is helpful in understanding this particular disorder.

People who fail to reach their goals and who therefore feel insignificant and insecure tend to desire protection from further hurt. I agree with Adler that most neurotic symptoms are best understood as moving the person toward safety. If I am too depressed to work, I cannot fail on the job. If I suffer from a compulsive disorder, my husband's rejection will be a response to my problem, not to me. Neurotic symptoms often have a rather complex etiology but are most easily understood by a "teleogical analysis" which asks: toward what goals are the symptoms directed? What is achieved through the symptoms? From what am I trying to find safety?

A woman once consulted me concerning severe, almost-continuous headaches which apparently had no organic basis but which had plagued her for nearly two years. By studying the consequences of the headaches, it became clear that they were having at least two definite effects. First, her mother was displaying a great deal of interest and concern in her because of the headaches, and second, her mother was terribly inconvenienced and very worried about them.

Further analysis suggested that my client's basic assumption involved the belief that she desperately needed her mother's love in order to be secure. She had encountered two obstacles en route to the goal: 1) a fear of failure which created anxiety and 2) an environmental block (her mother, who had in some ways rejected her) which produced resentment. The headaches relieved her fear of rejection by eliciting attention, and they also served as a safe expression of hostility toward her mother. To openly discuss her relationship with her mother would have been too threatening, and to verbally express her anger would have risked further rejection. The symptoms therefore moved her toward a safe but costly resolution of her problems. When my client understood the reason for her headaches, we then discussed her wrong belief that she needed her mother's love in order to be secure. As she slowly began to grasp the love of the Lord, she began to initiate the break in inappropriate dependency. Over a period of three months her headaches disappeared.

Paul tells us that the essential element in transformation is renewing our minds. Skinner renews circumstances. Rogers renews feelings. Glasser renews behavior. Analysts renew the personality. Christ renews minds. The basis of all transformation is to think differently, to believe differently, to change your basic assumptions. About what? Clients must understand that their significance and security as a contingent personal being depends exclusively on one's relationship to Christ.

The big problem, of course, is grasping that biblical insight in a way that really transforms us. To tell a depressed person that "Jesus loves you" usually elicits about as much interest as informing someone who is starving that a balanced diet is important for health.

How, then, can we change the thinking of our clients and ourselves in a way that touches people's deepest inward parts where it really counts? Let me illustrate. A man consulted me concerning his habit of uncontrollably lashing out at people who in any way crossed him. How do you go about helping him? Insisting that he control his behavior in accord with biblical standards had produced nothing but frustration. He was a sincere Christian who for years had been trying to behave more graciously but experienced consistent defeat. He was at the point of wondering whether God really existed, and if He did, whether He cared about him at all.

My first concern was to communicate that I accept him. Since my acceptance would be meaningless until he knew that I understood how he felt, I simply tried to empathize with him, to enter at least a bit into the emotional pain he felt. He began to share the hurt he experienced at the hands of his harshly rejecting mother. He then shared his deep fear of being rejected again. We discussed his present reactions to the experience of rejection, how perhaps he was lashing out in a defensive attempt to protect himself whenever he felt threatened.

At that point I began exploring his basic assumptions

about what constituted security. Massive rejection as a child had taught him that rejection hurt and it hurt badly. He came to approach life with the idea, the guiding fiction, that he could not exist as a secure person in the presence of any criticism or rejection. His central problem, to my way of thinking, was a false assumption—the belief that he was worthless unless he was totally loved by everyone. He believed that any rejection rendered him hopelessly insecure. Now that simply isn't true. A person's security rests on the love of Christ and His atoning work on the cross, by which He can forever accept anyone who trusts in Him as Savior. But because my client unconsciously believed that his security rested on the absence of rejection, he evaluated any current rejection as terrible, he felt angry toward those who were stripping him of his security, and he lashed out.

He understood that the Lord loved him, but he had never thought through the relevance of His love to an individual's need for personal security. He was still chained to other people, depending on their love, and furious with them for letting him down so often. When I explained to him that his security in Christ made him free from *needing* acceptance from everyone else, his response was, "Swell, now how do I stop getting mad?"

It is at this point that counseling cannot proceed without a commitment to believe what God says. Resistance often becomes a problem because the sin nature is thoroughly committed to unbelief. This particular man, however, did agree that the Scripture was true and that he would cooperate in a program to make it *experientially* true in his life. I then instructed him to write on a three-by-five card the sentence, "All I need to be secure is Jesus' love, and I have it; therefore I have all that I need to respond in any situation as a secure man." Whenever he felt angry, he was to picture his mind as a tape recorder and consciously thrust into the recorder a tape which played this sentence over and over. Then—and here is another critical point in counseling which often takes a while to work through—he was to choose deliberately, by an act of his will, to say something kind to his attacker, believing that he had all he needed within him to do so. He was to choose this behavior regardless of how he felt.

After the first week he reported that he would say a few gracious things but only through gritted teeth. He still felt furious. After several weeks of religiously following the program, he burst into tears in my office and said, "For the first time in my life, I can really believe that Jesus loves me." Further therapy helped him come to the point where he could express his anger acceptably, without a bitter spirit, in an attempt to constructively deal with problem relationships.

The entire process of counseling can be sketched in a simple seven-stage model.

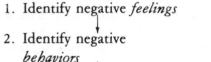

1. Identify negative *feelings*

2. Identify negative *behaviors*

3. Identify wrong *thinking*

4. Teach right *thinking*

5. Secure commitment to right *thinking*

6. Choose right *behavior*

7. Enjoy *feelings* of significance and security.

It seems to me that this model lays down a broad form within which there is considerable room for freedom in technique and approach. Rogerian reflection is useful at Stage 1. Adlerian lifestyle analysis is helpful at Stage 2. Stage 3 can sometimes be facilitated by free association, dream analysis, and historical tracing. Cognitive restructuring, cognitive dissonance theory, and rational-emotive procedures are all appropriate at Stage 4. Gestalt techniques, straightforward moral persuasion, and contractual agreement may help in Stage 5. Behavior modification, psychoactive drugs, and hypnosis have a place in Stage 6. And Stage 7 is the sabbath—sit back and enjoy what has happened. Rest in the wonderful feelings of realized significance and security.

THE PLACE OF THE LOCAL CHURCH
IN BIBLICAL COUNSELING

Wouldn't it be nice if it all worked that smoothly? The truth of the matter is that counseling rarely proceeds quite so nicely. Many Christians are struggling to reach wrong goals without understanding their motivation. But even when people realize that they are wrong in the belief that they need things like approval or success to become worthwhile, it requires a long, slow process to really effect the renewing of our minds. A neat formula approach to counseling carried out in the Christian counselor's office will rarely produce the desired results of real maturity.

One reason why our counseling efforts so often do not really reach the final stage of enjoying the results is because we are failing to use a major God-given resource as effectively as we should. I am speaking of the local church.

If we agree that a person's basic personal needs are significance and security, it can be seen that the input of the local church becomes critical in promoting personal maturity. Significance comes from understanding that I belong to the God of the universe, who is directing my life as a part of the most important project going on in the world today, the building of the church of Jesus Christ. I can really make a difference on my world for eternity. I can have impact.

Pastors and congregations need to stop thinking of the pastor as endowed with all the gifts and as responsible to do all the work of the church. Paul teaches in Ephesians that pastors are to equip the saints for the work of the ministry, so that they too can enjoy the thrilling significance of contributing to

God's eternal purposes. Let me illustrate how this actually worked.

A man in my home church was utterly miserable a year ago. His marriage was on the rocks, he felt depressed, and he was losing his grasp on God. Although he was able to keep functioning and to pretend that he was a happy Christian, he felt alone, inadequate, and hopeless. In this past year he has come to see himself as a minister, building up other people in the local body, sharing with them what he knows of the Lord by leading a small, group Bible study, and helping his wife develop spiritually by loving her as Christ loved the church. He has grasped something of his significance as a minister in a local body who can make a dent in other people's lives for eternity. Today he is a vibrant, excited, whole Christian, still battling depression sometimes, but growing stronger all the time.

Local churches are not only uniquely designed to provide a vehicle for meeting significance needs, but they are also a natural resource for developing Christian security. What a tragedy that in so many churches fellowship is reduced to sitting next to another believer for one hour a week, sharing a hymnbook, shaking his hand, and glibly commenting, "Nice sermon today, wasn't it?" God designed local bodies to experience close, open, deep relationships. Meaningful Christian fellowship is where I share a burden and you help me, where I bring you food when you're sick, where we get together during the week to encourage one another, where we discuss problems with our kids and seek God's wisdom, where I know you'll accept me no matter what I do. Meaningful Christian fellowship goes a long way toward meeting security needs.

In an effort to narrow the distressingly wide gap between the ideal and reality, I have organized the Institute of Biblical Counseling (IBC), a counselor training program to help local churches become communities where personal needs can better be met. IBC offers training in three levels of counseling based on the seven-stage model I have already presented.

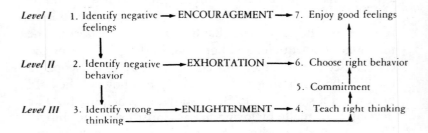

LEVEL I—*Counseling by Encouragement*

Every member of the body needs to be trained in Level I counseling: how to be more sensitive, how to listen, how to communicate care.

LEVEL II—*Counseling by Exhortation*

A group of mature believers can be taught biblical principles for handling common problem areas and can be trained to help people approach difficulties biblically. Current training opportunities in Level II counseling involve approximately thirty-five to forty hours of classroom training.

LEVEL II—*Counseling by Enlightenment*

A few selected Christians in each local church could be trained in perhaps a six-months-to-a-year training program to handle the deeper, more-stubborn problems which don't yield to encouragement or exhortation.

Counseling people who desperately need significance and security in an environment which potentially provides both—the local church—is an exciting possibility. Counseling in that setting should help us to better grasp that Jesus Christ (the second Person of the sovereign, triune Godhead as revealed in the inerrant, infallible, objective Word of God) is the foundation of all counseling that is truly biblical. He alone can meet our deepest personal needs.

10

DISCIPLESHIP COUNSELING

Gary R. Collins

Several years ago the editor of this book was listening to a series of lectures on discipleship. It is difficult to remember whether the lectures were especially stimulating or very boring, but I do know that my mind began to wander. Jesus instructed believers to "make disciples," and for years I had acknowledged this in my Christian life. But, I wondered, did the Great Commission, so central to Christianity, have any relevance to my work as a psychologist—especially my counseling work? This caused me to reexamine my entire approach to people helping and led to the book *How to Be a People Helper* (Santa Ana: Vision House, 1976). It is from this volume that the following chapter is excerpted and reprinted.

It is not to be implied that "discipleship counseling" is a unique approach to Christian counseling. Rather, it is a summary of existing knowledge about counseling basics and an attempt to show how these can be related to and built on the basic teachings of the Bible, especially the Great Commission.

What is a Christian counselor? Does the Christian have different goals in counseling from the nonbeliever? If he or she takes the Bible seriously, will that influence what the counselor does with counselees? Can there be a biblical approach to counseling which allows for the individual personality differences of counselors, the uniqueness of each counselee, and the variety of problems that are encountered in a counseling situation? Must a Christian counselor throw out all of the counseling theories and techniques that secular therapists have developed and shown to be effective? Is there a uniquely Christian approach to counseling?

These were some of the questions which concerned me when I received my doctorate in clinical psychology and went to work in a university counseling center. I had a diploma to prove that I was trained as a counselor, but I didn't feel very competent in spite of all my education at some very reputable graduate schools. As a Christian it seemed that I ought to be doing something other than rigorously following the secular methods that I had been taught, but I didn't know what to do that was different. Employed by a state university, I could not say much about religion to my counselees and still keep my job, but I also knew that the gospel of Jesus Christ had something to say to these lonely and frustrated kids who were coming to my office. Often I thought back to a paper that I once had written as a class assignment. The paper was titled "The Effectiveness of Psychotherapy," and in it I had concluded (after reviewing a great deal of published research) that counseling didn't work very well. Obviously this conclusion didn't do much to boost my morale as a young psychologist just out of graduate school!

During my year in that counseling center I think I helped a lot of people, and my employer appeared to be happy with my work. But I wasn't satisfied. After several months on the job I decided that teaching was more my gift, and so I left the counseling center and went to work in the psychology department of a growing college in Minnesota. Teaching was a very rewarding experience, but I still harbored my insecurities about counseling. Then I met Paul Tournier, the famous

Swiss writer (see chapter 3), and for the first time I began to see something of the potential of Christian counseling.

Tournier is a humble, godly man who has helped hundreds of people in his counseling work and probably thousands through his books. We may not agree with all of Dr. Tournier's conclusions, but in writing a book about this man[1] I saw an individual whose counseling is effective. As a people helper, he takes the Bible seriously, is compassionate, consistently demonstrates Christian love, and recognizes that every counselee is in some way unique. Although he resists anyone thinking that he has a theory, Tournier nevertheless has developed a biblical approach to counseling.

But others have proposed different approaches which also claim to be biblical. This confuses a lot of people. How can we be Christians, they ask, and have such a variety of counseling systems, all of which claim to come from the Bible? We should remember that counselors, like theologians and Bible students, are fallible human beings. We see things from different perspectives. Committed Presbyterians disagree with committed Baptists on some very basic issues—yet all may be Christian. There are different biblically based approaches to preaching (homiletics) or Bible interpretation (hermeneutics) even though each may be faithful to the Word of God. The same is true in counseling. Because of these differences we learn from each other, recognizing that we will never have the perfect theory of counseling until we get to heaven, and then counseling will no longer be necessary.

So long as we remain on earth, however, if we are to take the Bible seriously in our counseling, we cannot ignore the Great Commission. To do so would be to leave out a major tenet of New Testament teaching. So important, in fact, is the concept of discipleship in Scripture that we might think of Christian counseling as something which also could be termed discipleship counseling.

ASSUMPTIONS

Discipleship counseling is an approach which is built on Scripture and seeks to begin with the Bible as its starting point. It is a view of counseling which recognizes the centrality of the Great Commission and has the discipling of others at its core. It assumes that the God who speaks through the Bible has also revealed truth about His universe through science, including psychology. Thus, psychological methods and techniques are taken seriously, but they must be tested, not only scientifically and pragmatically, but also against the written Word of God. Discipleship counseling uses a variety of methods, depending on the counselor's personality and skill and on the counselee's needs, personality, or problems.

The goals of counseling are to help people function more effectively in their daily lives; to find freedom from spiritual, psychological, and interpersonal conflicts; to be at peace with themselves and in a growing communion with God; to develop and maintain smooth interpersonal relations with others; to realize their fullest potential in Christ; and to be actively involved in becoming disciples of and disciplers for Jesus Christ. The approach is expressed in terms of six general principles.

SIX PRINCIPLES

1. *In any counseling relationship, the personality, values, attitudes, and beliefs of the counselor are of primary importance.* In writing to the church at Galatia, Paul instructed the brethren to "restore" (or bring to a state of wholeness) any individual who was having personal difficulties (Galatians 6:1). Apparently the Galatians had some of their number who were lapsing into sin and having problems because of this. These men and women were of concern to the apostle, but notice who was to help them: "you who are spiritual."

In chapter 5 of Galatians we read the well-known listing of

those traits that characterize the spiritual Christian: love, joy, peace, patience, kindness, goodness, faithfulness, gentleness, and self-control (Galatians 5:22,23). The spiritual individual is also an individual who has values that are in conformity with the teachings of Jesus (Galatians 5:24), is led by the Spirit of God (v.25), and is not self-centered, a troublemaker, or impressed with his or her own importance (v.26). These were to be the characteristics of the good counselor who is described in Galatians 6.

In addition, notice that the restorer-counselor is gentle (Galatians 6:1), a person who may be firm with the counselee but is always compassionate; he or she is alert (v.1) to the temptations that come when one is involved in an intimate counseling relationship; is involved with the counselee (v.2), so much so that the counselor for a time bears the counselee's burdens with the pain and inconvenience that this might bring; is humble (v.3), recognizing the source of a counselor's strength and not acting in a superior, holier-than-thou manner; is self-examining (v.4), so that the counselor has a realistic self-appraisal and avoids comparing himself or herself to others; is responsible (v.5) for bearing burdens in his or her own life and helping the counselee to do the same; is willing to learn (v.6) from the counselee and at times to accept payment for services; is aware of God and spiritual influences in human behavior (vv.7,8); is patient (v.9) even when the task is long and arduous; and is desirous of doing good (v.10) not only to Christians but to all people, "especially to those who are of the household of faith."

This is a long and somewhat overwhelming list. The standards for a good counselor are high, but they are attainable standards. They characterize any Christian who is walking in close fellowship with Jesus Christ. It does not follow that the committed believer automatically is a good counselor; learning of skills is important too. But the person who follows Jesus Christ develops characteristics that might be summarized in the one little word *love,* and that is important for counseling.

All of this is consistent with psychological research on the counseling relationship, research which shows that the personal traits of the helper are as important to good counseling as are the methods which he or she uses.[2] These several research studies have shown that effective counselors succeed not so much because of their theoretical orientation or techniques; they succeed because they possess empathy, warmth, and genuineness.

Empathy comes from a German word *einfulung,* which means to "feel into" or feel with. Most of us have had the experience of sitting in the passenger's seat of a car and pushing our foot on the floor when we perceive a need to slow down. At such times we are feeling into the driver's situation and feeling with him or her.

In counseling, the effective helper tries to see and understand the problem from the counselee's perspective. "Why is he so upset?" we might ask. "How does she view the situation?" "If I were him, how would I feel?" The counselor wants to keep his or her own objective viewpoint intact but realizes that one can be more helpful if he or she can also see the problem from the counselee's point of view and let him or her know that we understand how our counselee feels and views the situation. The counselee, in turn, realizes that someone is trying to really understand, and this builds better rapport.

Warmth is somewhat synonymous with caring. It is a condition of friendliness and consideration shown by one's facial expression, tone of voice, gestures, posture, and eye contact, and by such nonverbal behavior as looking after the counselee's comfort. Warmth is a manner which says, "I care about you and am concerned about your welfare." Here as in so much human behavior, actions speak louder than words. The counselor who really does care about people won't have to advertise this concern verbally. It will be apparent for all to see.

Genuineness means that the counselor's words and actions are consistent. He or she tries to be honest with the counselee, and avoids any statements or behavior which could be viewed as phony or insincere. According to one writer, the genuine individual is spontaneous (but not impulsive or disrespectful), consistent in one's values or attitudes, not defensive, aware of one's own emotions, and willing to share oneself or one's own feelings.

Jesus showed empathy, warmth, and genuineness, and the successful Christian counselor must do the same. It is possible, however, that each of these can be overdone. We can show so much empathy that we lose our objectivity, so much warmth that the counselee feels smothered, and so much genuineness that the counselor loses sight of the counselee's needs. The helper, therefore, must frequently examine his or her own motives for helping. As helpers, our own needs will be met in the helping relationship, but our primary task is to help others with their problems and struggles to grow.

2. *The counselee's attitudes, motivation, and desire for help are also important in counseling.* At some time most counselors have had the frustrating experience of trying to work with someone who is stubborn, uncooperative, or disinterested in changing behavior. To work, for example, with a rebellious teenager who is sent to be "straightened out" or to counsel a depressed person who believes that he or she "will never get better" is to work with individuals whose attitudes will have to change before real helping can occur. When the counselee does not want help, fails to see that a problem exists, has no desire to change, or lacks faith in the counselor and the counseling process, then counseling is rarely successful.

God created us with free will, and it is no more possible to help an unwilling counselee to grow psychologically than it is to help a nonbeliever to grow spiritually against his or her will. In counseling, as in witnessing, such resistance must be acknowledged and the counselee helped to see the value in making changes in his or her own life. Counseling is a process of assisting another person to change and grow, but such growth is easiest when the counselor and counselee work together on the task. The counselee is the best-informed individual in the world when it comes to his or her own situation. The counselee knows the problem, how it feels, and what has not worked in bringing about change in the past. The counselor and counselee must both use this information together.

Of course, it should not be assumed that the person who needs help is always resisting in a stubborn manner. Sometimes people are scared. It is hard to talk about one's own failures or problems, and sometimes the counselee doesn't even know what is wrong. To tell another person about one's personal life can be risky, since we might be criticized or rejected. Then there is the attitude of frustration or self-condemnation which some counselees feel because they haven't been able to solve their problems on their own. All of these can interfere with the helping process, and thus the counselor's job is to help the counselee relax and "open up."

For best results, the counselee-helpee must really want to change, must expect that things will get better with the counselor's help, and must show a willingness to cooperate even if the counseling process is painful. Stated somewhat differently, it is important for the counselee to have an attitude of hope when he or she comes for help.

Jesus emphasized the value of this in His healing ministry. He commended the hemorrhaging woman for a faith which restored her to health (Mark 5:34). He healed two blind men because of their faith (Matthew 9:29), and He cured an epileptic boy whose father believed in the Master's powers (Mark 9:23-27). In contrast, when Jesus was in His hometown, not very many people were helped because they didn't believe in His healing powers (Matthew 13:58). It could be argued, perhaps, that faith as described in the Scriptures is different from hope and expectation, but the writer of the Hebrews links them together (11:1). Terms like faith, hope, expectation, belief, and motivation can all be used somewhat interchangeably because they all convey the idea that when a counselee desires to improve and thinks that he or she will get better, this very often happens—sometimes in spite of the counselor's techniques.

3. *In counseling, the helping relationship between counselor and counselee is of great significance.* As every counseling student soon learns, good rapport is an essential for successful counseling, so essential that one writer has even described counseling as primarily a helping relationship between two or more people.[3] Sometimes we call this relationship a counseling interview, a therapy session, an encounter, or a "good talk between friends," but in every case people are together in some kind of a relationship, working together on a specified problem.

Helping relationships differ in both their nature and their depth. When two people come together they do not leave their personalities, values, attitudes, insecurities, needs, feelings, perceptions, and abilities at the door. These enter into the relationship, and to the extent that people are different, it is likely that no two people ever relate together in a way that is duplicated elsewhere. Consider, for example, how Jesus related to people. He didn't have the same kind of relationship with them all. With Nicodemus it was intellectual, with the Pharisees it was confrontational, with Mary and Martha it was more relaxed, and with the little children it was warm and loving. Jesus recognized individual differences in personality, needs, and level of understanding, and He treated people accordingly. Counselors who try to treat all of their counselees in the same way fail to build good rapport because they are making the mistake of thinking that all people are alike. All people are not alike, and this must be recognized both in the relationships that we build and in the methods that we use.

Jesus not only dealt with people in different ways, but He also related to individuals at different levels of depth or closeness. John was the disciple whom Jesus loved, perhaps the Master's nearest friend, while Peter, James, and John together appear to have been an inner circle with whom the Lord had a special relationship. Although they were not as close as the inner three, the other apostles were His constant companions, a band of twelve men who had been hand-picked to carry on the work after Christ's departure. In Luke 10 we read a group of seventy men to whom Jesus gave special training. Following the resurrection He appeared to a larger group of five hundred, and then there were crowds, sometimes numbering in the thousands, many of whom may have seen Christ only once and from a distance.

The closeness of Jesus to His disciples might be illustrated by the following diagram. Jesus is in the center. John, His closest friend, is at 1, the three are next in nearness (2), then the twelve (3), the seventy (4), the five hundred (5), and finally the crowds (6) at the outer reaches of the circle.

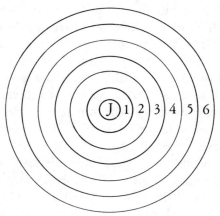

Most of us have this kind of relationship with others. Some people are close, while others are farther removed. We assume that in counseling or discipling we must always develop a close relationship, but it may be that such relationship either can be in-depth or can be more superficial.

Each one of us is surrounded by circles of people. A few, perhaps one or two friends and the members of our family, are very close. Others are a little further removed, and some are on the outer fringes touched by us only casually. The counselor does not strive to be the counselee's best friend. Counseling is a relationship that certainly may involve friendship, but it exists for another purpose—to have the counselor assist the counselee with a problem. At times, the relationship may be very close, near the center of the circle, with intimate, even two-way, sharing of emotions, concerns, and needs. On other occasions, the relationship may not be as deep. Perhaps the counselor and counselee see each other for one session, talk about the counselee only, or chat briefly about some relatively minor problem. It is even possible for the counselor to help others from a distance—by giving a public lecture on mental health, for example, or writing a helpful book. Sometimes, therefore, we help people on a one-to-one basis, sometimes we work in a group, and at times we may even help people whom we never meet face-to-face.

Every counselor-counselee relationship is in some sense unique. Each relationship depends on the personality of the people involved, the nature of the problems being considered, the depth of discussion, and the psychological closeness of the counselor to the counselee. Counseling is a helping process, but the helping involves a relationship. The better the relationship, the more successful the counseling.

4. *Counseling must focus on the counselee's emotions, thoughts, and behavior—all three.* In many of the secular and Christian approaches to counseling there is an emphasis on either emotion, thinking, or behavior, but rarely on all

three together. Albert Ellis's Rational Emotive Therapy, for example, refers to both thinking and feeling in its title, but the therapy deals almost exclusively with how the counselee thinks. In contrast, Carl Rogers puts most emphasis on the feelings of the counselee and makes little attempt to analyze what is happening intellectually. Many of the learning approaches emphasize behavior change and maintain that the counselee's feelings and thoughts are of minor importance—so minor, in fact, that "treatment" sometimes occurs without the counselee's even being aware that it is taking place.

When we look into the Scriptures we see that feeling, thinking, and behavior are all of great, perhaps equal importance. Consider first the *emotional*. Jesus Himself wept on at least two occasions, and sometimes got angry. He did not deny feelings, nor did He condemn people for experiencing and expressing their emotions. Clearly He was sensitive to the feelings of others, such as His sorrowing mother at the time of the crucifixion or the parents who brought their children to see the Lord but were rebuffed by the overprotective disciples. It is possible to overemphasize feelings in a counseling relationship, but it is also possible to stifle or deny them. Jesus did neither.

There were times, however, when He put more emphasis on *rational* thinking. Thomas was very much inclined to doubt, but Jesus dealt with these intellectual questions in a rational way. He did not ignore Thomas or criticize him for a lack of faith. Instead, when the disciple doubted, Jesus supplied the evidence. Following the resurrection Thomas had said, in essence, "I won't believe unless I can see with my eyes and touch the hands of Jesus with my fingers." As they met later, the Lord said to Thomas, "Reach here your finger and see my hands; and reach here your hand and put it into my side; and be not unbelieving, but believing" (John 20:27). In a similar way, when John the Baptist doubted during his last days in prison (Matthew 11:2-6), Jesus provided the rational facts which were needed. On numerous occasions He carried on intellectual debates with the religious leaders of His day, and He discussed apologetics with Nicodemus in a debate which may have gone far into the night.

But Jesus also was very concerned about sin and sinful *behavior.* He told the woman taken in adultery to change her behavior and to sin no more, He instructed Mary to change her hectic lifestyle, He advised the rich young ruler to be less selfish, and He told two quarreling brothers to stop being so greedy. Repeatedly in His sermons and discussions with individuals, people were confronted by Christ with their sinful, self-centered behavior and were instructed to change.

The emphasis on emotions, thinking, and behavior is seen in the Book of Acts and on through the New Testament epistles. Repeatedly, believers were held responsible for their own actions, but there was never any hint of overemphasizing behavior to the exclusion of feeling and thinking. Feeling, thinking, and acting—all three are important in the Scriptures, and each must be considered in counseling. As shown in the diagram, each is in contact with the others. When we have emotional problems, for example, our thinking and actions are affected. We cannot emphasize one part of this diagram while we ignore the other two parts.

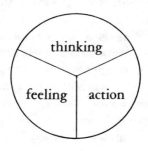

COUNSELING TECHNIQUES

5. *Counseling involves a variety of counselor skills.* This word "skills" might be viewed from two perspectives. On the one hand there are the counseling techniques—things like listening attentively, watching carefully, or questioning wisely as the counselee describes the problem. These refer to *what one does* in counseling. They are skills which can be learned by the counselor-helper.

For maximum effectiveness, counseling must also have direction. The counselor and counselee must have some goals in mind, and at least the counselor should have some idea about how these goals can be reached. This moving toward a goal might be called the process of counseling. It refers to *where one goes* in a counseling relationship.

Numerous books have been written to describe counseling techniques. The list of techniques varies from author to author, but most writers agree that in order to understand and help another human being the counselor must listen carefully, question wisely, give support or encouragement, and gently confront counselees with their sin, with their inconsistent behavior ("You say you love your wife but are mean to her"; "You claim to like sports but you never play"), with their self-defeating behavior ("You want to succeed, but you set your standards so high that you are certain to fail"), or with their tendency to evade issues ("You say you want to grow spiritually, but every time this issue comes up you change the subject").

Basically counseling is a special form of teaching. The counselee is learning how to act, feel, and think differently; the counselor is the teacher.

Teaching, of course, can occur in a variety of ways. It may involve instruction, giving advice, or telling the counselee what to do. Very often, however, such verbal direction has little impact on a counselee. It is usually more effective if a counselor can show by his or her behavior how to live or think more effectively; can give praise, encouragement, or other reinforcement when the counselee shows improvement; and can work with the counselee as he or she makes decisions, takes actions, and evaluates what is being done to change.

All of counseling techniques describe what the counselor does in his counseling, but equally important is the question of goals. Where is the counseling going and what does it seek to accomplish? This refers to the process of counseling.

This is a big topic of debate among professional counselors. Some see counseling as a highly complex procedure, but more-recent writers have simplified the process considerably. Egan,[4] for example, lists four stages: attending to the counselee and building rapport; responding to the counselee and helping him or her to explore feelings, experiences, and behavior; building understanding in both counselor and counselee; and stimulating action which is subsequently evaluated by counselor and counselee together.

A psychologist named Lawrence Brammer[5] has a longer but similar list: opening the interview and stating the problem(s); clarifying the problem and goals for counseling; structuring the counselor relationship and procedures; building a deeper relationship; exploring feelings, behavior, or thoughts; deciding on some plans of action, trying these out, and evaluating them; and terminating the relationship.

To a large extent what we do in counseling will depend on the type of problem, the personaliteis of the counselor and counselee, and the nature of their relationship. Building on the suggestions of Egan and Brammer, I would suggest that the counseling process has at least five steps, all of which are clearly illustrated in the Bible.

> a) Building a *relationship* between counselor and counselee (John 6:63; 26:7-13; 1 John 4:6).

> b) *Exploring* the problems, trying to clarify issues and determine what has been done in the past to tackle the problem (Romans 8:26).

c) *Deciding* on a course of action. There may be several possible alternatives which could be tried one at a time (John 14:26; 1 Corinthians 2:13).

d) Stimulating *action* which the counselor and counselee evaluate together. When something doesn't work, try again (John 16:13; Acts 10:19,20; 16:6).

e) *Terminating* the counseling relationship and encouraging the counselee to apply what he has learned as he launches out on his own (Romans 8:14).

COUNSELING AND DISCIPLESHIP

6. *The ultimate goal of counseling is to make disciples and disciplers of our counselees.* This statement could be greatly misunderstood. It seems to imply that counseling is concerned only with spiritual matters or that the most important goal is to "get people saved" rather than to help them with their problems.

To clarify this sixth principle let us think for a moment of the Christian physician. Like every other believer, he too has a responsibility to be making disciples, but in the emergency room he does not pull out his Bible and start preaching. He starts with people where they are hurting. He demonstrates the love of Christ through his actions and concerns, realizing that the alleviation of suffering is honoring to Christ and often a step toward evangelism (Proverbs 14:31; Matthew 10:42). The physician does not avoid talking about spiritual matters, but this is not the major part of treatment.

In the discipling process there are at least five steps. We must make contact, witness verbally, bring people to the point of decision, help them to grow as disciples, and teach them to disciple others. Much has been written about evangelism and witnessing, but only recently have we seen an emphasis on disciple-building.[6] The counselor is concerned with both, but several conclusions are important.

a) The counselor may come into a life at any point in these five steps. He or she may deal with a nonbeliever who has never heard the gospel, or may counsel with a mature saint who has been growing as a disciple and discipler for many years. Where do we get the idea that our counseling must be restricted to believers? "While we have opportunity," the Scriptures state, "let us do good to *all men,* and especially to those who are of the household faith" (Galatians 6:10).

b) The counselor may take the counselee through all five stages or may be present for a short time, making a few influences in his or her life and then moving out while someone else takes over. Sometimes one person makes contact and even does some counseling, another person witnesses, someone else leads the person to Christ, and the discipling is then taken over by others. Each of our lives is touched by a host of others. As counselors we need not be possessive of our conselees, assuming that we alone can help.

c) The spiritual can be introduced too quickly and too abruptly. Some counselees have been turned off in the past by well-meaning but pushy Christians who have rushed in to present the gospel or to give minisermons on how to live better lives. The counselor must be sensitive to the Holy Spirit's leading, but at times he or she might not even mention spiritual things at all. Sometimes a low-key approach to discipleship is the best way to begin.

d) Counseling, like discipleship, involves the whole body of Christ. In Romans 12, 1 Corinthians 12, and elsewhere we read that the body exists for mutual support, help, burden-bearing, and edification. We have settled too quickly into the idea of a "one-on-one" type of counseling. The church must be a healing community which supports the work of individual counselors and the growth of counselees.

e) Discipleship counseling is concerned about the whole person. When I first presented the concept of discipleship counseling in a public lecture, one man criticized this as an approach which seems to be interested in a person's spiritual well-being and nothing else. Certainly the Bible does not break humanity down into segments; to say that we have two, three, or more parts is a carry-over from Greek philosophy which is not supported by Scripture. A human being, instead, is a unity who has no such thing as a strictly spiritual need, solely psychological abnormality, a social conflict, or a purely physical illness. When something goes wrong with one aspect of the unified person, the individual's whole being is affected. A healer may specialize in medicine, psychotherapy, or spiritual counseling, but each must remember that there is no sharp line between the spiritual, emotional, volitional, or physical in humans. One symptom may cry for healing, but at such a time the entire body is off-balance. We must not deal with the spiritual and forget the person's psychological needs. They go together, and the counselor who forgets this does the counselee and the Lord a disservice.

These then are the principles of discipleship counseling. They concern the importance of the counselor, the attitude of the counselee, the counseling relationship, the importance of feeling, thinking, and actions, the use of helping skills, and the ultimate goal of Christian counseling: bringing others to maturity and wholeness in Christ and helping them to be disciples and disciplers.

FOOTNOTES

1. Gary R. Collins, *The Christian Psychology of Paul Tournier* (Grand Rapids: Baker, 1973).
2. R.R. Carkhuff, *Helping and Human Relations: A Primer for Lay and Professional People, Volume I, Selection and Training* (New York: Holt, Rinehart and Winston, 1969); C.B. Truax, "Therapist Em-

pathy, Genuineness, and Warmth, and Patient Therapeutic Outcome" in *Journal of Consulting Psychology,* vol. 30, 1966, pp. 395-401; and L.M. Brammer, *The Helping Relationship: Process and Skills* (Englewood Cliffs, NJ: Prentice-Hall, 1973).
3. Brammer, op. cit.
4. G. Egan, *The Skilled Helper* (Monterey, CA: Brooks/Cole, 1975).
5. Brammer, op. cit.
6. R.E. Coleman, *The Master Plan of Evangelism* (Old Tappan, NJ: Fleming H. Revell, 1963); N.A. Henrichsen, *Disciples Are Made—Not Born* (Wheaton: Victor Books, 1974); and C. Wilson, *With Christ in the School of Disciple Building* (Grand Rapids: Zondervan, 1976).

11

THREE-DIMENSIONAL PASTORAL COUNSELING

Paul L. Walker

Much of the significant work in the field of Christian counseling has come from pastors and others who counsel within the local church. Writers such as Boisen, Hiltner, Clinebell, Oates, and others have been associated with the development of pastoral counseling as a discipline, but thousands of parish pastors have learned to apply counseling skills to persons in need who come to the church for help.

In one chapter, it would be impossible to summarize the various approaches to pastoral counseling. As the writer of this chapter suggests, there are "nearly as many approaches as there are counselors." Instead, we have invited one successful pastoral counselor to share his perspectives on counseling in the church.

Paul L. Walker has served for almost twenty years as pastor of the Mount Paran Church of God in Atlanta. After completing his seminary education, he received a Ph.D. in counseling from Georgia State University. In addition to his pastoral duties, he teaches, and he has written several books, including *Counseling Youth, Understanding the Bible and Science,* and *Courage for Crisis Living.* This chapter was prepared especially for this volume.

In Margaret Mitchell's novel *Gone with the Wind,* Will Benteen delivers an oration at Mr. O'Hara's funeral which states the case of many people in our churches and communities. Will says, "Everybody's mainspring is different. And I want to say this—folks whose mainsprings are busted are better dead."

Because of strained and broken mental and spiritual mainsprings, the pastor of our day is called upon to adapt his pastoral ministry to dealing with specific persons who approach him for help with specific problems. This necessitates pastoral counseling and suggests that the pastor give close attention to a three-dimensional model of counseling: 1) the pastor as shepherd-leader, 2) the pastor as facilitator, and 3) the pastor as an agent for therapeutic change.

THE PASTOR AS SHEPHERD-LEADER

The pastoral role is not an easy one. It involves multiple activities, but the successful pastor is the one who is able to integrate these into a unified function as the shepherd-leader who sincerely cares about the spiritual and personal growth of his parish. In this role the pastor seeks to lead persons toward the achievement of positive adjustment to God, to themselves, and to other persons. Thus, within this broad context we can define pastoral care as the pastor's oversight of the personal and family needs of his people.

This definition is derived from the ministry of our Lord Himself, for His ministry was not so much program-centered as it was person-centered. He valued the religious-institutional program only as it served the needs of persons. Thus, whenever ritualistic demands and ecclesiastical observances conflicted with personal needs, those needs took top priority. In every sense of the word Christ cared for others, and He put aside long-standing traditions to set people free to live a new life in His kingdom (Luke 4:18; John 8:31-36; Matthew 23:4; Luke 11:46; Acts 15:10; Galatians 5:1). In this regard notice the following:

1. *He recognized people at the point of need.* He ate with publicans and sinners (Matthew 9; 10:1-13; Luke 19:1-10). He was attentive to the needs of a Syrophenician mother (Mark 7:24-30). He was willing to talk with a Samaritan woman (John 4:4,9,27).

2. *He related to people in spite of tradition.* He treated a case of adultery with understanding and forgiveness (John 8:1-11; compare Leviticus 20:10). He touched people who were diseased and dead (Mark 1:41; compare Leviticus 13:46; Mark 5:13; compare Numbers 19:11,13). He ignored such customs as the prescribed hand-washings and customary fastings (Mark 2:18 ff.). He often broke the Sabbath (Mark 1:21, 2:23 ff.; 3:1 ff.; Luke 13:10; 14:1; John 5:8,9, 9:14). To put it succinctly, Jesus said, "The Sabbath was made for man, and not man for the Sabbath" (Mark 2:27).

3. *He responded to people in a therapeutic context.* In fact His entire ministry was characterized by love (Luke 6:1-35), compassion (Matthew 9:36; Luke 13:34,35), concern (Mark 9:24,25), tenderness (John 8:1-11; Matthew 12:20), noncoercion (Matthew 13:58; Luke 16:30,31), and optimism (Mark 10:27).

In a word, Christ epitomized the shepherd-leader image of the pastor in loving concern for his people.

In the epistles, Paul the apostle exhibits a similar role:

1. *He emphasized affection, love, and friendship.* (Romans 9:1-3; 2 Corinthians 6:11; 7:3-9; 11:2,29; 1 Thessalonians 2:7,11; 3:6,8; Galatians 4:19; Philippians 4:1).

2. *He exercised profound concern for the individual in spite of administrative overload* (2 Corinthians 11:28; Romans 16).

3. *He encouraged edification as an overarching aim second only to evangelism* (Romans 14:19; 1 Corinthians 8:1; 10:23; 14:3,4,5,12,17,26; 2 Corinthians 13:10; Ephesians 4:7-16,29).

4. *He exemplified a noncoercive approach that viewed peo-*

ple as equals and not objects (1 Corinthians 1:10; 16:15-18; Philippians 3:15).

5. *He engendered empathy, tactfulness, sensitivity, and honesty toward the attitudes and reactions of others* (Acts 26:29, 1 Corinthians 9:19-27; Philemon 1:14-20).

6. *He enlisted balance, wholeness, and sound-mindedness in the maturity of Christ.* He advocated arriving at the completeness of personality (Ephesians 4:13) in such areas as thought (Romans 12:3), attitude (2 Timothy 1:7), and overall development Titus 1:8; 2:2).

In the image of Christ, Paul also exhibited the shepherd-leader image of pastoral care.

However, inherent within this shepherd-leader role is the ministry of counseling, and emerging from effective pastoral care it may be defined as follows: *pastoral counseling is a way of facing problems together with a needy person toward a goal of gaining new understanding and developing new responsibility whereby constructive solutions can be worked out by appropriate action.* This means as shepherd-leader the pastor initiates counseling in the following areas.

1. Pastoral counseling should offer an opportunity for complete and open confession to God by the person without fear of the counselor's blame, hostility, or betrayal of confidence.

2. Pastoral counseling should offer a deepening meditative introspection by the person to bring the unconscious into the conscious and a positive exertion of the will to master the emotions.

3. Pastoral counseling should offer a means of lifting the person's self-esteem so that he sees himself as a person of intrinsic value and worth to be treasured rather than a thing to be manipulated or degraded.

4. Pastoral counseling should involve a dependence upon the Holy Spirit in which the counselor is freed from the temptation to play God, and the person is enabled to grow in grace

as he accepts the counselor as a fellow human being interested in his welfare.

THE PASTOR AS FACILITATOR

Counseling is not done by an object or a blank screen. Pastoral counseling calls for modeling behavior and Christian maturity by an effective Christian pastor. The pastor brings himself with his strengths and his weaknesses into every counseling session. In essence the pastor strives to develop a facilitative personality characterized by spiritual maturity, if he is to counsel efficiently.

Becoming a facilitator means the following: a) the pastor lives effectively himself; b) the pastor relates to people in a constructive and genuine manner; c) the pastor endeavors to achieve an accurate and empathic understanding of people's feelings and experiential level; d) the pastor learns to create a climate of acceptance and positive regard for people regardless of the circumstances or the situation; e) the pastor learns how to be assertive and confrontive in an appropriate and nurturing attitude; f) the pastor develops a response style that enables feelings, facilitates action, and maintains respect and confidence; g) the pastor seeks to model the Christ ideal as a shepherd-leader who truly cares and wants to help.

With these concepts in the forefront, the question of *process* arises. "What counseling technique is appropriate for pastoral counseling? What professional resources can be utilized?"

While investigation reveals nearly as many approaches as there are counselors, one approach that has been meaningful in an eclectic sense as a theoretical framework for pastoral counseling is known as Adlerian counseling.

This approach emphasizes the socioteleological aspect of man as a social being with a social purpose. In the broadest sense the Adlerian framework stresses that man is a free agent with creative ability which he utilizes to set his own goals and ultimately to find his place in the social group. Within this framework, counseling becomes a family affair, and it works on the premise that "psychopathology in an individual may be an expression of family pathology, and the conviction that seeing a family together may offer advantages over seeing its members individually."[1]

Thus, counseling in the Adlerian sense becomes an uncovering and interpreting process with four overlapping but distinguishable phases.

First, there is the *relationship* phase, which includes the establishment and maintenance of a proper counseling relationship involving trust, respect, understanding, and the anticipation of success.

Second, there is the *analysis* phase, which includes a psychological investigation of the dynamics which lead to an understanding of the family's present problem situation. It involves a clarification of lifestyle and an exploration of the family constellation with regard to birth order, sibling rivalry, and parental interaction.[2]

Third, there is the *interpretation* phase. This aspect of the procedure involves discussion and explanation of motives, intentions, and goals. The aim is learning through insight into the individual client's family's private logic. Emphasis is placed on "action" and "purpose" rather than "why" and "feelings."

Fourth, there is the *reorientation and reeducation* phase. At this point, specific means of promoting changes and improvement are utilized. A type of mirror technique is employed to aid the individual client or family in becoming aware of its power, its ability to make decisions, and its freedom to choose direction. The ultimate aim is redirection of mistaken goals and restoration of self-faith and self-worth of each person in the family unit.[3]

In this context the main point for consideration is that each group situation presents its own dynamics and calls for appropriate procedures by the counselor. Some operational guidelines for Adlerian family counselors are as follows.

1. *The counselor works with as many family members as are available.*

Whenever possible, all adults in a household are drawn into the counseling session. However, reluctance on the part of one parent or other significant adult may make this prohibitive; thus the counselor works with those who are willing to come and tries to draw others into the counseling relationship.

2. *Discussion and counseling deal with the dynamics that operate in the family.*

In this regard the child's behavior is considered as part of an interpersonal conflict involving all of the family members and the prevailing situation. The "problem" child may not be the problem at all; it may be parent, grandparent, sibling, or a combination of these. Thus counseling consists of interpretations of exposed familial interpersonal dynamics and of suggestions of methods for dealing with each problem.

3. *The counselor is aware of the unique aspects of the varying group settings and processes.*

Because of the multilevel groups, different processes are at work. Consequently, the counselor is called upon to be sensitive to the needs of all concerned. He finds himself in the role of maintaining a calm atmosphere of objectivity for the discussion of mutual problems in a democratic spirit of respect while at the same time giving attention to such details as seating arrangements and appropriate interventions to insure involvement and participation of individuals in groups that may possibly reach as many as one hundred persons. To function in such a diverse setting is not an easy task; it calls for flexibility, sensitivity, outgoingness, poise, confidence, courage of convictions, and the willingness to assume responsibility of serving as an interpreter and a guiding agent in the psychological process of change.

4. *The counselor employs specific techniques for appropriate situations.*

In some instances psychodrama as developed by Moreno[4] is utilized to facilitate reorientation of the child, or a music therapist may intensify the corrective effectiveness of the counseling process.[5] In those instances where the entire family is interviewed before the observer/participant group, an opportunity is presented for observation of the family unit interacting. An atmosphere is sought wherein a discussion of mutual problems in a democratic spirit of respect can be conducted with a goal of better understanding and the development of a technique known as the family council. The family council is a procedure instituted by the family for the continuation of the corrective approach learned in therapy. The council meets at home at regular intervals and is guided by agreed-upon principles designed to foster free expression, balanced family equilibrium, and education in a democratic relationship.[6]

BASIC ASSUMPTIONS

At this juncture adaptation is the key, and modification within the evangelical framework as a must. In fact, if the church and psychology are to travel together, certain basic assumptions are necessary if we are to avoid complete secularization and mere humanism.

These presuppositions, common to both psychology and ecclesiology, include the following convergency points.

1. *All truth comes from God.* If either psychology as a science or ecclesiology as a program fails to see its origin as theocentric, humanism results, and both psychology and ecclesiology are rendered sterile.

2. *Transactional theology is a valid framework for behavioral change.* While both transaction/relational

theology and psychology share the goals of mature personal development and a productive lifestyle, the importance of the redemptive reconciliatory transactions of God in Christ, appropriated by faith and subjectively experienced, must nevertheless be accepted as the essential thrust for complete transformation with eternal significance. Anything short of this in either ecclesiology or psychology becomes a behavioral technique that may bring greater comfort but fails to provide ultimate meaning.

3. *Man is created in the image of God.* Psychology takes a three-dimensional stance toward the nature of man. The behaviorists say he is a reactive being; the psychoanalysts say he is a reactive being in depth; phenomonologists say he is in the process of becoming. In reality, man is all three, but he is also something far greater—he is made in the image of God. This in turn posits a spiritual dimension of man that must be shared and cultivated if psychology and the church are to collaborate.

4. *Man has an eternal destiny.* To be sure, it is important to make the most of life on earth in terms of healthy personality and facilitative relationships. However, unless both psychology and the church deal with the problem of values, death, and eternal existence, the central thrust of the resurrection and the focal point of the second coming are lost in a here-and-now epistemology devoid of a then-and-there eschatology. Becoming too well-adjusted to this world is to miss the point of the paradoxical tension with its eternal consequences. As Paul puts it, ". . . we are looking all the time not at the visible things but at the invisible. The visible things are transitory: it is the invisible things that are really permanent" (2 Corinthians 4:18 Phillips). As a consequence, "We are hard-pressed on all sides, but we are never frustrated; we are puzzled, but never in despair. We are persecuted, but are never deserted: we may be knocked down but we are never knocked out!" (2 Corinthians 4:8, 9 Phillips).

5. *The Holy Spirit is an active agent in personal growth.* If the Holy Spirit is at work in the world (as we claim), then His intercessory work cannot be minimized (Romans 8:26). This means that any therapeutic relationship within a Christian context should give credence to this spiritual resource. Obviously, such an assumption is outside the scope of psychology as a science and is often ignored by the rather secularized trends of ecclesiology, but coupled with the Christian commitment of a person with psychological skills, the Holy Spirit becomes a potent force for behavioral change.

In short, before psychology can be incorporated in a collaborative function in the most complete sense, it too, along with ecclesiology, must come by the cross and under the Lordship of Jesus Christ.

THE PASTOR AS CHANGE AGENT

Research has shown that the degree to which certain relationship variables are present determines the degree to which therapeutic change and help occurs. These variables include empathy, congruence, respect, concreteness, and confrontation. When these are placed in a scriptural framework and utilized in the relationship between a pastor and a troubled person, the stage is set for spiritual enrichment and genuine behavior change.

Empathy, based on Ephesians 4:31,32 and 1 Corinthians 13, means entering the person's private world and communicating that one understands, cares, and is willing to help. Empathy is intense sensitivity to another person's feelings and experiences.

Congruence is based on 2 Corinthians 3:18 and suggests that the pastor be himself in an honest and forthright manner. It means being what one really is at the particular moment in an open and flexible attitude devoid of bias and exploitative motives.

Respect, based on 1 John 1:7-10 and 2:1,2, calls for the pastor to "prize" the person as being of extreme value and work regardless of the situation.

Concreteness is based on Ephesians 4:29 and involves the importance of fluent, direct, and simple speech patterns. It connotes clarity, interpretation, and opportunities for honest feedback.

Confrontation, based on 1 John 2:3-6, offers the opportunity for assertive and direct behavior that promotes constructive action and effective resolution.

However, if these variables are to be present in the counseling relationship to the degree that the pastor can truly function as a therapeutic change agent, then it is important that the pastor make a thorough analysis of his own role as counselor, the parishioner's role as client, and the counseling process in function.

Counselor

First, there is the *introspective* dimension, in which the pastor surveys his cultural consciousness, becomes aware of his own value structure, and strives to develop a genuine, unprejudiced concern and positive regard for the client's perception and potentiality for change.

Second, there is the *process* dimension, in which the pastor revises his basic assumption in keeping with scriptural attitudes, and then functions in a variety of roles and behavior models to meet the needs of a variety of clients. Thus, although he may operate out of a general framework, yet he takes the stand of a specialist and utilizes the relationship variables and multiple techniques to bring about effective behavior changes in the achievement of a more productive, satisfying life on the part of the client.

Third, there is the *content* dimension, in which the pastor pursues the type of training that will enable him to function as a referral agent, a supervisor of nonprofessionals within his own parish, and a helping agent committed to the goals of enabling the client to strive for self-exploration, a sense of control, the development of interpersonal skills, and the acceptance of responsibility

Client

In view of the foregoing, certain inferences need to be made by the counselor concerning the client if therapeutic change is actually to occur.

First, the client might best be viewed by the pastoral counselor within the framework of a *coping model*. This means that above and beyond the limitations and deprivations which have stymied the personal growth of the person there is yet an ability to solve problems. Consequently, the client is approached as having the capacity to bring both personal and faith resources to bear upon an obstacle or frustration in the environment. The client possesses ego strength and potentiality to be strengthened by the Holy Spirit. He has the capacity to maintain inner integration or to find ego-unity under stress or difficulty.

This concept views the client as a self-coping organism capable of actively dealing with any limit situation encountered in the environment or any problem to be solved as posed by the environment. This model proposes a positive view of the client and attempts to tap the potential inner strengths and spiritual resources available for appropriate decision-making.

Second, it is observed that the pastoral counselor's role might best be perceived within the framework of an *experiential model*. This means that in relating to the client, attention should be given to the counselor's own intrinsic value structure. He must move beyond his professional expertise to an internalization of the relationship variables (empathy, congruence, unconditional regard) as a continuing way of life. As a result, the effective counselor relates to the client as one who actively cares and is willing to become experientially involved in the person's plight. Such a view of the counselor's role requires a willingness on the counselor's part to counsel at the point of need beyond traditional counseling practices. It implies greater risk-taking, innovation, and involvement by the counselor and necessitates a counselor function as friend, stimulator, evocator, resource person, coach, fellow-believer in the power of Christ, and mediator between the needs of the individual and the demands of the situation.

This places the counselor in the general role of a helping agent who shows active care for the client's external situation and engages in a communication process which speaks to the client's inner needs. In this sense the counselor strives to achieve and experience the elements comprising the whole person as a physical, emotional, and spiritual being.

Counseling

Finally, it is observed that the counseling process might best be expressed within the framework of a *spiritual-socio-behavioral model*. The point here is to develop a context such as Adlerian counseling which allows for flexibility and variation. In a specific sense this model emphasizes a more individualized and personalized approach comprising the following ideas: a) the establishment of a unique relationship with the individual client; b) the development of an individualized profile of each client determining a specialized ongoing process; and c) the utilization of all major theories of personality and counseling together with varying group and individual counseling strategies under the lordship of Christ and relevant to the individualized profile: e.g., trait-factor approach for vocational needs; analytic and self-actualizing approaches for more verbal, literate, and introspective clients; learning theory and behavioral approach as an action-oriented strategy interacting with varying degrees at all levels to bring about movement toward desired outcomes.

As illustrated in the following diagram, the spiritual-socio-behavioral model as it is here described proposes a counseling process between a counselor operating from an intrinsic value structure characterized by a biblical lifestyle, the relationship variables as a way of life, and a client with self-coping capacities to solve problems and maintain ego strength. In the dynamics of this interaction, a) a unique relationship is established; b) an individualized profile is developed; and c) a personalized process is engineered toward specific client goals.

Counselor   *Client*

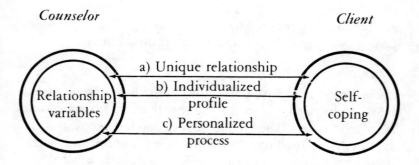

In summary, pastoral counseling is one facet of the pastoral ministry that is generated by effective pastoral care. Counseling is a necessity in this age of anxiety and broken mainsprings if the church is truly to minister to persons and individual needs. Thus, to be effective, the pastor must learn to function in a three-dimensional model of shepherd-leader, facilitator, and agent for therapeutic change.

FOOTNOTES

1. Group for the Advancement of Psychiatry, *Treatment of Families in Conflict,* (New York: Science House, 1970), p. 30.
2. D.C. Dinkmeyer, *Guidance and Counseling in the Elementary School* (New York: Holt, Rinehart & Winston, Inc., 1968).
3. T. Dreikurs and M. Sonstegard, ''The Adlerian or Teleanalytic Approach'' in G.M. Gazda, ed., *Basic Approaches to Group Psychotherapy and Group Counseling* (Springfield, IL: Charles C. Thomas, 1968).
4. J.L. Moreno, *Psychodrama* (New York: Beacon, 1946).
5. A. Starr, ''Psychodrama in the Child Guidance Centers'' in R. Dreikurs, R. Corsini, R. Lowe, and M. Sonstegard, eds., *Adlerian Family Counseling* (University of Oregon: University Press, 1959); and R. Dreikurs, ''The Dynamics of Music Therapy'' in M. Bing, ed., *Music Therapy* (Lawrence: The Allen Press, 1954).
6. R. Dreikurs, R. Corsini, R. Lowe, and M. Sonstegard, eds., *Adlerian Family Counseling* (University of Oregon: University Press, 1959).

12

LOVE THERAPY

Paul Morris

Perhaps the most basic theme in Christianity is the love of God. He *is* love, and He *demonstrated* love when He created human beings in His image, gave us the freedom to sin, and sent His son to die for our sins. In talking to His disciples, Jesus told them to "love one another" as He loved us—unselfishly and unconditionally. "By this shall all men know that you are My disciples," He added, "if you have love one for another."

In this chapter, the author criticizes professionalism in counseling, especially when it is technique-centered and devoid of love. He argues that Christian counseling should be a form of "love therapy" in which an attitude of Christian love permeates the helping relationship, and takes precedence over the application of specific techniques. Basing his approach first on the Bible and then on the writings of Glasser and Janov, the author proceeds on the assumption that "all human behavior stems from the need to love and be loved."

Paul Morris is a graduate of Bob Jones University and Grace Theological Seminary; he received his Ph.D. from the California Graduate School of Theology. A former pastor and subsequently the director of a counseling center in Garden Grove, California, he currently is National Training Director for Prison Fellowship, in Washington, D.C. This position involves in-prison seminars, speaking, and development of counselor-training programs.

This chapter was prepared specifically for this book, although it draws on earlier writings by Dr. Morris, including *Love Therapy,* published in 1974 by Tyndale House Publishers.

The first thing I had to do was take a number. "Your first name, please." The perky girl behind the counter could not have been more than nineteen. She did not ask for my surname or my title. I was dressed in my best pin-striped suit. For all she knew I might have been a senator.

"Thank you, Paul. Sue will be with you in a moment." I sat down. In a few moments, Sue emerged dressed in a tight black T-shirt and jeans. "Hi, Paul," she oozed. "Would you follow me, please?" She indicated a chair for me. I sat down and relaxed while she did her thing on me with extraordinarily nimble fingers. "There you are," she murmured; "Carol is ready for you now." I sat down in another chair, having traversed the distance arrayed in a long white robe.

"And you are Paul." It was not a question. It was a condescending statement of fact. In about twenty minutes Carol had worked her magic on me, and as I slipped on my coat and tightened my tie, the mirror on the wall told the whole story. I had just had my hair cut by "professionals." The sweet young thing who had taken my money and given me my number was a professional. The black T-shirt who shampooed my hair was a professional. And Carol, bless her heart, was a professional. By the time I had been shunted to her, I was so intimidated I fell all over myself trying to tell her how I wanted to look.

But did I look fine? Yes, indeed. Not bad for only $14.50 (plus a tip for Sue and a tip for Carol). And you can bet that I left the Hair Movement that day even feeling like a professional. Would I come back? Not on your life!

You are, today, a professional dishwasher if you do it for a living and use a certain kind of soap. For $25 an hour, you can hire a professional to fix your leaky faucet. Or if you want your grass cut, you may want to try out your local professional lawn service. Modern society today has created, in a word, a Professional Monster, not the least of which is found in the psychotherapeutic and "caring" communities.

We have reached the point in our technocratic lust where we can hire a "professional" to care about us. These professionals are probably the most ludicrous of all, and in some respects, in their own ominous way, the most parasitic and dangerous of them all.

Now being a "pro" in the caring professions is not half bad, except for the fact that those they propose to care for often make the mistake of thinking that their very own "professional" has joined the Trinity. Also, others who are no small potatoes in caring are so intimidated by the professional establishment that their caring takes the form of referral to another professional. After all, who would let his mother cut his hair when Carol and Sue are around?

Also, being a psychologist or psychiatrist provides a certain amount of job security. One has arrived. One has paid his dues when he has a Ph.D. or M.D. behind his name. What would you expect after eight to ten years of college and graduate school, passing those state boards, and accumulating those five thousand hours of supervised experience? When you finally get your license to practice, there's no stopping you. You are a professional. You can now charge people $2.50 per minute for caring.

Since you have arrived, you now have the ability to change the rules. In the forthcoming third edition of the DSM *(Diagnostic and Statistical Manual for Psychiatric Disorders)* we discover that there is no more neurosis. This is not to say that the professionals have discovered a new vaccine which prevents or cures neurosis. This is not to say that the pathology of neurosis has been rendered medically obsolete. The writers of the new bible for the psychiatric community inspired by that Great Psychiatrist in the sky have made the decision that from the day the new DSM is released, there shall be no more neurosis. There shall be "disorder" instead. And it was so.

Can anyone wonder that when the state draws up legislation governing these great scientific disciplines, they consult the professional oracle itself for guidelines and expertise in lawmaking? When lawyers and judges want to determine whether a man was insane when he killed someone 2½ years ago—you guessed it—they consult the oracle who testifies under oath that it was so. After all, he was there and he had his trusty DSM as a faithful, inerrant guide. Of course, the defense has oracles of their own who will testify under oath that the prosecution's oracles are wrong, quoting chapter and verse from their DSM. Then, naturally, the court must decide which oracle is the true oracle, which is usually evidenced by the one which is the most persuasive, or with the most "professional" credentials, or who has been oracling the longest time. The life of the alleged murderer hangs, meanwhile, in the balance.

The professionals in the psychiatric community have established this wondrous credibility by their faultless cure rate and their magical potions like thorazin, or their amazing procedures like electroshock and lobotomy. They are so proficient that patients keep filling their hospitals for treatment. This creates an overcrowded condition because therapy is often protracted, and thus the waiting hordes are given a new designation: they are called "incurables." They are "helped," of course, by the administration of assorted psychotherapeutic drugs like Thorazin, which turns them into unconscious zombies. They are so benumbed that they are unaware that they have a problem. Such treatments are given the name "Chemotherapy." After all, it cures cancer, so why not psychosis?

If the above narrative has an unsettling effect, we may be comforted that there are some psychiatrists who believe that their "science" is illegitimate.[1] They recognize that they are helping very little, if at all. And they are advocating abolishing the specialty and retraining as neurologists. Such refreshing honesty should become the ministerial establishment.

Are we to infer that there are "professionals" among the Body of Christ? You better believe it! Just ask anyone who has had eight to ten years of academic training, and has had to endure five thousand or more hours as an associate or assistant minister, or worse yet, the minister of youth and music! Just ask anyone who has been before an ordination board. It doesn't make any difference if he is a pastor of a church with a cast of thousands or a handful, smaller than a Sunday school class. The pastor is still a professional who will care for you on a one-to-one basis, provided it does not conflict with his executive duties, and also provided that you are a person of consequence.

Some men of the cloth, however, concern themselves only with "spiritual" problems, leaving the "psychotherapeutic" problems to the more competent hands of the psychotherapeutic professional. "Referring to a professional," they call it. This would not be so bad if it were not for the fact that many ministers are at least on a par with a counseling professional, and some are substantially more effective in the helping skills.

THE CRY IN THE WILDERNESS

Set against this backdrop of professional demagoguery is the need of the patient. Picking their way through the morass of white coats and silver ankhs, stumbling around the halls of the mental hospitals, wandering disoriented through the jungles of clinics, psychotherapists, and ministers, their cries can be heard. They are the cries of people who need help. Good substantive help. And there are plenty of them.

> *Poem by John Witmer*
> You followers of the bearded Christ
> and you of the Carpenter
> and you of the twelve-year-old Philosopher—
> hold your talk at Easter-Christmases,
>> you back rowers, and morning onlys,
>> and 5 days of chapel already
> Fighters for ecumenical support of Indian Bill 12,
> unprejudiced suburbanite who's never eaten chili,
> seekers of Truth and Life and The Way,
> PLEASE LISTEN!
> When you retreat from your Crusades
> and pull back from your Causes
> and finally have time for somebody,
> have time for me;
> I need somebody to love me.*²

The trauma of the human condition is no respecter of economics. It crosses the lines of the poor and the rich and all the shades in-between. Most go unaided through life; stumbling, lurching, disoriented, unhappy, and miserable, they fall over the lip of the grave out of everybody's way.

In a small town in California there is an honest-to-goodness gold mine. There is gold there, but the mining has stopped. The reason for this is that it has become too expensive. The cost of mining has exceeded the value of the gold. Conse-

---

*Used by permission of Tyndale House Publishers. See footnote 2.

quently, millions of dollars of gold lie in the earth untouched.

Society is a bit like this. Inside of each one of us there is the infinite worth of the human spirit and soul. But there is so much to wade through to get to it that the cost of doing so has become prohibitive. There are so many problems. There is so much unresolved pain, so much personal disorder and chaos, that an economy-minded society will not spend what it takes to mine the wealth. Consequently, incredible value to men in general is lost. It lies forever buried under the trauma . . . buried under a mountain of professionalism.

This is why it is so important to make the point that there is a mandate here. A mandate which screams to be recognized. A mandate to which government has been sensitive (albeit politically) but is incapable of adequate response. A mandate for which whole systems of professional support have been created, which succeeds only in *aggravating* the cry and *enlarging the mandate*. It is the mandate which calls for the one prerogative which only the Body of Christ can effectively meet—but not in their church buildings and denominational structures. The mandate is expressed in the groans of the derelict, the crazed wail of those designated as "insane," the whimper of the suicide victim as he stares down at curious onlookers two hundred feet below. It is the cry of young John Witmer, "I Need Somebody to Love Me!"[3]

> As I have loved you, so must you love one another.
> By this shall all men know that you are my disciples, if you have love one for another (John 13:34,35).

This is the single command of Christ that the church has ignored more than all the others combined. It is time for us believers, for the Body of Christ, to reclaim our prerogative, our prerogative to care, our prerogative to love.

THERAPEUTIC PHILOSOPHY

This is the starting point and indeed the therapeutic force and healer—genuine, open, honest loving and caring. Without it, all of the mental hospitals, outpatient clinics, psychosurgery, electroshock, chemotherapy, psychotherapy, Gestalts, Transactional Analyses, and Primal Screams in the world will not help. All are sounding brass, and all of the various therapies in the world (including Nouthetic) and seminars (including Erhard's and especially Gothard's) will not take away one scab from the face of human trauma without the healing essence of love.

One of the most satisfying dimensions of being created in the image of God is our ability and our need for love. God is love, the Scriptures tell us. He is the Source from which it comes, the Fountainhead from which it springs. It is inconceivable that One so rich in love should have a need for it Himself. In the minds of some, to suggest that God has a need is to conclude that God is insecure in Himself. Yet Jesus declares that the first and great commandment is to *love thy God!* If God has no such need, why is our love so important to Him?

What kind of person, therefore, would make an effective counselor? The most basic quality is the ability to love, and to be able to accept a mutuality of loving involvement with one's client. This includes, of course, the professional establishment, but is certainly not limited to it.

Counseling itself is an ability, a skill native to the person capable of loving. Since the love of God is central to His character and essence, the same must be true of the Holy Spirit, otherwise known as the Comforter, the "Paraclete," "One called alongside." Called alongside for what? Called alongside for support. Called alongside for empathetic enablement.

"Paraclete," of course, is one name for the Holy Spirit and what He does. It is found elsewhere in the Bible in verb form.

Romans 12:8 names it among the other abilities (skills) which we understand to be a partial list of what has come to be known as the "charismatic gifts," which is to say that paracleting is to be understood as the gift of counseling. This skill, then, is something given from God. It cannot be "acquired" in the classroom.

This is not to say that the study of the behavioral sciences is unproductive or unnecessary. Such study better acquaints the gifted counselor with the needs of his clients and the mechanical procedures of meeting those needs. But the most highly trained academician, or a psychiatrist with impeccable credentials, is sometimes the world's worst therapist. I suggest that it is because his motivation did not come from the right place. It does not stem from caring, loving involvement. Whatever the professional motivation, without this quality of love, it does not come from God, and is therefore inefficient.

What precisely is Love Therapy? It is the incarnate therapeutic illustration of a loving Comforter and enabler. It is not authoritarian, brusque, or in any way "obedience-oriented." It is the therapist asking himself the question, "How would Jesus treat this person?" Its objective is, "Peace be unto you; My peace I give you . . ." and on *rare* occasions, "Get thee behind me, Satan; thou savorest not the things that be of God!" But the latter is never suggested until the former is, in the mind of the patient, a clear option.

Love Therapy is the total involvement of the personality of the therapist in the therapeutic process.

Love Therapy is biblically based. To say that this is a "biblically based" therapeutic procedure is not to say merely that it is a biblical orientation, or that the Bible is used as a springboard, or that the Bible is pedantically implemented. Love Therapy finds its philosophical focus in the mental and emotional health principles found in the Bible. Rarely (if ever) is a Bible verse quoted in the presence of a patient, but it is very much in the mind of the therapist as he skillfully employs its healing quality in therapy. If this sounds like a subtle form of psychological quackery, let me say that the most enduring of psychological principles which have been discovered by the eminent psychotherapists are found in the Bible! From Freud's (Ps. 4:4) psychoanalysis to Gestalt, to Janov's Primal Scream—all of these, plus many others, have contributed to my own composite, to that which I have designated as "Love Therapy."

Years ago when I was a young pastor just beginning to twitter my psychotherapeutic wings, among the many books I read was Bill Glasser's *Reality Therapy*. When I read this book, it dawned upon me that what he was saying was verbatim what the Scriptures taught: loving involvement with a focus on responsibility. The thought that an extremely effective psychiatrist used clearly articulated biblical principles in his therapy greatly intrigued me. I began to study Freud, Jung, Adler, Mowrer, Rogers, and others. I made a significant discovery: that a biblically supportive argument could be made for every demonstrable principle which these eminent theorists found to be true.

I have always had a gift for synthesizing things into a distillate, so I did it. I assembled all of the data that my research provided into a biblical/psychological base, and I began to construct a therapeutic procedure.

THERAPEUTIC PROCEDURE

Diagnosis. By "diagnosis," it is crucial to understand that we do *not* necessarily mean that the therapist must arrive at one of the disorders suggested in the DSM. We have already seen how these "disorders" are fluid in their dimensions and definition, (i.e., "no more neurosis"). Further, such designations tend to cause the patient to act out his malady, once he has been branded as a "_____," or whatever. Glasser, Mowrer, and others have demonstrated that these designations are ineffective in therapeutic procedure, and often counterproductive.

The objective in diagnosis as I see it is to understand and have a firm grasp of the patient's symptoms, and be able to recognize the subliminal force which causes the symptoms. Psychological testing is helpful in this regard, but it is not definitive. Of far more importance is the patient's history. With regard to testing and history-taking, we depart sharply from Glasser's approach. His system (also Arthur Janov's) provides for neither.

But just listening to the patient talk about his life, childhood, parents, education, employment, etc., provides enormous banks of data for the therapist's understanding of just what he is facing in therapeutic procedure. It also provides needed information for the therapist if he intends to employ one of the cathartic techniques.

Objectives. Obviously, the objective in any therapeutic procedure is permanent healing. However, this is visionary. "Permanent" healing is impossible. There is no vaccine against depression, neurosis, or psychosis. In the same way that one may break his leg again, or experience a recurrence of cancer, given the right set of circumstances, one may have another psychological dysfunction. But the same is true for anyone. None of us is exempt from the possibility of behavioral disorder.

However, the healing of subliminal tension and symptomatic phenomena most certainly is possible. Homosexuality, for example, can be "cured." Or shall we say that the neurosis which produces it can be cured. (See *Shadow of Sodom*, by Paul D. Morris, Tyndale House Publishers.) Depression and anxiety can be relieved. Psychosis and thought-disorder can be corrected so that an individual can live responsibly. Sometimes, as in the case of glandular dysfunction, medication can effectively control emotional instability. But it is a medication which treats the glandular dysfunction and not the psychological disorder itself.

The objective in psychotherapy is not to produce a "normal" human being from a heretofore "abnormal" one. It is rather to enable a person who is living irresponsibly to adjust his behavior pattern to a responsible one. It is to assist him in living a life more in keeping with the biblical norm—which is not, let me hasten to say, some rigid adherence to a religious code of conduct. It is rather the establishment of an emotionally satisfying, loving relationship with God, with oneself, and with other human beings. It is to help one understand his place in the overall plan of things and to help him realize that there is a rationale for his living in a world of pain.

Implementation. Before any kind of implementation can take place, and before any substantive progress can be made in the therapeutic process, *involvement* must be achieved. That is to say, a loving relationship must be established with the patient with sufficient strength to generate and warrant controlling *influence.* By "controlling" we do not mean "manipulation" in its worst sense. Instead, we mean the achievement of influence with the client so that he or she will in fact do what is requested and will believe that something is true simply because someone who is implicitly trusted says that it is true.

This places the therapist in an awesome position. He or she must know the Scriptures intimately. Further, he or she must understand what it means to enjoy the Lord and to live happily in relationship with Him.

When one is faced with a patient sitting in a chair opposite him, certain things are assumed. First is that the patient has come to him because he knows that he needs help. He is plagued with the thought of "What is wrong with me?" His marriage may be in shambles, or his children may be incorrigible. The point is that *something is wrong* in his own evaluation, with his lifestyle, and maybe with him personally.

After the patient has ventilated (told his story) sufficiently, which may take anywhere from one to five hours, a history must be taken. If done adequately, this will take another two to three hours.

There are three basic methodologies which I use in the *Love Therapy* approach. Remember that the uniqueness of Love Therapy is not so much in the technique or method used as in the attitude or emotional framework of therapy. In terms of mechanics, what follows is not so different from other forms of therapeutic technique.

Insight and Guidance. Insight therapy has been around for years. It is based on the premise that once a patient is able to intellectualize his problem he will be able to objectify it, see it for what it is, and draw upon his own resources to correct it. This is what happens when a parishioner goes to see his pastor for counsel. This is what happens when we share our problems with those whom we respect and who will listen. It is seeing one's problem through the eyes of another person whose objectivity will not be colored by emotional rationalization.

Like all other forms of therapy, this form assumes the basic responsibility of the counselor. The counselor will listen and provide insight into the patient's problem, will suggest valid and invalid emotional postures, will point out weaknesses and strengths relevant to the situation, and will provide positive guidance and "counsel." He will register his "opinion" or thoughts with the counselee regarding the nature of the latter's difficulty, with the hope that the counselee will opt for his counsel and adjust his behavior accordingly.

This method is effective if the following conditions exist.

1. The counselor has established influence with the patient. He is "involved" with the counselee enough so that his "opinions" not only have merit with him, but are strong enough to coerce behavior. This is not to say that the thoughts expressed by the counselor are in themselves strong,

or expressed in any kind of demanding or authoritarian manner. But it is to say that the relationship he bears with the counselee is powerful enough to warrant adherance to his guidance.

2. The patient's problem is not so deep that it cannot be corrected or relieved at the conscious level. Insight therapy is relatively useless on a patient whose problem has effected a dysfunctional lifestyle. If the patient does not know what is wrong with him, or is incapable of adjustment when corrective measures are provided for him, his problem stems from neurosis or psychosis. No amount of insight, guidance, or counsel will help him. He needs to be dealt with on a deeper level.

Programmed Cathartic Regeneration (PCR). Since writing *Love Therapy* (indeed, while writing it), I have been developing a psychotherapeutic method which I call PCR. It is not to be distinguished from the basic concept of Love Therapy, but is viewed as an expansion of the same idea. Freud said that all human behavior was based in the sexual impulse. It is my contention that all human behavior stems from the need to love and be loved. I will not take time here to demonstrate this, but I want to make the point that what follows is a definite attempt to get a patient past his subliminal dysfunction to a place of loving comfort. The object is to resolve dysfunctional pain while at the same time creating three-dimensional love in the patient: self-love, others-love, God-love.

PCR is a program by which a patient is caused to lie down, relax, and get in touch with himself physically and psychologically. In a semihypnotic state he is guided through a series of imaginary scenarios designed to stimulate catharsis (emotional reliving). This catharsis is regenerative and therefore healing. Arthur Janov (*The Primal Scream*) rightly presumes that psychosis/neurosis is formed at the subliminal level. The reason one becomes mentally irresponsible is because of unresolved conflicts that have taken place over the course of a lifetime and have built up "head" until one becomes affected by it. The object of the therapeutic process is to to get to this underlying pain, resolve it by catharsis, and thus provide space for healing. However, in my opinion, Janov does not take it far enough. Love must be introduced as the healing catalyst. Love is the progenitor of responsibility formation. PCR is an intricate process which provides this.

As a patient is resolving pain cathartically while being guided through an imaginary scenario, a scenario designed to help the patient feel the love of God (or of someone significant to him), healing is implemented. Often dramatic emotional results occur. Given enough time and enough experiences with this sort of thing, it is always curative. It requires a certain amount of professional skill and should not be attempted by nontrained therapists.

Group Therapy. Again, group therapy can be conducted on the insight/interaction level, or the PCR level. I simply want to mention here that a therapeutic process involving a group is highly constructive. There is substantial value in hearing the experiences of others and relating them to oneself, and having the opportunity to share one's own experiences in the arena of the loving support of those around him. Actually, the therapist's role is (or should be) minimal here. The group is *intrinsically* therapeutic. The therapist's role in the group is to facilitate rather than to lead or to attempt to provide a responsible norm.

RESTRUCTURING THE CHRISTIAN MIND

This is no small task, to be sure, but a crucially necessary one! Frankly, I do not think there is another religion so psychologically crippling as Christianity wrongfully applied. I argue with others that Christianity is not a religion. It is a relationship. But I hasten to add that this is what it should be. All too often, it is not. Here are some examples of so-called Christian thought that bring people to the therapist's office:

"I am nothing. A big zero. Christ is everything."

"I must ask forgiveness every time I sin, because if I don't I will not be forgiven."

"I must concentrate on becoming more holy." (Meaning: I must do everything I can and be constantly concerned about eliminating sin in my life.)

"I must continually seek for the will of God for my life."

"I must never get angry."

"I must never swear."

"I must never do anything to break God's law."

"I must be constantly obedient to God."

"I must make Jesus the 'Lord' of my life."

"He must increase and I must decrease."

"Not I but Christ."

"My righteousness is but filthy rags."

"His thoughts are greater than my thoughts."

"I must be constantly aware of and on guard for satanic influence in my thought-life."

"I am not worthy."

"My will is not His will."

"My thoughts are natural, human, and therefore always wrong."

"If I don't pray and read the Bible, I will be out of fellowship."

"When I pray, my prayers never get past the ceiling. Therefore something is wrong with me."

"I know I must be filled with the Holy Spirit, but I don't know if I am."

"I must speak in tongues, or I am not saved, or I am not a Spirit-filled Christian."

"A Christian is always happy and joyful."

"Christ is the answer for every problem."

The problem with all of the above is that they are all true—almost! By *almost* I mean that there is an element of truth in each of them, but somehow this "element" has become lost in the froth of unrealism, and every single one of the above statements is totally devoid of love. If I understand the Bible correctly, love is the prime force and essence of Christian living.

Wrong thinking almost always results in wrong feelings and wrong actions. People who have a demanding, austere concept of God and what He requires of them never measure up to those demands, either literally or in their own minds. In practice and in their feelings they have completely lost the meaning of grace. Their lives are one constant struggle of the frustration of that grace. Therefore, there is a desperate need for Christian people to get back to the basics of divine/human relationships. There is a desperate need in the hearts of most believers to understand God within the framework of genuine trust and love.

Modification of theology is called for. People need to feel the love of God and to feel love for Him in return. People need to understand the scope of forgiveness, the depth of atonement. People cry out to be recognized by God. They should be told that He does recognize them and that they are important to Him, and that because of this they should feel important to themselves and to others. They should know that they are autonomous, that they have an individual purpose and destiny, and that God is responsible for their achieving it and for their Christian growth. They need to fully realize the immense power of belief—how that the "filling of the Holy Spirit" depends on it, indeed their entire relationship with God depends on it; their regeneration depends on it. There is so much, so very much that the Christian has at his disposal. But he needs to be made aware of it and shown how to tap into it.

There is so much in the Bible that is therapeutic and fulfilling. But so many people who come to my office are suffering emotionally because they are suffering theologically. I do not provide them with the "chapter and verse," but I do provide them with a relaxed, realistic theological view. I do plug them into the immense resource of emotional, mental, and spiritual power available to one who enjoys a healthy relationship with God. Problems and painful irregularities—even sin—is discovered to be part of the patient's growth processes. And when there is unexplainable loss, persecution, disparity, or stress without apparent reason, they come to understand that God hurts with them—not just vicariously, but in actuality.

Ruth Carter Stapleton suggests that God is capable of "healing the memories." She is 100 percent right! Stapleton has discovered the effectiveness of bringing one to realize that a loving, gentle Christ who understands and comforts is far more capable of healing than a demanding, guilt-association, punitive God. The more love of Christ we feel in our hearts, the healthier we will all be. The more acceptance we feel from God, the more we feel accepted by ourselves and others. The more our thoughts are aligned with and *involved* with a loving, responsible God, the more our own thoughts will resemble responsibility, and the more satisfying life will be.

FOOTNOTES

1. See, for example, E. Fuller Torrey, *The Mind Game: Witchdoctors and Psychiatrists* (New York: Emerson Hall, 1972).
2. John Witmer, *Rappings* (compiled by Robert Webber) (Wheaton: Tyndale House, 1971).
3. Ibid.

13

INTEGRITY THERAPY

John W. Drakeford

O. Hobart Mowrer, research psychologist at the University of Illinois and past President of the American Psychological Association, probably would not refer to himself as a "Christian counselor." But Mowrer has had a great influence on Christians. His book *The Crisis in Psychiatry and Religion* (published by Van Nostrand in 1961) created a mild uproar among professionals. Mowrer argued that personal problems are the result of sin, that psychotherapy really involves the "problem of values," that guilt is a crucial issue in helping people, and that "Freud and his works are the 20th Century equivalent of the Devil." Mowrer sharply critized the church for turning counseling over to psychiatry and complained that theology is "undisciplined verbiage" out of contact with "human realities." He then went on to challenge church leaders to take a more active involvement in counseling. He wrote, "the Church must become concerned, in a new and more vital way, with the problem of mental illness. No longer should it take a position of subservience to a profession which, by its own admission, has failed to solve this problem; instead, it must approach the problem . . . in terms of religion's own great insights and authority."

Jay Adams (see chapter 8) was greatly influenced by Mowrer, and so was John Drakeford, author of this present chapter. As a Christian, a counselor, and a seminary professor, Drakeford has introduced Mowrer's concept of "Integrity Therapy" to the church, has developed these concepts to a greater degree of sophistication, and has attempted to integrate these concepts with more familiar Christian doctrines. The present chapter, which was written especially for this book, draws on some of Drakeford's earlier writings to produce a summary of Integrity Therapy as a Christian approach to counseling.

John W. Drakeford, a native of Australia, is professor of

Psychology and Counseling at Southwestern Baptist Theological Seminary in Fort Worth, Texas, and is Director of the Baptist Marriage and Counseling Center. His several degrees include an M.A. from Texas Christian University, a Th.M. from Brite Divinity School, and a D.R.E. and Ed.D., both from Southwestern Baptist Theological Seminary. He is the author of over twenty books, including *Integrity Therapy, Counseling for Church Leaders,* and *People to People Therapy.*

John Wesley sat down in the year 1748 to writer a letter to his friend Rev. Perronet, the Vicar of Shoreham in Kent. The letter, which in typical Wesley fashion was published later as a tract titled *A Plain Account of the People Called Methodists,* gives a fascinating glimpse into the way in which Wesley's followers were organized. In the course of the letter he speaks of the work of the lay assistants. Among other things, he says, they are to meet with the United Society, the Bands, the Select Society, and the Penitents once a week and to visit the classes once a quarter.[1]

This statement ushers us into the complex organization of early Methodism. As will be seen by the accompanying chart, the entities set up by Wesley included a group called the Band, in which the members met together. In these groups the participants met to "confess their faults one to another," and one of the conditions of joining was that a participant should be willing "to speak each of us in order freely and plainly, the true state of our own souls and the faults we have committed in thought, word, or deed, and the temptations we have felt since our last meeting."[2] They were led by a layman who supervised the group, made sure that they started on time, and set the example by first speaking of "his own state" and then asked other members of the group searching questions concerning their states, sins, and temptations.

A number of features of group life emerge from a study of the Wesley movement.

1. The Wesleyan groups recognized the importance of in-

dividual differences and provided group experience at various levels. There was association at the society levels, examinations and discussion of behavior at the class-meeting level, and the use of self-disclosure at the band level.

2. Laymen came into a new day in Wesley's groups. High churchman though he was, Wesley gradually gave a large place to laymen and used them in his groups. As improbable as it must have seemed in his day, he also used women leaders in some of his groups.

3. Differing patterns of leadership were utilized within the groups. At the society level the leader addressed the group; in the class meeting he questioned the members one at a time. In the band he "modeled" by telling of "his own state," then called for a response from the others. At the select-society level the group became almost leaderless.

4. The practice of self-disclosure became important. Wesley suffered much criticism because of his commitment to "confession." Despite the problems it brought, Wesley continued to insist on the procedure and answered all the complaints with telling arguments. "Confess your faults to one another" (James 5:16) was probably his most frequently used verse of Scripture.

5. Wesley developed some interesting training programs for preparing leaders for their duties. His programs of supervision have a strangely modern sound.

6. Wesley was a student of the primitive church, and he claimed that he was trying to follow as closely as possible the practices of the early Christians. Thus he became an eighteenth-century bridge for Christians seeking to study early Christianity.

7. Many of the basic books on group counseling look back to 1905 as the starting point for group counseling, when J.H. Pratt held classes for his tuberculosis patients. But an unbiased observer must conclude that the band in Wesley's movement was in many ways a group-therapy experience one hundred fifty years before the modern practice commenced.

THE STEPS OF GROUP LIFE FOR AN 18TH-CENTURY METHODIST

(Few societies were actually as highly organized as this. It represented the ideal.)

SOCIETY

1. Open to all wishing to "flee from wrath to come."
2. Prescribed rules of conduct.
3. Admission by ticket, which could be withheld.
4. Stewards cared for finances.
5. Many activities for members.

CLASS MEETING

1. Originally for collecting money.
2. Focused on behavior of members.
3. Both sexes present.
4. Lay leader questioned each member about spiritual condition.
5. Criticism about leaders led to training program.
6. Became most influential group in the movement.

BAND

1. Purpose "to confess faults one to another."
2. Divided by age, sex, marital status.
3. Leader "modeled role" by first telling "his own state."
4. Leader asked other band members "searching questions."
5. Emphasis on "confession" led to criticism.
6. Members lived by strict rules even covering dress.
7. Special meetings for all the band members.
8. Leaders also met periodically.

SELECT SOCIETY

1. Were inner group seeking "perfection."
2. This was not a static condition.
3. Members motivated development of individual talents.
4. They were to be a model for the rest of the society.
5. They had few rules but insisted on confidentiality.
6. Wesley himself invited close interaction.
8. These groups soon disappeared from Methodism.

PENITENT BAND

1. For the people who had failed and needed help.
2. Made special application their individual circumstances.
3. Leader applied "threats" and "promises" of God.

The Wesley groups were a monument ot John Wesley's administrative ability. He managed to maintain a threefold emphasis in his work of fervent evangelism, social concerns, and a variety of group experiences; he may give us a clue as to the place of counseling in evangelical churches today.

PEER MUTUAL SELF-HELP PSYCHOTHERAPY GROUPS

This discussion of Wesley's groups may prepare the way for consideration of the Peer Mutual Self-help Psychotherapy Groups. The most outstanding of these is probably Alcoholics Anonymous, which historically stems back to the Oxford Group. As Bill W., one of the founders of the movement, said, "The early Alcoholics Anonymous got its ideas of self-examination, acknowledgment of character defects, restitution for harm done, and working with others straight from the Oxford Group." These ideas characterized the Oxford Group when it was an evangelistic organization emphasizing the changed life. In the process the individual passed through a series of steps: confidence which comes from speaking truthfully about one's life, confession, conviction, a sense of wrongdoing, guilt, conversion, acceptance of an altered way of life, and continuance in helping of others as the individual himself has been helped.

A very important part of the Oxford Group was something generally referred to as "modeling," and called by Buchman "sharing for witness." In this process the group member told about his own personal struggles with life, the sins he may have committed in the past, and the way in which he discovered victory over them. In this way it was hoped that the person being approached would see the example of "change" and would embrace the group's philosophy.

An example of Buchman's philosophy of "sharing for witness" is seen in a conversation in which he said, "You don't know what to do with your sins. I use mine. I drive them like a team of horses. They are my entry into the hearts of other people. Telling them honestly where I have failed often helps them to be honest about themselves."

Then he added, "That doesn't mean telling all about yourself all the time, in private or in public. That is wrong. Dead wrong. But you must learn to live free from the pride that is not ready to tell anybody about yourself if, in guidance, you see it will help him. Never tell anything to someone else which involved a third party."[3]

Alcoholics Anonymous took these principles and applied them to the specific problem of the alcoholic, and from the success of Alcoholics Anonymous there have sprung a whole variety of organizations trying to help people with some of the most difficult problems that beset the human personality. These include psychosis and neurosis, drug addiction, alchoholism, obesity, gambling compulsions, and criminality. In a study[4] of a number of these groups I discovered the following elements that many of them had in common.

1. *Socialization.* There are no wallflowers in self-help groups. Whether he likes it or not, the newcomer is pushed into close association with his fellows. A characteristic saying is, "We alone can do it, but we cannot do it alone."

2. *Responsibility.* One self-help group member describes a procedure which is fairly typical: "No one is admitted until he's gone through a tough, emotionally bruising interview. He's forced to look at the miserable condition of his life and face the unhappy truth that he *caused it himself.* He learns to quit blaming others and to start behaving himself as an adult."

3. *High standards.* In contrast to many of the modern schemes of therapy—so permissive in their attitudes toward the client—the self-helpers set high standards for their members and sometimes make heavy demands upon them.

4. *The use of slogans and epigrams.* Alcoholics Anony-

mous has a number of slogans, such as "Easy does it," "A day at a time," "But for the grace of God." Slogans such as these give the member an easily remembered statement of a facet of their philosophy that can be easily recalled when needed.

5. *Lay leadership.* Most self-helpers are a little apprehensive about professionals. Sometimes they grow to think of them as friends, but they jealously guard their lay leadership. The leaders in self-help groups are generally those who once passed through the same experience as the people they are trying to help. The evidence all indicates that they have good reason to be proud of the accomplishments of the laymen.

6. *Self-disclosure.* Most self-helpers have some type of self-disclosure experience. One drug-group member tells of his experience: "Honesty is stressed here, because we are all big liars, very dishonest. It's very hard for people to learn to be honest. There's a fear within us about telling the truth in a situation that might make us look bad. And that's not really necessary here. It's gotten to a point now that if I tell someone a lie I have to go back to him and tell him I lied. I really feel guilty. I have to back off and say, 'Hey, it didn't exactly go like that, this is what happened.' This all came from people stressing honesty to me."[5]

7. *Activity.* Life is one long rush in self-help groups. When A.A. says, "Take it easy," they don't mean sit still, for they are going to run the alcoholic off his feet. In some groups life is one constant hectic round of meetings, classes, and conferences. It sometimes seems as if they are determined to fill up every waking moment of the member's life with so much activity that he won't have time to get into trouble.

8. *Modeling.* What has now come to be called "modeling the role" or "role model" is found in many of the self-help groups. Put into simple terms, it means that the leader gives a practical demonstration of the way he wants the group member to act within the group milieu.

The A.A. member goes to visit the desperate alcoholic who has issued a cry for help. He doesn't lecture him; he just tells his own story of his battle with alcohol and how he found a way out of it all. If the alcoholic is convinced, he attends the meeting, where he is bombarded with a barrage of personal experiences. "I am an alcoholic," "I have been dry for three years," "The fault never was with me," "I always blamed somebody else," "I discovered the program works," "I did the stupidest things."

The frustrated alcoholic begins to feel better. He inwardly says, "These are my people. They too have been defeated and they found a way out of it—by following the plans. Maybe there is hope for me if I will try it."

One evaluation by a professional makes interesting reading: " . . . it is likely that more people have been and are being helped by Peer Self-help Psychotherapy Groups than have been and are being helped by all types of professionally trained psychotherapists combined, with far less theorizing, analyzing, and for much less money."[6]

INTEGRITY THERAPY

Against this background we can turn to a consideration of Integrity Therapy, which is firmly embedded in the Peer Mutual Self-help Psychotherapy Group movement, so much so that it has sometimes been referred to as A.A. in civilian dress. The basic theorizing has been done by O. Hobart Mowrer, who now refers to his movement as Integrity Groups. Integrity Therapy may have moved in a slightly different direction, and I do not want Dr. Mowrer to be held responsible for what I write about his basic theory.

The basic assumptions of Integrity Therapy are:[7]

1. Integrity Therapy rejects all deterministic theories which make one a victim of heredity or environment. Every individual is responsible for his or her own life and exercises

this right by making one's own decisions.

2. Each individual has a conscience, or value system. When this conscience is violated, one becomes guilty, a condition which is not a sickness but a result of individual wrongdoing and irresponsibility.

3. A common reaction to personal wrongdoing is to cover up and deny its existence. In this secrecy, guilt gives rise to symptoms which may be so severe as to upset life's balance.

4. As secrecy causes trouble and separates us from our fellows, so openness with "significant others" is the road back to normality.

5. Openness takes place with increasing numbers of "significant others," and progresses in ever-widening circles as the individual learns to live authentically with his or her fellows.

6. By itself, however, openness is not enough. The guilty individual is under an obligation to make restitution appropriate to the acknowledged failure in his or her life.

7. The only way to become a whole person is not only to remain open and make restitution but also to feel a responsibility to carry the "Good News" to others.

These principles have a close resemblance to a series of biblical ideas, as is seen in the following chart:

EXPERIENCE	SCRIPTURE STATEMENT (KJV)	REFERENCE
Human failure	There is no difference, for all have sinned, and come short of the glory of God.	Romans 3:22,23
Responsibility	So then every one of us shall give account of himself to God.	Romans 14:12
Conscience	The Gentiles, which have not the law . . . are a law unto themselves, which show the work of the law written on their hearts, their conscience also bearing witness.	Romans 2:14,15

EXPERIENCE	SCRIPTURE STATEMENT (KJV)	REFERENCE
Concealment	When I kept silence, my bones waxed old through my roaring all the day long.	Psalm 32:3
Parading virtue	And why beholdest thou the mote that is in thy brother's eye, but considerest not the beam that is in thine own eye? Or how wilt thou say to thy brother, Let me pull out the mote out of thine eye; and, behold, a beam is in thine own eye? Thou hypocrite, first cast out the beam out of thine own eye, and then shalt thou see clearly to cast out the mote out of thy brother's eye.	Matthew 7:3-5
Confession	He that covereth his sins shall not prosper, but whoso confesseth and forsaketh them shall have mercy.	Proverbs 28:13
Relationships	If thou bring thy gift to the altar, and there rememberest that thy brother hath aught against thee, leave there thy gift before the altar, and go thy way; first be reconciled to thy brother, and then come and offer thy gift.	Matthew 5:23,24
Sharing	Confess your faults one to another.	James 5:16
Activity of faith	Your work of faith. Fight the good fight of faith.	1 Thessalonians 1:3 1 Timothy 6:12
Restitution	When a man or woman commits any of the sins that men commit by breaking faith with the Lord, and that person is guilty, he shall confess his sin which he has committed; and he shall make full restitution for his wrong, adding a fifth to it, and giving it to him to whom he did the wrong.	Numbers 5:6,7 RSV
Involvement	Go home to thy friends, and tell them how great things the Lord hath done for thee.	Mark 5:19

THE RATIONALE FOR A
GROUP METHOD

It will be seen that Integrity Therapy is a group technique, a fact which seems to upset certain evangelical Christians, though it is a mystery to me why this should be. Christian fellowship both within and without churches is one of the highlights of the Christian experience. Life within a church generally involves a number of group experiences in Sunday school, prayer gatherings, and church worship services. Moreover, the New Testament teaches Christians to "Confess your faults to one another."

There are a number of good reasons why group counseling is to be preferred to individual counseling.

Group counseling highlights relationships. If we accept the idea of the crucial place of relationships in the development of personality, and that the troubled individual has gotten out of relationship and isolated himself from his or her fellows, it will follow that therapy will aim at reversing this process. A one-to-one counseling experience provides a starting point, but no more than that. Continued over an indefinite period, individual counseling may become a discussion of secrets shared by two peopole, but it will still be a secret. The process must proceed further. So the group becomes the means by which the counselee enters into a whole new series of relationships.

A good counseling group builds trust and confidence. Many counselees will maintain, "I cannot talk in the presence of a group; it would be impossible for me to bare my soul before a number of other people." Yet the experience of one counseling center, which functioned on a one-to-one basis for a long period before switching to group practices, has been that people are more open before a group than they were in one-to-one counseling. Many women particularly discussed very intimate and personal matters much more freely than they ever did in individual counseling.

All of this was confirmed in Yalom's study,[8] which showed that "Feeling more trustful of groups and other people" was among the factors which participants in group therapy considered to be significant. This seems to be a common reaction to group life.

Groups frequently build self-esteem. In a good group the member soon discovers that he or she can help someone else. A capable leader recognizes that even though the subject may not have his or her own problem completely under control, nevertheless he or she can help someone else. Therefore the leader works to move the group member into deeper group situations. As the group member makes a first feeble effort at helping others, he or she gradually becomes aware of new abilities. One's sense of self-esteem grows. Life begins to look better. In helping someone else, the group member has helped himself.

Group experiences provide feedback. In the process of presenting his problem to the group, the counselee encounters a variety of reactions and feedback from the other members. Because of these responses he is able to see his difficulty from a number of different points of view and can take a look at it from a new perspective.

Group counseling provides experiences of interaction. The skillful leader of a group carefully controls the dynamics of the group, bringing them to bear on the members of the group. Isolation is probably the biggest single problem people face today. It is very easy to give counsel like, "You should move toward people," but then the counselee can merely give his or her shoulders a helpless shrug. Once within a group, the sensitive leader can bring the "forces" of group interaction to bear upon individual problems.

Group counseling increases the leader's effectiveness. In a day when counselors frequently find themselves struggling to meet the demands for their services, group counseling opens the way for a much more effective use of the counselor's time.

In the time which would be given to one person, the counselor finds that he or she can effectively help six to nine people.

Counselors also find help from an unexpected quarter. Experience in the group becomes a type of in-service training, and many of the participants learn the skills of leadership and move up to become assistants to the counselor. This greatly facilitates the work of the group.

One final factor is lack of transference. Psychoanalysts have long claimed that positive transference, in which the client came to love the analysts, was a necessary part of therapy. My personal experience has shown, instead, that transference may be a test of a counselor's maturity. In the area of pastoral counseling, particularly, the profession is strewn with counselors whose effectiveness has been reduced and marriage compromised because of an emotional involvement with a neurotic counselee. Rather tragically, this separation from a spouse is sometimes rationalized on the basis, "She didn't continue to grow with him." A group moves away from both positive and negative transference or affection, thus saving the counselor from experiences that have been the Achilles' heel of the counseling profession.

COUNSELING WITH AN INDIVIDUAL

Counseling is a relationship experience, and it begins when two people sit down together and discuss a problem in the client's life. In Integrity Therapy the counselor begins with what we call an Intake Interview. It passes through several stages.

1. *Listening to the counselee.* Most troubled people have a sense of isolation, a feeling that no one is interested in them, a fear that life is getting out of hand. With this in mind the counselor spends time listening to the troubled person. He or she says, "Tell me all about it," and then gives the counselee

undivided attention, without interrupting. Periodically the counselee may be encouraged with such statements as "Yes," "Go on," "Tell me more." The counselor may ask a question, but it will be open-ended, never a question that can be answered with "yes" or "no." A good rule of thumb is to spend two-thirds of the available time listening.

2. *Emphasizing personal responsibility.* When someone gets into difficulty the easiest thing to do is to blame someone else. It makes us feel better if some other person caused our difficulties.

In counseling, an attempt is made to get a client to quit blaming others. He or she is asked, "Yes, but what did you do?" Sometimes we point out that our strong points are O.K., and that it is the weak points that need working on. One of our favorite sayings is, "A man is never stronger than when he's admitting his weaknesses."

Sometimes a biblical allusion will help. God, speaking to Paul, said, ". . . my strength is made perfect in weakness" (2 Corinthians 12:9). Paul himself stated, "When I am weak I am strong," (2 Corinthians 12:10).

3. *Modeling.* Modeling has been called the heart of Integrity Therapy. The word "teach" means to "show," and modeling is a way in which the counselor shows the counselee how he or she should respond. It means using an experience in our own life that may help our counselee. The procedure is seen in the following case.

John S. is telling the counselor about his malaise. He is depressed and just doesn't feel well, and he says the only reason he can think of is that his supervisor at work is giving him a hard time.

The counselor responds, "I think I understand how you feel and I know the tendency we all have to blame others for the way we feel. But I have found that when I feel bad it generally comes because of what I have done rather than what others have done to me.

"A few Sundays ago I was driving to Sunday school. We were running late and I was fussing at my wife and kids. Held up at a traffic light, I was behind another car. The light changed to green and the other driver was slow to move. I started honking at him. As soon as I could I sped past him.

"I drove into the church parking lot, and as we were getting out that car came driving in. The driver was apparently a member of our Sunday school. I didn't enjoy the Sunday school lesson that morning, and I had a horrible headache. I found out that when I act badly I feel badly."

"Is there any possibility that my experience has any parallel to yours?"

The counselor has successfully built a bridge to his counselee by making him feel he is talking to someone who has had his own problems and who therefore understands. He has also nudged his counselee toward facing his own personal irresponsibility and has made it easier for his counselee to become open.

4. *Signing the contract.* In one counseling center the newcomer is invited to join the therapy groups and to sign a contract stating that he will come for at least six weeks.

CONTRACT

Understanding that Integrity Therapy has an implication of honesty and commitment, I undertake to become a part of a therapy group meeting each_____at_____. I further make this a commitment to attend for at least six weeks commencing_____and continuing until_____.

NAME_____

ADDRESS _____

PHONE _____

WITNESS _____

---

5. *Introduction into the group.* The interviewer takes the newcomer into the group and helps him to get started in the group experience.

MARRIAGE COUNSELING

Using the Integrity Therapy technique for marriage counseling requires a slight adaptation. In the initial interview it is our practice to take husband and wife separately. This may be accomplished by starting with both of them together. Then, after discovering which partner is the more ready to talk, the other person returns to the waiting area. Following the interview with the more voluble one, we talk with the second partner. Modeling will also be done differently. It should focus on relationships, with the counselor relating an incident about his or her own failure in the area of relationships.

STRUCTURING A GROUP SESSION

In order to get a group started properly it is important to structure the group. This can be done by the leader making a statement which could take the following form.

He or she might say, "We want to welcome you here this evening. So that there will be no misunderstanding, I want you to know some of the principles under which this first group operates.

"First, we are gathered here under *the covenant of confidentiality*. This means that no one repeats outside the group anything that is said as we are gathered here. Every individual tells his own story—not someone else.

"Second, there are no spectators—only participators. Everyone here is under an obligation to participate. If you have just come to have a look, then you are in the wrong place.

"Third, we have all failed. There are no perfect people in

our groups. We don't discuss our strong points—we speak about our weaknesses. We have a saying, 'A man is never stronger than when he is admitting his weaknesses.'

"Fourth, before we can tell anybody what he should do in his situation we must 'earn the right.' We earn the right by admitting our own failures before we tell anybody else his failures.

"Fifth, because we are operating under the 'covenant of confidentiality' it is not necessary that we know each other's last names, so we will function on a first-name basis.

"Sixth, our group will run for two hours. We comence at 7 P.M. sharp and we try to stop exactly at 9 P.M. , so let us use the time wisely."

We do not have the space to go into the details of group dynamics involved in an Integrity Therapy group; the interested reader is referred to my book *People to People Therapy.*[9]

Integrity Therapy is a counseling technique that has been built on a carefully formulated theoretical foundation and has been widely researched. To the original formulations of O. Hobart Mowrer, sometimes called an unfinished symphony, has been added the ultimate experience in resocialization, a right relationship with God. Emphasizing the biblical ideas of values, personal responsibility, openness, and restitution, it utilizes groups (the time-honored technique of church life) and provides a large place for nonprofessionals, thus allowing lay men and women to exercise their God-given gift for helping their fellows in the process of loving their neighbor as themselves.

FOOTNOTES

1. *The Works of John Wesley, Vol. XIII* (London: Wesleyan-Methodist Book-Room), pp. 248-68.
2. Ibid., pp. 272-73.
3. Peter Howard, "The Result Is a Miracle" in O. Hobart Mowrer, ed., *Morality and Mental Health* (Chicago: Rand McNally & Company, 1967), p. 426.
4. John W. Drakeford, *Farewell to the Lonely Crowd* (Waco: Word, 1969).
5. Paul Martin, "Integrity Techniques in Alcoholism and Drug Addiction" in O. Hobart Mowrer, Anthony J. Vattano, and others, *Integrity Groups: The Loss and Recovery of Community* (Urbana: Integrity Groups, 1974), p. 238.
6. Nathan Hurvitz, "Peer Self-Help Psychotherapy Groups and Their Implications for Psychotherapy" in Mowrer, Vottano, and others (ibid.), p. 153.
7. John W. Drakeford, *Integrity Therapy* (Nashville: Broadman Press, 1967), p. 9.
8. I.D. Yalom, *The Theory and Practice of Group Psychotherapy* (New York: Basic Books, Inc., 1970).
9. John W. Drakeford, *People to People Therapy* (San Francisco: Harper & Row, 1978).

14

POPULAR APPROACHES TO COUNSELING

Gary R. Collins

Where do people turn for help when they have problems? Probably many turn to friends who are immediately accessible, empathetic, able to understand the needy person's situation and style of life, unaware of professional jargon, free of cost, and willing to help. Many needy people also turn to magazine articles, books, self-help groups, radio and television programs, cassette tapes, and popular seminar speakers.

It is difficult to know how much these popularizers have influenced Chrsitians over the years. Liberal elements of the church, with their greater willingness to accept psychology, probably have been sympathetic to the populizers, whereas the theological conservatives may have been more resistant and skeptical. During the past couple of decades, however, all of this has changed dramatically. A number of dedicated people have appeared, each of whom in different ways has combined a popular form of psychology and a biblically related religion into self-help formulas which are widely dispensed through lectures, books, and cassette recordings. Keith Miller's *A Taste of New Wine*, published in 1965, heralded the coming of the Christian popularizers, but more recently, others have attracted large followings. Some of these people, like the Swiss writer Paul Tournier, deal with a variety of topics and appeal to liberal and conservative Christians alike. Others, such as Charlie Shedd or Walter Trobish, attract more limited audiences and restrict their subject matter to a few basic topics, such as sex or marriage. Some are primarily speakers, some are writers, and many do both.

Many of the popular speaker-writers have had formal training in psychology, while others have little or no training in this field and even flaunt their lack of psychological expertise.

This chapter discusses the popular approaches, evaluates their influence, and suggests some guidelines for examining their effectiveness. Written by the editor of this book, it is a revision and expansion of "Popular Christian Psychologies: Some Reflections," an article which first appeared in the *Journal of Psychology and Theology*, Volume 3, Spring 1975, pages 127-32.

The popularizing of psychology is not a recent phenomenon. For many years, magazine writers, newspaper columnists, sales managers, preachers, and numerous others have attempted to apply the conclusions of psychology to a variety of human problems. The advice from these popularizers has often shown considerable deviation from the established findings of scientific psychology, but thousands of people have been influenced nevertheless. And while popular speakers and writers have dispensed their brand of self-help psychology, other nonprofessionals have formed mutual-aid groups composed of needy and sometimes frustrated people who band together to help each other.

Professional counselors often are amazed by these popular approaches to problem-solving and sometimes are inclined to criticize or dismiss them as being simplistic, potentially harmful, and of no importance. It must be recognized, however, that perhaps millions of people follow the teachings of popular, advice-giving leaders and uncritically accept their conclusions on such significant issues as how to rear children, have a better marriage, cope with depression, mature spiritually, get along with people, succeed at work, or have a more satisfying sex life. Millions more are involved in self-help groups in which participants help one another to stop drinking, adjust to widowhood, prepare for heart surgery, cope with cancer, or deal with a host of other life stresses.

These popular movements, including Christian nonprofessional approaches, are exploding in number, variety, and acceptance.[1] All of this suggests that they must be meeting human needs that neither the church nor the counseling professions are meeting. In any book discussing Christian counseling, therefore, we must look at these popular movements seriously and examine them carefully. In the paragraphs which follow we will consider the popular self-help groups, the popular self-help books and writers, and the popular speakers. We will examine the common elements in these approaches, the common appeal in each, and the common message that seems to pervade nonprofessional systems. We will consider some implications for Christian counselors and conclude with practical guidelines for evaluating popular approaches, especially popular Christian approaches to helping.

THE SELF-HELP GROUPS

The term "self-help group" is widely used but somewhat misleading because these groups really comprise a growing movement of "mutual-aid." Katz and Bender, whose recent book is one of the first to analyze the self-help movement, define these groups as

> . . . structures for mutual aid and the accomplishment of a special purpose. They are usually formed by peers who have come together for mutual assistance in satisfying a common need, overcoming a common handicap or life-disrupting prob-

lem, and bringing about desired social and/or personal change. The initiators and members of such groups perceive that their needs are not, or cannot be, met by or through existing social insituations. Self-help groups emphasize face-to-face social interaction and the assumption of personal responsibility by members. They often provide material assistance, as well as emotional support; they are frequently 'cause'-oriented, and promulgate an ideology or values through which members may attain an enhanced sense of personal identity.*2

Self-help groups often are characterized by compassion, an attitude of acceptance, common needs and experiences, self-reliance, informality, similar beliefs, hope, a desire to help others, and (frequently) a resistance to what the participants view as the cold, ineffective, and expensive influence of professional counselors. In short, these groups really embody a very basic and ancient principle for meeting the stresses of life: people must help one another in times of need.

Although the self-help, mutual-aid group phenomenon is widely accepted in the secular world, several writers have argued that the movement really has its beginnings in the Judeo-Christian traditon.3 The New Testament repeatedly instructs us to encourage, support, pray for, teach, comfort, care for, and otherwise help one another. Early Wesleyanism had a small group-mutual-support emphasis, and the controversial Oxford Movement of the last century was clearly a religious phenomenon. It is probable that the Oxford Movement gave rise to what surely is the most effective and best-known of self-help groups: Alcoholics Anonymous—a group

---

*Used by permission of the publisher, Franklin Watts, Inc. See footnote 2.

which still has strong religious connotations. More overtly spiritual are the innumerable small Bible-study, prayer, and sharing groups that have grown up in neighborhoods, educational institutions, business offices, homes, and churches throughout North America.

Professional counselors, including Christian counselors, have not always viewed these groups with acceptance or enthusiasm. While it is probably true that some professionals feel threatened (especially when it becomes apparent that the groups often have a clearer understanding of problems and a better "cure rate" than the professionals), it is also true that many professionals are concerned about potential dangers in the self-help groups. Such groups may discourage or prevent people from getting needed professional help, may encourage unhealthy dependence on other group members, may fragment the society as each group "does its own thing," or may put pressure on people who fail to improve in spite of their involvement in the group. A more serious concern for Christians is whether these groups (including some Christian groups) foster a self-centered philosophy which leaves no place for dependence on Christ, but instead looks to human resources, in the form of a group, to meet all of our needs.

In spite of these criticisms, the groups continue to proliferate. Time will tell whether this is a passing fad or a new return to the old attitude of people helping people.

THE SELF-HELP WRITINGS

Many people look to books and magazine articles for help in coping with the stresses of life. Current best-seller lists often include books which offer easy answers and "never-fail" formulas for asserting oneself, building a better marriage, succeeding in life, losing weight, finding lasting happiness, and solving a variety of problems. The titles are catchy and sometimes as blatant in their promises of success as a book titled *You Can Cope: Be the Person You Want to Be Through Self-Therapy*.

In spite of the proliferation of these books and the seemingly insatiable public desire for self-help formulas, few if any research studies have attempted to evaluate how or even if the self-help volumes bring changes in the lives of readers. In a survey of seventy of these books, one psychologist concluded that self-help authors frequently:

— convey the expectation that change is possible and likely to occur;
— convey the message that every problem has a solution;
— help the reader identify and elaborate problems;
— reassure readers that their problems are common and not evidence of abnormality;
— convey a four-part formula for solving problems (try it, evaluate it, modify it, then try it again); and
— provide a new language for organizing and explaining behavior. Words such as "pathological" or "abnormal" are eliminated and replaced with less threatening concepts such as "games people play," "biorhythms," and "erroneous zones."[4]

Many of the self-help books and articles make people aware of their problems and give reassurance that others experience similar stresses. It is probable that many people benefit from such help, especially those readers who are relatively well-adjusted, able to analyze their problems with some degree of objectivity, and capable of the personal commitment and discipline needed to apply self-help principles.

Regretfully, however, not all consumers of self-help advice fit this description, and it is probable that many are confused rather than helped by the books and articles, which provide conflicting explanations of life problems and contradictory pathways to success and happiness. At least four characteristics of many self-help books make them especially dangerous.

Simplistic assumptions. Every counselor knows that life is complicated and that human problems rarely have simple solutions, but this is not the message of the self-help writings. Many imply that there are easy answers to the stresses of life and that solutions to life problems can come by following a simple recipe. For example, in a widely read Christian book on depression, the author writes "of one thing I am confident, you do not have to be depressed. . . . I am convinced that by using the formula in this book, you can avoid ever being depressed again."⁵ Such promises are misleading, grossly simplistic, and potentially harmful. They discourage people from seeking needed counseling help, and insure the arousal of guilt, greater discouragement, and bewilderment when the formulas do not bring the promised relief. Like diets, these happiness formulas may work for a while, giving people a temporary lift, but almost always they are followed by another "letdown" and the search for a new formula.

Unrealistic expectations. Many of the books and articles create unrealistic expectations about how people should feel, what life should be like, and how problems should be solved. One writer calls this "magic-think"—the tendency to cling to magical beliefs that "If I do what the formula says, I will be happy." Perhaps this is in no place more apparent that among believers who assume that their Christianity holds a magical formula for earthly satisfaction. In contrast to biblical teachings, these Christians are convinced that problems will disappear if they "pray hard enough," "trust enough," or "believe enough." When the prayers are unanswered, they try harder, afraid to face the devastating fact that their theology may be wrong or that their expectations may be unrealistic.

Self-condemnation. Self-help formulas often imply that problems are self-caused and self-cured. This assumption leads people to be overly self-critical, especially when the expected success and happiness is not forthcoming. There is a tendency to ignore the influence of circumstances that are beyond one's own control, and there is a reluctance to seek help from counselors, physicians, pastors, and others who could bring more certain and lasting relief.

Self-condemnation is most likely to follow the reading of books or articles which make glowing promises of success and which imply that a lack of success is the reader's own fault. According to one writer, this principle is best exemplified not in self-help books, but in a self-help group—Weight Watchers.

> The great majority of Weight Watchers are not pathologically obese women, but ordinary women who are striving desperately to fit into socially determined norms of feminine beauty. The prime Weight Watcher tactics—ridicule and humiliation—are superbly designed to enforce the notions that (1) the "overweight" woman is despicable and unsexy, and (2) that all women are self-indulgent, childlike creatures.[6]

What is said here of women could apply equally to men. The self-help approaches teach that one's own behavior can be changed and that failure to change is cause for castigation and self-condemnation. While the self-help emphasis on personal responsibility is admirable, the implied intolerance of personal failure can be destructive.

Egocentric emphasis. Within recent years, one of the most

widely purchased self-help books instructed readers how they could "Look Out for Number 1." Another book told people how to "Win Through Intimidation," and others have given guidelines for helping people "get to the top" in their businesses and careers.

These books illustrate what may be the most dangerous and erroneous aspect of self-help writings—the assumption that happiness and success come to people who focus their attention and energies on themselves and their own achievements. This narcissistic, self-centered viewpoint is widely accepted in our society. It emphasizes hedonistic pleasure, immediate gratification, and self-fulfillment in place of concern for others, duty, self-denial, responsibility, and commitment to God. This philosophy, which shines through the pages of Christian books and articles as well as those that are more secular, tells us to "trust ourselves and do our own thing," but it fails to realize that true happiness comes when we have meaningful relationships with God and with other human beings.

In a period of history when life is stressful, people are confused, and printed materials are both inexpensive and readily available, the self-help books and articles can have tremendous potential for helping those in need. Such media aids bring enlightenment and meaningful insight when they are consistent with biblical teaching, are psychologically sound, and are free of unrealistic promises or simplistic formulas. They can be a useful adjunct to counseling and at times they can even make counseling unnecessary. But many of these books, including so-called Christian books, can also be harmful, and the Christian reader must be cautious in recommending and applying what the self-help books and articles proclaim.

THE POPULAR SELF-HELP SPEAKERS

For centuries, speakers (including teachers and preachers)

have attempted to help people by giving instruction, guidance, and advice from the public platform. With the invention of the radio and the development of television the influence of the spoken word became even more powerful, but within the past decade two additional developments have expanded this verbal influence considerably, especially in the Christian world—the popularity of seminars and the widespread availability and use of cassette tapes.

Although there are some exceptions, the speakers on these tapes or seminar programs (and probably the popular writers as well) appear to have at least nine characteristics in common. In presenting this list there has been no attempt to make value judgments. The following characteristics may or may not be good, but they give a clue as to the reasons for the popularizers' appeal.

Relevance. Each of these movements focuses on issues which are of personal concern to people: marriage, loneliness, failure, phoniness, sex, etc. Most of these issues are presented along with case histories or personal illustrations which stimulate interest and make it easy for the listener or reader to identify with the topic being discussed.

Simplicity. In general, the popularizers avoid references to theory, technical terms, or the extreme complexity of human behavior. Simple explanations are given for problem behavior, along with simple solutions. Adams, for example, lists only two causes of human problems: sin and organic malfunctioning. The latter is best treated by a physician, the former by an ordained pastor who confronts the counselee with the sin in his or life.[7]

Practicality. Most of the popularizers give specific advice telling people precisely what to do in order to cope with a problem. These formulas or principles of behavior often are accompanied by success stories which are used both to demonstrate that the formulas have worked with others in the past and to create the expectation that they will work again in the future.

Avoidance of the academic. Although they often borrow ideas from other writers, the popularizers give the appearance of being disinterested in scholarly debate. They make little reference to books, journals, or other authorities, avoid numerous footnotes, often have no index in their books, and do not qualify their conclusions as would writers in more scholarly literature. In general, the popularizers are more concerned about people than about research, theory, theology, or academics. This person-emphasis is, of course, very appealing to audiences.

Communication skills. Each of the popularizers is a good communicator. Using simple, understandable language, they present clear, explicit messages. Very often several channels of communication are used, including books, speeches, pamphlets, radio broadcasts, and cassette recordings. This multimedia approach creates maximum exposure, which in turn contributes to the popularity of the speaker and his or her message.

Personal appeal. All of the popularizers possess attractive personalities which are appealing to their followers. There are, of course, large individual differences among the popular leaders, and because of this they do not all attract the same followers. Bill Gothard, for example, seems to be liked for his casual manner, humility, and sincerity; Keith Miller is attractive because of his honesty and open attitude; Marabel Morgan is humorous and spices her material with references to sex; Jay Adams is a dynamic and powerful speaker; Paul Tournier is a grandfatherly type of person whose deep interest in people shines through all of his writings and speeches. Each of these people is appealing in a unique way, and each has a following centering around the personality of the leader.

Biblical orientation. The popularizers differ from each other theologically, and while some (like Gothard) refer to the Bible frequently, others (such as Bruce Larson) mention it less often. Nevertheless, each takes the Scriptures seriously, and all attempt to apply Christianity to life in a way that will help others. This acknowledgment of the importance of Christianity undoubtedly attracts people who would fear or otherwise avoid a strictly secular psychology.

Reactionary nature. Each of the popularizers is dissatisfied with something. Adams, for example, opposes secular psychology; Miller resists phoniness in the church and static Christianity; Tournier began his writing career by opposing a form of medicine which ignores the spiritual and psychological nature of man; Larson resists "deadness" both in the church and in the lives of Christians; Peale and more recently Schuller have resisted "negative thinking" and the attitude which says "I can't." The spirit of opposition to some injustice of faulty thinking doubtless attracts followers who are equally dissatisfied and willing to join with a leader who is seeking to bring change for the better.

Uniqueness. Each of the popularizers has something unique—a fresh new writing style, a new message, a way of presenting an idea. Many of the principles for living are not especially new, but they are presented in a uniquely creative way, and this probably accounts for much of the popularity.

THE APPEAL OF THE POPULARIZERS

Why are these popular secular and Christian psychologies flourishing today? Many of the leaders in these movements have little or no training in psychology, and some are untrained theologically. Nevertheless they attract great numbers of followers who are looking for practical advice about psychological and spiritual matters. In the absence of research in this area we can only speculate concerning the reasons for the popularity of these leaders, but probably the characteristics as listed in the above section explain part of the appeal. One might wonder, however, why so many popularizers have come into prominence within the past decade.

Perhaps a part of the answer lies in the current state of the society. The 1960s were years of great social unrest in America. Assassinations, riots in the streets, increases in crime, decreases in morals, turmoil in the universities, an unpopular war abroad, an apparent breakdown in the family unit, widespread dissatisfaction with the traditional church— all of these doubtless created a widespread attitude of discouragement and insecurity. The political corruption, ecological crisis, and economic problems of the 1970s have further shaken our faith in the future and made people especially receptive to anyone who brings a message of hope and confidence.

This is precisely what the popular Christian psychologies have proclaimed: as we move toward the last years of this century, the assurance of stability, hope for the future, concise practical answers to the problems of life, and a promise of success in coping with stress. This message is presented clearly, often authenticated by appeals to Scripture, and supported by numerous case histories and testimonies which demonstrate that the popular psychologies do, in fact, "work."

Coupled with this message of hope is a formula for action. People are urged to apply principles in a practical way, taking action at a time when to do nothing would be painful and depressing. The popularizers each imply that his or her solution is superior to the techniques that people have used in the past, and thousands have jumped on what they perceive as a "winning bandwagon."

The enthusiasm of these followers also contributes to the leaders' popularity. Many make no apparent attempts to attract disciples, but each has a band of enthusiastic disciples whose devotion helps to create controversy around the leader.

Such adulation and controversy attract more people, especially those who are curious. Enthusiastic followers are also verbal in their testimonies and most willing to recommend their leader's writings and ideas to others. By word of mouth the popularity spreads.

THE POPULARIZERS' MESSAGE

It is possible, perhaps, to dismiss the popular movements as fads which will fade as quickly as they arose. But even fads must arise for some good reason. By their prevalence and widespread popularity the movements discussed in this chapter have demonstrated that there are human needs which are not being met elsewhere. People who join self-help groups, flock to seminars, or read the self-help books must have questions which are not being answered in their churches or schools. Such people want help with their marriages, child-rearing, spiritual growth, or interpersonal relations, and they are turning to the popularizers for answers.

One of the clearest messages that comes from the Christian popularizers, therefore, is that the local church has failed to show people how their faith can be applied to the practical problems of life. Bill Gothard, for example, has a sincere concern for pastors and a deep respect for the local church, but the fact that his seminars have existed is living proof that the local congregations have failed to provide guidance in practical Christian living.

It is difficult to place the blame for this failure. Perhaps the seminaries are at fault for teaching a dead orthodoxy which leaves the graduate proficient in Greek and Hebrew but profoundly ignorant of basic human needs and interpersonal skills. Perhaps church leaders are to blame for ignoring the ways in which Scripture speaks to the needs of individuals. Perhaps individual Christians are guilty for taking their Christianity so lightly that, like the believers in Corinth (1 Corinthians 3:1-6), people today have remained spiritual babies, following after a variety of "expert" leaders who spoon-feed their followers with predigested answers that can be swallowed with no need to chew over ideas. More feasible, perhaps, is the conclusion that we are living in an age of experts, when things are so complicated that people have learned to look to specialists in human behavior for help with the problems of daily living.

Why, however, are the specialists in most cases untrained in psychology? Might it be that the professionals are partially at fault for leaving the popular field to others? We have learned in graduate school that psychology is a science which is best applied in the classroom, counseling room, or laboratory. We have tended to look askance at people like Joyce Brothers who popularize psychology, but when untrained persons like Ann Landers or Tim LaHaye appear on the scene, we are also critical because their advice is simplistic and lacking in sophistication. The problem may not be so much with the popularizers who are trying to help people or with the followers who are seeking answers. The rise of the popularizers may be largely because professionals have avoided a needy area—that of helping Christians and others to cope with the stresses of the twentieth century and to live abundant and balanced lives. The popular Christian psychologies, therefore, present both the church and the professional counselor with a challenge. If we disagree with the popularizers, our task is not so much to criticize as to rise up and do a better job.

For the professional such a challenge is extremely risky. By dabbling in the popularization of psychology, the professional loses respect and prestige among academic colleagues, and any move in this direction is almost certain to bring criticism, misunderstanding, and charges that we are oversimplifying complex human behavior. Fortunately, some professionals are moving in this direction anyhow—men like

James Dobson, Bruce Narramore, and Quentin Hyder. The alternative is to leave the popular field to those who are psychologically untrained and unaware of the harm that they might be doing.

IMPLICATIONS FOR CHRISTIAN COUNSELORS

How does the Christian counselor, especially the professional, influence the people who currently follow popularizers? As a start, let me make four suggestions.

First, we must earn a hearing. To do this our professional degrees help, but we must also demonstrate a deep and sincere devotion to Christ, a belief in the authority of Scripture, a genuine interest in people, and an ability to communicate on a popular level. Not everyone can meet these criteria, but they are essential prerequisites for any professional who hopes to reach the popular marketplace.

Second, we ourselves must write and speak about practical issues in a clear and concise way which nevertheless does not overlook individual differences or the complexity of behavior. Our work must be consistent with the teachings of Scripture and as psychologically sophisticated as possible.

Third, we must focus our efforts on at least two fronts. We must appeal to the *layperson*, helping him or her to cope with the problems in life and showing how to reach fellow believers through a process of peer counseling. Then we must help the *pastor* to counsel more effectively and to deal more efficiently with the needs of the congregation. The church leader must be shown the importance of preventive psychology (using the church to prevent problems from arising in the first place or to arrest budding problems before they get worse). He or she must be helped to see how psychology can clarify one's understanding of the Scriptures and how it can help in the practical nature of the ministry.

Recently, a pastor's wife offered the opinion that people,

especially professional people, who disagree with the conclusions of Bill Gothard are simply jealous of his success. While there might be an element of truth in this analysis, it doubtless would be much more accurate to conclude that the professionals are distressed over the potential harm that can come when psychologically untrained persons dispense psychological advice on a massive scale. The popular Christian psychologies do not pose a threat so much as they present a stimulus for professionals to enter a field which we have too long neglected.

Finally, the Christian counselor must help untrained people to evaluate the popular approaches to counseling.

EVALUATING THE POPULAR APPROACHES

When faced with an ever-increasing number of theories, opinions, books, articles, speakers, and advocates of self-help groups, even the professional finds that it is easy to get confused and perplexed about who or what is right. How, then, can the popular approaches be evaluated and utilized in ways that will maximize help and minimize harm? Let us consider eight suggestions.

1. Test the conclusions against the Scriptures. Is the Bible an authority or merely a springboard for the popularizer's own ideas? Does the writer-speaker use good hermeneutics or does he or she snatch verses out of context to prove a point?

2. Test the conclusions against the findings of psychological and related research. This is a difficult assignment for the layperson, but the professional can be aware of recent scholarly trends and can help untrained persons evaluate the popularizers psychologically.

3. Examine the qualifications and characteristics of the popularizer. Is he or she speaking or writing in an area for which he or she is qualified by training or experience? Of course, God does not always work through highly skilled or

educated people, but those who write or speak on personal topics have a responsibility to present ideas which are consistent with Scripture and sensitive to the findings of careful scholarship. The popularizer's qualifications should be examined carefully.

4. Spend some time trying to summarize the major tenets and basic assumptions of the system. These assumptions (about the nature of persons, the nature of the universe, the existence of God, the authority of the Bible, the nature of right and wrong, for example) are not always stated clearly, but they influence the advice and formulas which are given.

5. Try to determine if the system is internally consistent or if it is weakened by contradictions and logical inaccuracies.

6. Examine how case histories are used. Are they illustrative, or does the popularizer use cases as major support for his or her conclusions? Remember, one can find a case history or personal experience to support almost any conclusion.

7. Be slow to attack personalities. Surely it is more important to evaluate and criticize ideas than to attack people whose life work is being scrutinized.

8. Remember that a popular approach can be partially correct. One need not accept a whole system to find ideas that are of value. Ask, then, if the system really works as well as its advocates claim. If not, is there anything of value in the approach? No one is perfect or correct all the time, but even the poorest self-help advocates may reach some conclusions which can be helpful to the Christian counselor and his or her counselees.

FOOTNOTES

1. This proliferation of self-help groups is documented by writers such as Glen Evans, *The Family Circle Guide to Self-Help* (New York: Ballantine, 1969); and A.H. Katz and E.T. Bender, eds., *The Strength in Us: Self-Help Groups in the Modern World* (New York: New Viewpoints, 1976).

2. From p. 9 of *The Strength in Us*, by Alfred H. Katz and Eugene I. Bender, copyright 1976 by Alfred H. Katz and Eugene I. Bender. Used by permission of the publisher, Franklin Watts, Inc.

3. See for example, John W. Drakeford, *People to People Therapy: Self-Help Groups—Roots, Principles and Processes* (New York: Harper & Row, 1978); and N. Hurvitz, "The Origins of the Peer Self-Help Psychotherapy Group Movement" in *Journal of Applied Behavioral Science, 12,* 1976, pp. 283-94.

4. Reported in Sol L. Garfield and Allen E. Bergin, *Handbook of Psychotherapy and Behavioral Change: An Empirical Analysis,* 2nd ed. (New York: Wiley, 1978), pp. 52, 36.

5. T. LaHaye, *How to Win Over Depression* (Grand Rapids: Zondervan, 1974), p. 12.

6. Barbara Ehrenreich, "Letter to the Editor" in *Social Policy, 4,* 1974, p. 56.

7. Jay E. Adams, *Competent to Counsel* (Grand Rapids: Baker, 1970). In a more recent book, *The Christian Counselor's Manual* (Nutley, NJ: Presbyterian and Reformed, 1973), Adams lists a third cause of problems, demon activity, but he dismisses this as being of no current importance, since the Devil is assumed to be bound at present.

15

CATHOLIC APPROACHES TO COUNSELING

Mose J. Glynn and Gary R. Collins

There is perhaps no such thing as a neutral, unbiased point of view on any subject, including counseling. Each counselor, like each reader, brings a perspective to the task of people helping, and this point of view at least partially determines what we observe and how we attempt to help others.

In the preface to this book, the editor noted that most of these chapters have been written to indicate "what is happening in the area of Christian counseling—especially the more conservative Protestant segments of Christian counseling." Although this is the perspective of the editor, not all of the authors would consider themselves to be theologically "conservative Protestants," and neither have we assumed that this is the major perspective among Christian counselors today.

The present chapter, for example, deals with Roman Catholic approaches to counseling. Unlike evangelical Protestantism, in Catholicism there appears to be less concern about finding an approach or approaches to counseling which are "distinctively Christian" or "distinctively Catholic." Nevertheless, much creative, practical, and thought-provoking writing has come from priests and other Roman Catholic counselors. This chapter is an attempt to survey some of this work of contemporary Catholic writer-counselors.

Mose J. Glynn is a former priest. He is a graduate of the University of Notre Dame, St. Mary of the Lake Seminary, and Luthern School of Theology at Chicago. Ordained to the Roman Catholic priesthood in 1967, he served both as a parish priest and as a faculty member at St. Mary of the Lake Seminary in Mundelein, Illinois. The coauthor of this chapter, Gary R. Collins, is editor of this book.

To write about Catholic approaches to counseling is a monumental task indeed—something akin to writing about "Protestant approaches" or even "psychiatric approaches." Catholic approaches to counseling are as diverse and changing as the Roman Catholic Church itself. Although there are similar theological beliefs, there also are wide-ranging differences which influence the ways in which Catholic counselors work.

Some Catholic counseling is *explicitly religious,* dealing with religious matters and sometimes using religious language and symbols. Other counseling is *explicitly secular but implicitly religious.* The techniques and subject matter may be similar to those of the secular counselor, but the values, assumptions, and goals are consistent with Catholic theology. Then there is Catholic counseling which is *exclusively secular.* The counselors and writers may be Catholic, but this is never discussed or acknowledged in their work, and sometimes it appears that secular assumptions are accepted without question. In addition, there are Catholic approaches which might be termed *popular.* As with non-Catholic writers, there are a number of Catholic authors whose popular writings have been used to help readers apart from counseling interviews.

Before considering each of these categories in more detail, it might be helpful to summarize some assumptions about human beings which would be accepted by most Catholic counselors.

1. Humans are dynamic, changing, existential beings. They are not static, fixed entities. They move through stages of growth, interacting with one another and with their environment. A child of two years is very different from a senior citizen. Both are persons, but existentially they are very different.

2. Human beings are social, interpersonal, and communal by nature rather than isolated and solitary.

3. Humans are holistic beings. They are not split into dichotomies of body and soul, intellect and will, reason and emotion. All of these qualities and characteristics are blended together in each person. Human beings are breathing, spiritual, emotional, intellectual, biological, interpersonal organisms. Sometimes people speak about individuals as though they are compartmentalized or split-level structures. That is inaccurate.

4. Human beings are free, responsible, and able to shape their future. They are not determined, as some strict behaviorists suggest. They are not "nonresponsible" as though they are totally controlled by forces outside themselves and exhaustively dictated by external pressures and forces. Of course, people are influenced by what happens outside themselves, but this influence does not take away freedom and responsibility. Outside influences set some limits on the possibilities of human freedom and responsibility, but human freedom and responsibility are both real.

5. By nature, human beings are good rather than evil, corrupt, or depraved. This is an optimistic understanding of human persons. It is opposed to a pathological understanding that sees man and woman as more or less sick or immoral. It is opposed to a pessimistic outlook on people. Paradoxically, although men and women are good and "graced," they do disgraceful things. This optimistic understanding of people emphasizes the intrinsic preciousness, dignity, and value of a human person.

6. Human beings are transcendent, living, and in relationship with God. They can have meaning beyond themselves. They are in communion with God and live for others as well as themselves.

7. Human beings live in a world where there is no radical separation between natural and supernatural, between nature and grace, between human and divine. An understanding of the world and human experience which puts people's actions and experiences into separate compartments labeled natural and supernatural is a distortion. To distinguish natural love and care from supernatural love and care is not assumed in a Catholic approach. People live in one world which is a gracious reality, divinely human and humanly divine.

8. In counseling, human beings reflect what might be termed "the principle of incarnation." This is the assumption that God is revealed in humans. Matter communicates spirit. The tangible contains the intangible. The visible bears the invisible. Human communicates divine. Jesus communicates God. Another person reveals Jesus and God.

The story is told of a young soldier who wired his mother a bouquet of roses for Mother's Day. He did this several months in advance in order to insure his mother's getting the flowers on time. Shortly after arranging to have the flowers sent, however, the soldier was killed and the mother was informed of his death. A few weeks later, when Mother's Day arrived, along came the roses and a note. For the mother, the son was present in the flowers. The visible, tangible, conrete roses represented the invisible, intangible, meaningful reality of the son. This illustrates the principle of incarnation in which human counselors represent and communicate the invisible reality of God.

CATHOLIC APPROACHES—EXPLICITLY RELIGIOUS

Catholic counseling which is explicitly religious refers to those approaches in which definite religious, biblical theological language and understanding directs the counseling. The counseling uses explicit religious terms and categories to understand the counselee's experience. Reference is constantly made to the counselee's relationship to God and to the church. A moral-ethical framework pervades. When sin is determined, sacramental confession and absolution is expected.

This approach is best illustrated when a priest makes a hospital visit. Assume, for example, that the patient-counselee-parishioner shares with the priest that he or she has not been attending weekly Mass and has not been married in accordance with the law of the Church. The priest listens, gets information, and determines how the marriage can be validated. He asks the parishioner if he or she is willing to validate the marriage according to Church norms. If so, the priest invites the parishioner to make a formal confession of sin and receive sacramental absolution. The counseling encounter becomes the prelude to a formal sacramental religious experience. The priest brings to the counseling relationship the religious symbols and thought of the Church's tradition.

This illustration is somewhat caricatured to emphasize the explicit religious thrust of the counseling encounter. This caricature is not suggesting that this priest is not a loving and caring person. The priest *is* caring and loving, and in counseling he uses listening and helping skills. He is knowledgeable of counseling theory and practice, but he emphasizes and responds from an explicitly religious understanding of the counselee's experience. He freely interprets and discusses the counseling issues, using biblical images and theological categories.

CATHOLIC APPROACHES—EXPLICITLY SECULAR, IMPLICITLY RELIGIOUS

Catholic counseling which is explicitly secular but implicitly religious refers to those approaches in which there may be religious and theological understandings of the counselee's experience, but this is not mentioned in the counseling session. Instead, psychological and human relational categories and terms are used in the verbal dialogue.

These approaches assume that psychological and interpersonal-relational secular categories are the equivalent of religious theological categories. Gregory Baum in *Man Becoming*[1] explains this equivalency somewhat as follows: both theologian and counselor are interested in the counselee's experience. The theologian identifies the counselee's experience as *sin*, while the counselor calls the same experience a *pathological resistance to human growth.* The counselor keeps the religious, biblical, theological understanding of the counselee's experience in his mind and heart, but does not make that understanding explicit in formal religous words and actions. Here, then, are approaches in which the counselor translates religious symbols into secular symbols to describe the human experience and help counselees.

Consider, for example, the case of a woman counselee who is having personal internal conflicts and is in the middle of a divorce proceeding. She describes the last seven years of her life as years of turmoil. She and her family have moved several times. Her husband has worked only haphazardly. All savings have been spent. Although she is working as a waitress, her husband has moved out. She has practically no money and soon will be divorced and facing a future still to be built.

The priest-counselor uses his counseling skills to listen and understand her. He verbally responds to her with psychological and human relational language. He speaks to her with the kind of language she is used to in her everyday, secular life. This counselor also listens to her with his theological and biblical imagination and symbols. In his own mind he may think of the story of the prodigal son. He does not tell her this, but his counseling manner and posture is that of the father toward his son. The counselor listens, reflects, understands, and responds with love, care, and genuine unconditional acceptance.

Yet the priest-counselor does not move the counseling relationship to a formal sacramental rite of reconciliation. Reconciliation and healing is assumed to be happening in the explicit secular mode of counseling, without having to become formalized in an explicit religious ceremony.

This approach is well illustrated in the writings of Charles Curran, who until his recent death was professor of Clinical Psychology at Loyola University of Chicago. An ordained priest and clinical psychologist (with a doctorate from Ohio State University), Curran wrote a number of books, some of which have titles that are revealing: *Personality Factors in Counseling, Counseling in Catholic Life and Education, Counseling and Psychotherapy: The Pursuit of Values,* and *Religious Values in Counseling and Psychology.*[2] A pioneer in Catholic counseling, Curran studied with Carl Rogers, was highly nondirective in his methodology, and openly acknowledged the influence of Seward Hiltner, Carroll Wise, Paul Pruyser, and other leaders in the pastoral counseling movement.

Curran saw counseling as a means by which counseles could "arrive at the integration of relgous values and so make religion personally effective." He believed that counseling could bring "a greater degree of religious maturity," and argued that "modern developments in individual and group counseling and psychotherapy, with all their evident weaknesses, yet offer religion one of the best approaches to modern man as he really is. . . . Awareness adapted from counseling therapeutic knowledge and applied to the religious situation can be significant and effective aids to religion."[3]

Unlike some of his more traditional colleagues, Curran was deeply impressed with the therapeutic value of both the Church and the community. He recognized that sermons could stimulate "self counseling," and he believed that counseling was an effective means of instilling and changing values.

CATHOLIC APPROACHES—EXCLUSIVELY SECULAR

Catholic counseling can also be carried out in an exclusively secular way. Such counseling makes no attempt to consider or to use formal religious and biblical terms or categories. There is no denial that the counseling process is religious, but counseling is seen as a secular endeavor using secular skills and categories. Formal religious issues and concerns are referred to a professional in religion, such as a minister or priest. The counselor is considered as a counselor and not as a priest-counselor or as a counselor-minister. The sacred and secular of human experience is not attended to or denied. The counselor avoids taking any formal religious role.

Perhaps the best example of this approach is the work of priest-psychologist-professor Gerard Egan. His creative work on interpersonal relations is well-respected, and his book *The Skilled Helper* [4] outlines a concise, clear, sophisticated approach to counseling and counselor training. A careful reading of Egan's books reveals almost no mention of religion or religious values. The counseling approach described in these books is completely secular, giving no hint of the author's theological training.

Writing several years ago in the *Catholic Educational Review*, a Marquette University professor noted that with some exceptions (such as Egan), there is

a continuing paradox of Catholics in counseling: Most . . . discussions center around the theories of Professor Carl R. Rogers. In one way this is fitting.

Rogers has been the pioneering genius in the field, beyond doubt. At the level of techniques and descriptive psychology, we are deeply in his debt. In another way, however, it is frustrating to be obliged to return continually to his naturalism as against our supernaturalism, his phenomenology as against our qualified dualism, and his somewhat vague relativism as against our critical realism. Is it not possible to build the theory of counseling on a more positive basis, rather than simply reacting to another school of thought? Is not our own theological and philosophical heritage rich and valid enough that it can combine with clinical data in a synthesis that makes its own case, independently of what anyone else happens to be saying? We should look much more to our own intellectual riches before hopping on every existentialist, Zen-ish, phenomenological, or beatnik band wagon that comes rolling along. . . .

A premise that 'anything goes' if it pleases the client is not compatible with Catholic thought. . . . Let the Christian . . . derive the theologico-philosophical facets of his own theory of counseling from his own heritage rather than chasing after the vagaries and anti-intellectualism of phenomenology, Zen Buddhism, and the other contemporary visitors to psychology's heterogeneous garden. Why should we exchange a precious pearl for a bit of gaudy costume-jewelry![5]

This writer's challenge has yet to be answered decisively by Catholic psychological writers.

CATHOLIC APPROACHES—PRIMARILY POPULAR

Within recent years a number of Catholic writers, mostly

priests, have written popular books of a psychological nature. Only three of these writers will be considered here.

Father John Powell is perhaps the best-known of these. Even the titles of his books arouse interest and poignant reflections: *Why Am I Afraid to Love? Why Am I Afraid to Tell You Who I Am?* and *The Secret of Staying in love.*[6] Illustrated with drawings and photographs, these books are thought-provoking and stimulating discussions of psychological issues, interspersed with subtle, but not overt, references to religion.

Father Earnest Larsen is a poet who writes about psychological topics in a style such as the following.

I'd like to ask you a favor.
It's about this friend of mine.
I'd like to tell you about her.
Her name is Bonnie.
She is built like Raquel Welch,
except she is only 19 and
    five feet tall.
The thing about Bonnie
is that she needs help. . . .
Bonnie lost her virginity
in seventh grade
(up at the lake during the summer).
Some virile hero
could boast how
"he scored."
Like I said, being
beautiful has its problems.
That made her distrust people,
every one of them.
Since she couldn't talk to anyone
    at home,
she kept it inside.
She keeps everything inside. . . .

Think right now,
all you guys, of
all the street corners, bars, schools, offices
where
countless women come and go
   believing
deep in their heart;
"There is no such thing as a
man
as he is described here."
There are only more or less
adolescent
baby makers who have no idea
what it means to REALLY
be present to someone
other than sexually.
Think of Bonnie
and all her sisters
messed up, maybe for life, by
   some idiot
proving his manhood,
and who have no chance of finding
human life
unless they do find a
man
who understands what it is to love,
to be present to someone.
If
Bonnie were to ask you,
   "Really,
   of all the males you know,
   how many are trying to live
   a life
   built around the ability
   to love?

How many real
MEN
do you know?"
what would you tell her?"
. . . As Eric Fromm says:
Love is an art
needing constant attention and effort.
Without this art
a person simply can't make it!
Not as a parent,
a husband or wife,
a mother or father—
simply
not as a human being.
Yet,
not only are there no schools to teach the
skill of love
(no formal schools anyway),
but even the basic elements of this skill
are ridiculed and put down.
Discipline, honesty,
courage, honor,
dignity and tenderness,
humility and patience—
all of these ingredients
necessary for the ability to
love
are so little valued.
ESPECIALLY FOR MEN.
And so few living within the culture
seem to even notice the difference.
Finally,
way back here at the end of the book,
we speak of God.
Are we just dragging him in

because we should?
Really,
we have spoken of nothing else.
The message of God
dawning in the darkness
to every male
is: *Be a man.*[7]

More intellectual and philosophical, perhaps, are the works of Father Henri J. M. Nouwen, currently on the faculty of Yale Divinity School. In his several books, including *With Open Hands, Intimacy, The Wounded Healer,* and *Reaching Out,*[8] Nouwen writes insightfully about psychological, spiritual, and counseling topics. The following is an example:

> Much of our world is similar to the acting stage on which peace, justice and love are portrayed by actors who cripple each other by mutual hostilities. Aren't there many doctors, priests, lawyers, social workers, psychologists and counselors who started their studies and work with a great desire to be of service but find themselves soon victimized by the intense rivalries and hostilities in their own personal as well as professional circles? Many ministers and priests who announce peace and love from the pulpit cannot find much of it in their own rectory around their own table. Many social workers trying to heal family conflicts struggle with the same at home. And how many of us don't feel an inner apprehension when we hear our own pains in the story of those who ask our help?

---

*Used by permission of Liguori Publications.
See footnote 7.

But maybe it is exactly this paradox that can give us our healing power. When we have seen and acknowledged our own hostilities and fears without hesitation . . . the tension can keep us humble by allowing us to offer our service to others, without being whole ourselves. . . .

We all want to be educated so that we can be in control of the situation and make things work according to our own need. But education to ministry is an education not to master God but to be mastered by God.**9

THE EXAMPLE OF EUGENE KENNEDY

It is rare to find a writer whose sensitivities and communication skills permit him or her to be equally adept at reaching lay readers, theologians, and professional counselors. Such an author is Eugene Kennedy, Professor of Psychology at Loyola University and former priest whose diverse works reach different audiences with equal success. Some of these books are primarily theological and unrelated to counseling.[10] Others, especially *On Becoming a Counselor* and *Sexual Counseling,* reflect Kennedy's Catholic background and beliefs but appear to be strictly secular in approach.[11] The books lack references to religious language or concepts.

On a popular level, Kennedy has written a highly acclaimed volume which discusses the building of self-confidence and which bears the arresting title *If You Really Knew Me, Would You Still Like Me?*[12] This book, like his writings on sexuality[13] and his biography of the late Chicago mayor Richard J. Daley, makes no claim to be religious.

**Used by permission of Doubleday & Company.
See footnote 9.

Kennedy's writings illustrate the diversity among Catholic counselors—a diversity which we have attempted to communicate in this chapter. A Catholic approach to counseling suggests a denominational, institutional exclusivity, but actually a Catholic approach is universal, beyond institution and denomination, diversified, only sometimes explicit in its religious references, and yet reflective of the tradition whose name it bears.

FOOTNOTES

1. Gregory Baum, *Man Becoming* (New York: Herder and Herder, 1970).
2. Charles A. Curran, *Personality Factors in Counseling* (New York: Grune & Stratton, 1945); *Counseling in Catholic Life and Education* (New York: Macmillan, 1952); *Counseling and Psychotherapy: The Pursuit of Values* (New York: Sheed and Ward, 1968); and *Religious Values in Counseling and Psychotherapy* (New York: Sheed and Ward, 1969).
3. Ibid., pp. 1, 24.
4. Gerard Egan, *Interpersonal Living* (1976); *You and Me: The Skills of Communicating and Relating to Others* (1977); and *The Skilled Helper* (1975); all published by Brooks/Cole, Monterey, California.
5. Robert B. Nordberg, "Is There Christian Counseling?" in *The Catholic Educational Review.* 1963, pp. 1-6.
6. John Powell, *Why Am I Afraid to Love?* (1967); *Why Am I Afraid to Tell You Who I am?* (1970); *The Secret of Staying in Love* (1974); and *Fully Human, Fully Alive* (1976); all published by Argus Communications, Niles, Illinois.
7. Reprinted with permission from *For Men Only,* copyright © 1973, Liguori Publications, One Liguori Drive, Liguori, MO 63057.
8. These books are published by Doubleday.
9. Excerpt from *Reaching Out,* by Henri J.M. Nouwen. Copyright © 1975 by Henri J.M. Nouwen. Reprinted by permission of Doubleday & Company, Inc.
10. See, for example, Eugene C. Kennedy, *Comfort My People* (New York: Sheed and Ward, 1968); and *The People Are the Church* (Garden City, NY: Doubleday, 1979).

11. Eugene C. Kennedy, *On Becoming a Counselor* (New York: Seabury, 1977); and *Sexual Counseling* (New York: Seabury, 1977).
12. Eugene C. Kennedy, *If You Really Knew Me Would You Still Like Me?* (Niles, IL: Argus, 1975).
13. Eugene C. Kennedy, *The New Sexuality: Myths, Fables and Hangups* (Garden City, NY: Doubleday, 1972).

16

OTHER APPROACHES TO CHRISTIAN COUNSELING

Gary R. Collins

In preparing an edited book, the compiler is always faced with some difficult decisions: what should be included, who should be invited to participate, what should be excluded, etc. As we have indicated in chapter 1, many people have made contributions to the field of Christian counseling, but in one volume it is not possible to include all of these as writers. In general, we have chosen to focus on those who are evangelical Protestants, but even here the field is large and growing. Previous chapters have emphasized some of the best-known writers and/or approaches to Christian counseling, but some readers surely will disagree with the editor's decisions concerning who and what is "best-known or most influential."

In the present chapter, therefore, the editor has attempted to summarize additional current perspectives which are significant but perhaps less prominent than those discussed in preceding pages. In time we may discover that approaches which are mentioned briefly here (or are not mentioned at all) will become more and more prominent. Other perspectives which now are widely accepted and influential will perhaps fade in their significance. This book and this chapter, therefore, represent one man's perspective on the current status of a dynamic and growing field.

There is always the danger of misrepresentation when one person attempts to summarize the work of another. Even the choice of a word or phrase could bias the presentation and unfairly distort the viewpoint which is being presented. In order to prevent this, a copy of this chapter was sent to the four people whose positions are summarized in more detail, along with an invitation to make corrections or suggestions for change. Their recommendations were considered carefully, although these counselor-writers in no way endorse what is written. It is hoped, however, that this chapter represents an accurate, although brief, summary of the approaches which are described.

Within the past decade, the field of Christian counseling has exploded in terms of influence and interest among lay people, church leaders, and professional counselors. With this burst of interest has come an outpouring of books, articles, and even several journals—all written from an evangelical perspective. Table 3 summarizes a number of these positions, along with suggestions for further reading.

In general, the positions listed in the table rely upon and are consistent with current psychological-psychiatric thinking. Most also seek to relate the Bible to counseling, although in some cases this appears to consist of little more than the citing of proof-texts from the Bible to add theological credibility to secular counseling perspectives.

Four recent additions to the counseling field have added a unique Christian approach, however. Although Ruth Carter Stapleton's concept of *inner healing* has been described as a "popularized Christianized form of psychoanalysis," many believers have found it to be helpful, especially because of its emphasis on prayer and the power of the Holy Spirit. Coming from a somewhat different perspective, Charles Solomon's Spirituotherapy also stresses the Holy Spirit's power to change people from within. Stanley Strong's *Christian Counseling is* based on more traditional psychology, although it has a strong biblical base. The Bible is even more central in the work of Waylon Ward, whose book *The Bible in Counseling* is heavily characterized by the giving of Bible-based homework assignments. Each of his positions will be summarized in this chapter.

TABLE 3
SOME OTHER APPROACHES TO CHRISTIAN COUNSELING

Author	Sample Writing	Dinstinguishing Features
Bustanoby, A.	"Rapid Treatment for a Troubled Marriage" in G.R. Collins, ed., *Make More of Your Marriage* (Waco: Word, 1976), pp. 108-22.	Bustanoby is a Christian marriage and family counselor with theological training. He advocates "rapid treatment" based in part on the work of Robert Carkhuff and George Bach.
Crane, William	*Where God Comes In: The Divine Plus in Counseling* (Waco: Word, 1970).	Written by a pastoral counselor, this is a summary of basic counseling techniques with a special emphasis on the influence of the Holy Spirit in counseling.
Day, Jerry R.	*Counseling* (Scottsdale: Christian Academic Publications, 1977).	A programmed text which is presented as a self-instructional course in counseling, based on Jesus Christ as a counselor model.
Estes, Arthur	*Bible Therapy: God's Help for the Joyless Christian* (New York: Vantage Press, 1973).	This book is described by the author as a "system of Bible-based and Bible-guided personal counseling . . . presented here for the primary purpose simply of stating that it has been found to work for me."
Hamilton, James D.	*The Ministry of Pastoral Counseling* (Grand Rapids: Baker, 1972).	A restatement of established counseling techniques.

Author	Sample Writing	Distinguishing Features
Hyder, O. Quentin	*The Christian's Handbook of Psychiatry* (Old Tappan, NJ: Revell, 1971).	A consideration of psychiatric topics, including mental illness, depression, anger, guilt, and counseling. Combines "worthwhile tenets of psychiatry" which "have been selected and integrated with long-proved directives of the Scriptures."
Koch, Kurt E.	*Christian Counseling and Occultism* (Grand Rapids: Kregel, 1965).	Perhaps the standard Christian work on exorcism and on counseling those who appear to be demon-possessed.
Lake, Frank	*Clinical Theology* (London: Darton Longman & Todd, 1966).	A massive work (1282 pages) subtitled "A Theological and Psychiatric Basis to Clinical Pastoral Care" written by a counselor who is well-known in Britain.
McLemore, Clinton W.	*Clinical Information for Pastoral Counseling* (Grand Rapids: Eerdmans, 1974).	A restatement of established counseling techniques.
Minirth, Frank B.	*Christian Psychiatry* (Old Tappan, NJ: Revell, 1977).	This is an overview of traditional psychiatry, drawing from secular sources, the Bible, and modern psychopharmacology. Describes man as being in "three distinct and separate parts."
Narramore, Clyde	*The Psychology of Counseling* (Grand Rapids: Zondervan, 1960).	An early restatement of basic counseling techniques, with Christian implications clearly stated.

Author	Sample Writing	Distinguishing Features
Reed, Bruce	*Christian Counseling* (Grand Rapids: Eerdmans, 1965).	This is a small booklet-study guide (50 pages), strongly biblical, and "intended to help in training Christians to serve Christ by accepting responsibility for one another."
Sall, Millard	*The Emotions of God's People: Helping Those Who Are Hurting* (Grand Rapids: Zondervan, 1978).	A currently perspective on counseling, written by a Christian counselor.
Skogland, Elizabeth	*Can I Talk to You?* (Glendale: Regal, 1977).	Written by a licensed family counselor, this is one of several books for laypeople. This book is subtitled "How to be a counselor, parent or friend of teenagers."
Smith, Bob	*Dying to Live: An Introduction to Counseling That Counts* (Waco: Word, 1976).	One of the founders of Peninsula Bible Church presents a "therapy of redemptive truth" based on a three-part view of man, and identification with Christ.
Tweedie, Donald F., Jr.	"A Model for Marital Therapy" in G.R. Collins, ed., *Make More of Your Marriage* (Waco: Word, 1976), pp. 122-33.	In this article the author, a professional counselor and former Fuller professor, describes what he terms "covenant therapy." He is also noted for his Christian interpretation of Frankl's logotherapy.
Welter, Paul	*How to Help a Friend* (Wheaton: Tyndale, 1978).	A well-written restatement of established counseling techniques.

Author	Sample Writing	Distinguishing Features
Wittman, E.C., and Bollman, C.R.	*Bible Therapy* (New York: Simon and Schuster, 1977).	Prepared by authors who are identified on the book jacket only as residents of New York City, this volume is primarily a quoting of verses from the King James Bible, each dealing with some personal problem (e.g. anger, frustration, loneliness).
Wright, H. Norman	*Training Christians to Counsel* (Denver: Christian Marriage Enrichment, 1977).	This is a creative manual for training Christians to counsel, written by a man who has been described as "the dean of evangelical writers on marriage and family relationships."

RUTH CARTER STAPLETON: INNER HEALING

When Freud developed his theory of psychoanalysis, he put great emphasis on childhood and on the ways in which early experiences influence adult behavior and thinking. As a counseling approach, psychoanalysis focuses on these childhood memories which, while buried in the unconscious, nevertheless mold present actions. An important goal of Freud's approach was to uncover these unconscious influences and bring them to conscious awareness, where they could be acknowledged and handled.

In the years following Freud a variety of other counselors built on his theories and sometimes wrote popularized versions of psychoanalysis. Missildine's *Your Inner Child of the Past* is an example. "Your childhood, in an actual, literal sense, exists within you now," Missildine wrote.

It affects everything you do, everything you feel. . . .
Whether we like it or not, we are simultaneously
the child we once were who lives in the emotional

atmosphere of the past and often interferes in the present. . . . In trying to be adults we mistakenly try to ignore our lives as children, discount our childhood and omit it in our considerations of ourselves and others.*[1]

As an approach to counseling, Missildine proposed that people be helped to identify, understand, respect, retrain, and learn to manage their "inner child of the past." But this popular approach was completely humanistic—based on the efforts of the counselee and counselor. God was neither mentioned nor considered.

The Christian concept of "inner healing" or the "healing of memories" went beyond Freud and Missildine, to emphasize the place of prayer, the influence of the Holy Spirit, and the importance of a healing community of believers. Although he never used the term "inner healing," Paul Tournier described an early version of this approach in his first book, written in 1940. This description from Tournier also reflects the psychoanalytic and Roman Catholic roots of the method:

> Christian confession, then, leads to the same psychological liberation as do the best psychoanalytical techniques. As I write these lines, I am going over in my mind an interview I had today with a Sister of Charity whom I shall call Florence. She had been sent to me by her superior.
>
> Without any preamble she admitted that her difficulty was that she did not know how to begin to tell me about the problems on her mind. So we began with some small-talk about her work. She is scrupulous, shy, gloomy, full of worries, especially

---

*Used by permission of Simon and Schuster, Inc. See footnote 1.

about her work, at which she is too slow. Her state of mind is a further worry to her, because she feels she is being a bad witness to Christ by being so lacking in joy. Then she has doubts about her vocation—doubts which take away the last positive prop on which she might lean. . . .

I hardly say anything. Her story goes, bit by bit, right back to the sources of her vocation, then to her childhood memories, to the premature death of her mother, and the moral barriers which separated her from her father. Then, all at once, she goes to a deeper level still. While I pray in silence, she tells of terrible emotional shocks suffered in childhood, which have weighed on her mind all her life. I cannot of course recount them here, but what I want to point out is that they are the sort of repressed memories which psychoanalytical technique sometimes helps to bring out into daylight, but never as quickly as this. . . .

When I thanked Florence for the trust she had shown in me by being so frank, she replied simply that what had made it possible was that she had come with me into the presence of God.

I then suggested to her that she should pray, to bring all these things from her past and lay them at the foot of the Cross. But she did not dare to pray aloud—and this too was a great obstacle to her in her service for Christ. After some minutes of silence, however, she found the courage to make this second decisive step. When she left my consulting room she was radiant, and had no further doubts about her vocation.**2

**Used by permission of Harper and Row Publishers. See footnote 2.

The more modern concept of inner healing has been described in several books written by Catholics,[3] summarized succinctly by David A. Seamands on two cassette tapes ("The Healing of Memories," available from Christian Counseling and Enrichment, 8000 East Girard, Denver, Colorado 80231), and popularized in two books by Ruth Carter Stapleton.[4] The approach varies somewhat, depending on the counselor-healer and on the counselee, but some assumptions and methods are generally accepted.

1. It is assumed that present problems often arise from traumatic "dark and painful memories" which are deep in the mind, but which influence our current behavior and interfere with our happiness.

2. Healing of memories involves "the experience in which the Holy Spirit restores health to the deepest area of our lives by dealing with the root cause of our hurts and pain. . . . Since Jesus Christ is the same yesterday, today, and tomorrow, he is able to go back into our lives and heal the traumatic episodes."[5]

3. There is a strong emphasis on the healing power of the Holy Spirit. Stapleton writes that:

> Some areas within our lives can only be healed by the power of the Holy Spirit. Psychiatrists bring a degree of healing by probing into the past and bringing understanding of our weak and vulnerable spots and our angry and fearful reactions, but only the Holy Spirit can move back into these areas and remove the scars.***[6]

A similar theme is presented by Father Michael Scanlon, who writes that the healer-counselor does not depend on his or her own diagnosis or wisdom, but expects that the Lord

---

***Used by permission of Word Books, Inc.
See footnote 6.

will reveal what needs to be known and what needs to be done in helping people.[7]

4. Counseling involves helping people to "find and expose repressed painful memories," which are then committed to Christ with the prayer that he will bring healing, love, and forgiveness in place of fear, hatred, hurt, and feelings of rejection.

Sometimes a process called "visualization" is used. Counselors are told to think about a painful situation from their past or a difficult personal relationship, and then they visualize Christ coming into the situation, bringing forgiveness, love, and strength.

5. Forgiveness is at the heart of inner healing. With Christ's help, counselees must learn to forgive others and to forgive themselves.

6. Prayer is also central to the healing of memories. The counselor, counselee, and often a body of believers all pray that there will be love, a willing surrender to Christ, and the inner healing of memories which so often leads to a "release from a common bondage to a perfect freedom."[8]

In one of her books, Stapleton describes the criticisms of a minister who challenged the scriptural basis of inner healing. "I don't claim to heal," she responded; "I only try to prepare the person to be receptive for the healing in order that any unhealed, crippling memory can be touched by the Great Healer."[9] Such an approach continues to be controversial, but in the opinion of Mrs. Stapleton and many others, there is nothing in this approach which contradicts Scripture or the teachings of Jesus.

CHARLES SOLOMON: SPIRITUOTHERAPY

More explicit, perhaps, and better-developed theologically is an approach developed by Charles Solomon and labeled *Spirituotherapy*—a term which has been trademarked by the

U.S. Patent office. Described by Solomon as "a new discipline to replace psychotherapy and psychiatry,"[10] this approach assumes that "Christian counseling . . . is leading another person in understanding and appropriating all that the Lord Jesus Christ is for all that he (the counselee) needs, both here and hereafter. . . . The object of counseling . . . is to bring those with whom we deal to maturity in Christ."[11]

Spirituotherapy holds that there seldom is such a condition as "mental illness," and neither is the counselor described as a therapist. He or she is a "spiritual guide" who is "called of God to this specific ministry of leading souls into a depth relationship with Jesus Christ." Spirituotherapy is "not so much a technique to be learned as a relationship to be shared." But the counselor "can only lead a person to spiritual depths that he himself has plumbed. To do this will demand a willingness to forsake and repudiate the role of therapist"[12] and to allow the Holy Spirit to work through the counselor to make changes in the life of the counselee who is willing to be changed.

Solomon quotes Scripture freely and illustrates his approach with a number of diagrams which are too detailed to be included here but which are shared, in part, with counselees. It is assumed, for example, that human beings consist of a "tri-unity" consisting of body (the physiological part by which we relate to the world through our senses), soul (the psychological part, including the mind, will, and emotions, with which we related to others), and spirit (the spiritual part of our makeup, by which we relate to God.) This is illustrated in the following diagram.

At the center of this being (where the question mark appears in the diagram) there is either the self (flesh) or Christ. Nonbelievers and many believers have a life centered around the self. This leads to theological error and may result in physical symptoms, and such psychological attitudes as inferiority, insecurity, inadequacy, guilt, worry, doubt, fear, and more serious problems such as schizophrenia, obsessive thoughts, and depression.

It is because self is at the center of the life, that all this conflict has developed and continues to grow. . . . *Self in control of the life is repugnant to God.* In psychotherapy, of whatever persuasion, self is strengthened to cope with those problems. Herein lies the basic problem with psychotherapy. With enough psychotherapy many of the symptoms will respond so that a person becomes better adjusted, with the symptoms either diminishing or leaving. But, in order to cope with them, better defense mechanisms are built and self becomes stronger. This is diametrically opposed to what God does, because God's way of dealing with self is that it must become weaker and weaker until its control is finally phased out. Self is reduced to nothing so that Christ can be everything. This is the process by which Christ becomes the center of life.

When Christ is in control the self, or flesh, no longer holds sway. . . . The mental and emotional symptoms are purged from the life; and, if all that has caused the conflict inside is gone, the resulting psychosomatic symptoms leave also.[†][13]

In Spirituotherapy, the counselee is viewed not as a patient needing treatment but as a person needing spiritual help. Most people have experienced childhood rejection,[14] and the counselor helps the counselee experience Christ's adequacy to meet every psychological need from within.

The first two hours of counseling are fairly well-structured. After some opening remarks designed to establish "an open, trusting relationship," the counselor inquires into the nature of the problem and then spends forty to fifty minutes taking a case history, which looks especially for past rejection and traumatic events. As this proceeds there must be an ongoing spiritual diagnosis, and at some time the counselor takes two to five minutes to explain the rejection syndrome.[15] Then, forty to fifty minutes are spent explaining the body-soul-spirit wheel diagram to counselees and using a line drawing to introduce the concepts of complete commitment to Christ and identification with Him. The counselee is encouraged to make a prayer of commitment and is instructed to "review the information covered in the last half of the interview prior to the next interview," and confirm the concepts from Scripture.

Further interviews are less structured. They begin with a discussion of the counselee's concerns of God's dealings with him or her, and continue with "about half counseling and half teaching." Counseling, therefore, involves two prongs: 1) the client's increased understanding of himself and how his *past* influenced his *present,* and 2) the client's understanding of his inclusion in Christ's death, burial, resurrection, and ascension, and how he can appropriate all that Christ is for all that he needs, thus freeing him from the past.[16]

---

†Used by permission of Charles R. Solomon and Tyndale House Publishers. See footnote 13.

Unlike many other writers, Solomon is honest enough to admit that his counseling doesn't always work, and neither does it always bring permanent change. There can be several reasons for this, including failure of the counselor to teach properly, failure of the church to provide follow-up support, failure of the counselee to keep "appropriating his identification with Christ," and, in all of this, Satan's opposition. Notice, however, that the failure is not with the system. Solomon, who cites a number of case histories to support the value of Spirituotherapy, believes that the system is correct because it is built on Scripture. Not all believers would agree, however, with the "victorious-life" exchanged-life theology on which this system is built. For this reason the approach remains surrounded by controversy but defended enthusiastically, especially by those for whom it has been personally helpful.

STANLEY STRONG: CHRISTIAN COUNSELING

Stanley R. Strong is Professor of Educational Psychology at the University of Nebraska in Lincoln. He is not well-known among evangelicals, in part because he has never written a book on counseling. In 1977, however, he served as guest editor of *Counseling and Values,* a professional journal which devoted one whole issue to Christian counseling. In a lengthy and stimulating article, Strong outlined his concept of what was called "Christian counseling in action."[17]

Christian counseling, writes Strong, is similar to secular therapies which assume that "people can control what they think." What they think can in turn control how they act and feel. Counseling is viewed as "an intensely personal experience where clients review much of their life in detail and face their deficiencies in full." The Christian counselor seeks to love the counselee, to model what he or she "expects the client to become," and to always remember that God is in control.

> Only God can heal the wounds. . . .I must
> believe that God uses what I am doing (even when
> I do it stupidly) in His plan for my clients. . . .It is
> His work, I trust that His will is to heal, that He
> will use my efforts, and that people who come to
> me are the ones He wishes me to see.[18]

Christian counseling, suggests Strong, involves three phases.

First, the counselor must "meet" the counselee, listening attentively to his or her reported difficulties, giving support, asking questions, and communicating one's desire to value and understand.

Second, counselees must be mobilized for change. The client "is helped to see that he or she is personally responsible for the problems he or she is encountering, that the problems are traceable to and directly caused by his or her own thoughts, beliefs, and perceptions, and that only he or she can and must change them. In this phase the counselor interprets, defines, declares, and exhorts."[19] The counselor also points out that sinful pride and selfishness are two major causes of personal distress.

Third, the counselee is helped to "adopt and integrate responsible loving in all areas of life." Counselees are helped to admit their fallibilities and sinfulness, are encouraged to confess their wrongdoings to God and to others, and are shown how to accept divine forgiveness. In all of this, counselees are encouraged to think and act responsibly in all situations.

Several concepts are mentioned repeatedly in Strong's approach.[20]

1. *Values.* Gone are the old theories which assumed that counseling could be morally neutral. It is now recognized that the counselor's views of right and wrong greatly influence counselees. As a courtesy to potential counselees, therefore,

the Christian should not hesitate to state his or her Christian values. To not do so explicitly is to do so implicitly, and this surely is unfair to counselees.

2. *Self-control and responsibility.* Counseling can be defined as the art of helping people control themselves better. The counselor serves as a coach, retained by the counselee to help him or her to take responsible action. At times this process can be helped along if the counselor and counselee can understand past events which influence present attitudes and behavior. The counselor can also strengthen the counselee's will to change and can challenge the popular notion that we are not personally responsible for our lives.

3. *Responsible loving.* Christianity is based on love which comes from God. The counselor must demonstrate this love and teach counselees how to love in accordance with biblical teachings.

4. *Forgiveness.* This is a key process and a major uniqueness in Christian counseling. In secular approaches, injuries and mistakes can only be repressed or forgotten, but Christ forgives and enables us to forgive others. To experience this forgiveness, however, we must admit failures and acknowledge that we are sinners in need of divine pardon. Such an admission is often resisted, and for this reason many people fail to experience the joy of being forgiven.

5. *Prayer.* This is described as an "essential part of Christian counseling," an influence which can be a powerful factor in healing. To begin and end a counseling session with prayer points to the need for God's wisdom, guidance, control, comfort, strength, healing, and will in counseling. In addition, the counselor silently prays repeatedly during the interview, asking the Lord for guidance and the ability to understand and help.

Strong has given some indication of how Christian counseling can be applied to those who suffer from anger, guilt, depression, and marriage problems, but his creative approach has yet to be developed in detail. Nevertheless, this is an attempt to present

> . . . ways that psychological knowledge can be used for healing in Christian counseling. The approach assumes that all knowledge, including scientific psychology, is a gift from God and can and should work in unison with His healing love to aid His people with their problems in living. The approach differs from other counseling approaches in that it is Christ-centered: The model of health is Jesus Christ. Christian counseling's methods and processes are applications of psychological knowledge to help clients achieve health after the model of Jesus Christ.[21]

WAYLON WARD: THE BIBLE IN COUNSELING

Like many other writers discussed in this book, Texas counselor Waylon Ward believes that Christian counseling can draw on secular psychology but must be based on biblical revelation. Unlike secular approaches, Christian counseling is unique in its:

— emphasis on the creation, fall, and redemption of the human race;
— belief in the Bible as the absolute standard of truth and guidebook for counselors;
— unique ultimate goal: to enable counselees to become more like Jesus Christ;
— belief that "through the indwelling power and presence of the Holy Spirit, the Christian counselor has a source of knowledge, understanding, and guidance that enables him to be more effective";
— emphasis on *agape* love;
— encouraging counselees to build a dependency on God;

—conviction that the Christian counselor should model or reflect the character of God to his or her client, and actualize the attributes of God through one's manner of living;

—unique support group—the "body of Christ" (i.e., other believers in the church):

—eternity perspective, which assumes that life does not end at death but continues eternally;

—unique attitude which views the past from God's perspective as presented in the Bible—a perspective which believes that Christ died for our sins, forgives, and enables every event to be seen in the light of His ability to use it for the believer's good; and

—flexible methodology which permits counselors to use different techniques, providing they are consistent with Scriptural absolutes.[††22]

Ward's "counseling model from the New Testament" reflects basic evangelical Protestant theology, including God's creation of human beings, our fall into sin, and redemption by Jesus Christ.

An excellent illustration of what the Christian counselor does is found in John 11. Jesus called Lazarus forth from the grave. He came out bound in graveclothes—linen wrappings that still re-

---

[††]Used by permission of Moody Press.
See footnote 22.

tained the stench of death. Jesus could have easily commanded those wrappings to drop off. Anyone who can raise the dead could surely remove graveclothes. But Jesus did not remove the graveclothes that bound Lazarus. Jesus told Lazarus's friends, who were standing close by, to do that. He involved others in the miracle of Lazarus.

The friends did not give life to Lazarus. They were simply the tools that God used to release Lazarus so that he could really live. So it is with a Christian counselor. The counselor does not give life—he is merely a chosen tool in the hands of the Life-Giver. Why God chooses to use such tools only He knows for sure, but the counselor can help set people free so they can really live. . . .

To be truly scriptural in the counseling approach, one cannot deal with a person's attitudes only. Behavior must also be dealt with. A truly balanced, Christian approach in counseling will help a person work to be transformed in thinking and feelings and behavior.[†††][23]

Ward's approach is presented in only a few pages of his book[24]. The major emphasis of his counseling manual focuses on the concept of homework. This involves completing questionnaires and sentence-completion forms, writing biographical sketches and sometimes letters, discussions with mates or other people, reading, listening to tapes, and the completion of study guides based on various passages of Scripture. About fifty of these are included in Ward's book, along with instructions for their use.

[†††]Used by permission of Moody Press.
See footnotes 22 and 23.

CONCLUSIONS

As Carlson has noted earlier in this book, the modern idea of counseling is not mentioned in the Bible. Nevertheless, five Greek words are used in the New Testament to convey the concept of counseling.

First, there is *parakaleo*, used in Romans 12:1, 2 Corinthians 1:4, and Romans 15:30 to mean to beseech, exhort, encourage, or comfort.

Second is the Greek word *noutheteo*, found in Romans 15:14, 1 Corinthians 4:14, and Colossians 3:16. The word means to warn, confront, or admonish.

The third word, *paramutheomai*, is used in 1 Thessalonians 2:11 and means to cheer up and to encourage.

Fourth, *antechomai*, used in 1 Thessalonians 5:14, means to cling to, hold fast, take an interest in, and hold up spiritually.

Fifth, there is *makrothumeo*, a passive verb which means to have patience and which is found in Matthew 18:26,29, James 5:7, and Hebrews 6:15.[25]

True Christian counseling is biblically based and can be as diversified as the biblical terms which are used to describe it. Books and articles on Christian counseling continue to roll from the presses, and more will surely appear in the future. This leads to the question of how one can evaluate present and future counseling approaches which are called Christian. It is to this that we turn in the next chapter.

FOOTNOTES

1. W. Hugh Missildine, *Your Inner Child of the Past* (New York: Simon and Schuster, 1963), pp. 13, 14.
2. Paul Tournier, *The Healing of Persons* (New York: Harper and Row, 1965), pp. 236-37. (First published under the title *Medecine de la Personne,* in 1940.)
3. See, for example, Dennis Linn and Matthew Linn, *Healing of Memories* (New York: Paulist Press, 1975); Agnes Sanford, *The Healing Gifts of the Spirit* (Philadelphia: Lippincott, 1966); and Michael Scanlan, *Inner Healing* (New York: Paulist Press, 1974).
4. Ruth Carter Stapleton, *The Gift of Inner Healing* (1976) and *The Experience of Inner Healing* (1977), both published by Word Books, Waco, Texas.
5. Stapleton, *The Gift of Inner Healing,* p. 9.
6. Ruth Carter Stapleton, *The Gift of Inner Healing,* copyright © 1976, p. 10; used by permission of Word Books, Publisher, Waco, Texas 76703.
7. Scanlan, *Inner Healing,* p. 32.
8. Stapleton, p. cit., p. 35.
9. Ibid., pp. 62-83.
10. Charles R. Solomon, *Handbook to Happiness* (Wheaton: Tyndale, 1975).
11. Charles R. Solomon, *Counseling with the Mind of Christ* (Old Tappan, NJ: Revell, 1977), p. 21. Used by permission.
12. Solomon, *Handbook.*
13. Charles R. Solomon, *Handbook to Happiness* (Wheaton: Tyndale, 1975), p. 60.
14. Solomon, *Counseling,* p. 42.
15. The rejection syndrome is described in Solomon's book *The Ins and Outs of Rejection* (Denver: Heritage House Publications, 1976).
16. Solomon, *Counseling,* p. 78.
17. Stanley R. Strong, "Christian Counseling in Action" in *Counseling and Values,* 21, February 1977, pp. 89-128.
18. Ibid., p. 105-6.
19. Ibid., p. 110.
20. Ibid., pp. 116, 117.
21. Ibid., p. 75.
22. This list is adapted from Waylon O. Ward, *The Bible in Counseling* (Chicago: Moody, 1977). The illustration of Lazarus was first suggested by Maurice Wagner.
23. Ibid., pp. 15, 16.

24. In his private practice, Ward attempts to combine biblical accuracy with psychological and professional excellence. He emphasizes a relational and insight-oriented approach.
25. Adapted from Frank B. Minirth, *Christian Psychiatry* (Old Tappan, NJ: Revell, 1977), pp. 37-38.

17

THE DISTINCTIVES OF CHRISTIAN COUNSELING

Gary R. Collins

What is Christian counseling? Is it merely counseling done by Christians? How does it differ from secular counseling? How can we evaluate Christian approaches to counseling? These are difficult questions—questions which have only been answered in part within the previous pages.

It is easy for Christians to read the different approaches to counseling and become confused. If we count both popularizers and writers in the counseling field, we have at least one hundred Christian (primarily evangelical) approaches to helping people. Many of these approaches are similar, with like presuppositions and goals. But there also are sharp differences, which sometimes lead the advocates to criticize and condemn, and frequently leave the casual reader bewildered and floundering. Is there no "right" approach? How *can* we help others?

It is beyond the scope of this book to tell the reader which is most correct and which systems are most in error. In the preceding chapters we have attempted to let the authors present their views without editorial comment. In this chapter, however, we seek to pull things together by identifying some distinctives of Christian counseling, by discussing some disturbing trends in current Christian counseling, and by presenting some criteria for evaluating present and future approaches to counseling. It is hoped that by applying these criteria the reader will be able to make decisions about the counseling techniques and theories which he or she can accept and use in helping others.

This chapter, written by the editor, was prepared especially for this book.

The history of medicine has been described as a path strewn with worthless remedies which once were thought to be helpful. Blood-letting, ritualistic incantations, various forms of physical torment, and the application or ingestion of almost every imaginable substance have characterized treatment over the years. Commenting on this a century ago, the compiler of the *Paris Pharmacologia* wondered: "What pledge can be afforded that the boasted remedies of the present day will not be like their predecessors, fall into disrepute, and in their turn serve only as a humiliating memorial of the credulity and infatuation of the physicians who recommended and prescribed them?"

In reading the preceding chapters, we might be inclined to wonder if some future observer might raise similar conclusions about contemporary Christian counseling. The field is large, growing, diverse, and complicated. It is populated by counselors and writers who may be sincere, compassionate people but whose personalities, theologies, psychological orientations, values, and personal experiences have led to a variety of sometimes-clashing counseling goals, assumptions, theories, and techniques—all of which are labeled "Christian."

This complex caldron of Christian counseling approaches has led to confusion, contradiction, and criticism. This in turn has the potential of harming counselees. While it may be true that secular approaches to counseling are even more diversified and confused, many believers would like to see greater unity and greater evidence of effectiveness among those who claim to be Christian people helpers. Perhaps increasing numbers of Christian counselors, counselees, students, pastors, and other people are asking basic questions about Christian counseling. What, if anything, are its distinctives? Is Christian counseling the same as "biblical counseling"? Which Christian approach is best, or are they all equally effective? How can the Christian approaches be evaluated?

Before turning to these and related questions, it must be

emphasized that no one writer can answer these questions to the satisfaction of all readers. The authors whose names appear in this volume would not all define "Christian" in the same way, and there might be a diversity of opinions not only concerning the basic ingredients of "Christian counseling" but also concerning whether there even can be a Christian approach or approaches to counseling.

Some counselors and writers have attempted to develop definitive theologically and biblically based approaches to counseling; others have started with secular theories and have proposed "Christianized versions" of transactional analysis, behavior modification, psychoanalysis, rational-emotive therapy, and other contemporary psychologies. A few Christian counselors have attempted to validate their approaches with biblical and/or empirical research, others have relied on personal experience to "prove" the effectiveness of their approaches, while still others have ignored or resisted any efforts to test the real value of a theory or techniques. A few Christian approaches and their developers have attracted bands of enthusiastic followers; most others have had limited acceptance and application. All of this could leave the nonspecialist confused and discouraged. It is little comfort to realize that the secular counseling world is even more diversified and disrupted.

When God created human beings He made us each unique. We are not robots who look alike, lack the capcity to think, and all act in the same mechanical way. Instead, we are individual human beings, varied in our personalities and intellectual capacities, inclined to sin, imperfect in knowledge, and prone to error. Even those whose lives are committed to Jesus Christ differ—sometimes substantially—in their opinions, their perspectives about society, and in their understanding and interpretation of Scripture. It should come as no surprise, therefore, that we have different attitudes toward people in need and different helping approaches, each of which may be built on a study of Scripture.

Because of this diversity it is unlikely that we will ever have one "true" Christian approach to counseling, any more than we can hope for one generally accepted approach to homiletics, church government, evangelism, or eschatology. In fields such as evangelism, preaching, Christian education, and counseling, the diversity of opinions and approaches might even be good. Because people are different, they are reached and helped in a variety of ways. Surely no one approach to counseling speaks to every problem and benefits every person. Jesus used different approaches with different people, and counselors today do the same. But no one of us can reach everyone like Jesus could. Our unique personalities permit each of us to be especially helpful to some people but not to others.

It is probable, therefore, that Christian counseling will continue to be a diversified field. Christian counselors must begin with a commitment to Jesus Christ and must build their theoretical approaches on solid theological grounds. We must encourage and challenge each other to evaluate our methods, conclusions, and assumptions, but we must accept the fact of individual differences and avoid petty arguments and criticisms, especially those that are based on personal opinions, a desire to build up some one theorist, and an apparent need to "prove someone else wrong."

With this background, let us look at some distinctives of Christian counseling, some disturbing aspects of contemporary Christian counseling, and some ways of evaluating Christian counseling.

DISTINCTIVES OF CHRISTIAN COUNSELING

In a popular article published several years ago, psychologist Bruce Narramore wrote that "you cannot have a vital relationship with Jesus Christ and continue to offer the same secular counsel as you did before you knew Him." Narramore then identifies five distinctives of Christian counseling:

The most fundamental distinctive of the Christian counselor is the fact that *he can lead a person to establish a personal relationship with the God of the universe* through His son, Jesus Christ. This relationship carries an influence through time and into eternity.

The Christian counselor holds the only truly satisfying solution to a meaningful philosophy of life. No Plato, Aristotle or Tillich can give to man the sense of meaning, destiny and purpose that is revealed in the Word of God.

A further distinctive of Christian counseling is the therapist's *reliance upon the Bible as a guideline for moral and ethical behavior.* A searching soul is not left to the whims of his imagination or "the counsel of the ungodly" to determine his standards. More than once I have counseled women who have previously been advised to throw off their inhibitions and seek out an adulterous affair to relieve pent-up emotions and neurotic conflicts. The truly Christian counselor engages in no such harmful and unbiblical counsel.

The Christ-centered counselor finds in the Word of God great truths of human adjustment: insights into the nature of man, his motivation, his defenses and ultimate resolutions of conflicts. Such insight is not available to the non-Christian, for this is *spiritually discerned* (I Cor. 2:14).

Finally, *the Bible has the only clear answer to the problem of sin and guilt.* No amount of rationalizing or soul pacification will cleanse the heart of a sinful man and fill his life with a sense of purity and fullness.*[1]

---

*Used by permission of *Psychology for Living*.
See footnote 1.

While this is a beginning overview of Christian counseling distinctives, it only hints at Christian assumptions, says little about Christian counseling goals, and does not mention techniques in counseling. Each of these must be considered as part of Christian counseling distinctives.

Assumptions. In a recent article, Ross S. Banister wrote that many Christian cunselors have sought to—

. . .find psychology in the Bible. This pursuit has often led to a simplistic psychology which then develops into a rigid system. We must remember that the Scriptures are not a complete textbook on psychology (or history). However, the Bible will verify or validate psychology (or history) wherever they converge. Coming to Scripture with inconsistent presuppositions drawn from psychology in order to find proof-texts is not a valid approach. Unfortunately many Christian counselors begin here. Having been introduced to secular models in their training, these counselors take their solely secular presuppositions to Scripture and seek conforming evidence. Anything can be 'proven' by this method—thus the conglomeration of counseling theory professed by Christians.

Integration of psychology and theology can only accurately begin at the presuppositional level. One's world view determines one's perception of reality. A Christian world view is absolutely crucial to how one studies and applies psychology.**[2]

In an earlier book it was argued that every psychological and counseling system begins with underlying assumptions or presuppositions.[3] These assumptions influence counseling

---

**Used by permission of LifeStyles.
See footnote 2.

whether the counselor is aware of this or not. Evangelical Christians, for example, generally accept the following basic assumptions, each of which should have an influence on our perception of people and on our goals and methods.

Concerning *God*, Christians believe in His eternal existence, sovereignty, omniscience, omnipresence, and omnipotence. He exists in three persons—Father, Son, and Holy Spirit—and is intimately acquainted with each person in the world. Secular counseling says little about God and usually assumes His nonexistence and/or noninvolvement in human affairs.

Concerning *the universe*, Christians believe that God created the universe (including its human inhabitants) and that He "holds everything together."

Concerning *humans*, Christians believe that we were created "in the divine image" but that we fell into rebelliousness and thus are sinners who need a Savior. Jesus Christ, God's Son, died for sinful human beings, making salvation or the new birth available to all who believe in Him. For such believers there is the promise of life eternal in heaven after death. Secular counseling, in contrast, says nothing about salvation, our ultimate destiny, or our relationship to God. We are valuable creatures who are loved by the Creator. The secular counselor may also assume human value, but many would agree with Fromm that we are "alone in a universe indifferent to our fate."

Concerning *epistemology*, Christians believe that the Holy Spirit teaches and guides, especially through the pages of God's inspired Word, the Bible, our infallible guide of faith and conduct. We also learn through such means as intellectual activities, the communion of Christians, and empirical research, although all of this must be tested against the unchanging truths of Scripture. The secular counselor dismisses the Bible's relevance and proclaims the superiority of science, but has no basis other than subjective experience for making ultimate decisions.

Concerning *pathology*, most evangelical Christians would

agree that our problems arise ultimately from sin in the human race and often from sin in the counselee's own life. Christian counselors differ, however, in the *extent* to which we believe that individual sin in the counselee's life may cause problems. We also differ in our views of the relative importance of individual responsibility and environmental influences as causes for problems. Secular counselors also debate the "responsiblity-environmental causation" issue, but almost none accepts the concept of sin as rebellion against God and as an important cause of pathology.

Concerning *guilt,* Strong has written that "a major difference between Christian counseling and secular counseling lies in the importance of forgiveness. In secular counseling, injuries and mistakes can only be "forgotten" and used as learning experiences. "But in Christ we can do much more than forget our mistakes. We can be forgiven our mistakes and we can forgive others theirs."[4]

Assumptions such as these, therefore, distinguish Christian counseling from non-Christian approaches, and in this respect Christian counseling is distinctive.

It must be added, however, that even though there are similar Christian beliefs about God, the universe, humans, epistemology, and pathology, there are also differences on these same issues—differences which depend on our theological positions. These theological differences may rarely be acknowledged, but they surely affect counseling. Paul Tournier and Jay Adams, for example, are both Christians and both Calvinists. Both would agree that humans are sinners and that Jesus Christ alone is our Savior. Tournier, however, is a universalist who believes that everyone will be saved; in contrast, Adams writes that "as a reformed Christian, the writer believes counselors must not tell any unsaved counselee that Christ died for him, for they cannot say that. No man knows except Christ himself who are his elect for whom he died."[5] Such theological differences surely influence counseling and account for some of the differences that exist even among evangelical Christians.

Goals. Counseling books often include similar lists of counseling goals: to help counselees change behavior, attitudes, values, and/or perceptions; to teach skills, including social skills; to encourage the recognition and expression of emotion; to give support in times of need; to teach responsibility; to instill insight; to guide as decisions are made; to help counselees mobilize inner and environmental resources in times of crisis; to teach future problem-solving skills; to increase counselee competence and "self-actualization," etc.

But what about the Christian? Does he or she have alternative or additional goals for counselees? Does the Christian counselor seek to

—present the gospel message and encourage counselees to commit their lives to Jesus Christ?
—stimulate spiritual growth?
—encourage the confession of sin and the experience of divine forgiveness?
—model Christian standards, attitudes, and lifestyle?
—stimulate counselees to develop values and live lives which are based on biblical teaching, instead of living in accordance with relativistic humanistic standards?

The Christian who makes these issues a part of counseling is in danger of being criticized for "bringing religion into counseling." Such criticisms sometimes come from non-Christians, but they also come from believers. To ignore such theological issues, however, is to build our counseling on the religion of humanistic naturalism, to stifle our own beliefs, and to compartmentalize our lives into sacred and secular parts. In Colossians 1:28,29, the Apostle Paul described his life purpose in a paragraph which could well guide the counselor and give an ultimate goal for Christian counseling:

We proclaim him, counseling and teaching

everyone with all wisdom, so that we may present
everyone perfect in Christ. To this end I labor,
struggling with all his energy, which so powerfully
works in me.[6]

Christian counseling shares many of the goals of secular
counseling, but the Christian distinctive is that his or her
goals concern the counselee's relationship to Jesus Christ and
the acceptance of Christian values.

Techniques. It has been suggested that all therapeutic
techniques have at least four common attributes. They seek
to arouse the belief that help is possible, to correct erroneous
beliefs about the world, to develop competencies in dealing
with social living, and to help counselees accept themselves as
persons of worth. To accomplish these ends, counselors consistently use such basic techniques as listening, demonstrating
interest, attempting to understand, and at least occasionally
giving some direction. Most Christian counselors would have
no problem with these four "attributes," and most use the
basic techniques that characterize all counseling. It has been
estimated, conservatively perhaps, that over ten thousand
counseling techniques are in existence, each of which is used
enthusiastically by at least one or two counselors.

The secular counselor is inclined to select techniques on the
basis of their pragmatic value. If a technique "works" it is used,
providing that no one is "harmed physically or otherwise." The
Christian, likewise, selects techniques which are based on
pragmatism (and thus he or she is similar to secular approaches),
but the Christian also tests techniques against the authority of
biblical teachings and (for many believers) against the conclusions of Christian theology. In practice, therefore, the Christian
a) accepts and uses many standard counseling techniques, b)
refuses on moral, biblical, and theological grounds to use some
techniques which are used by secular counselors, and c) may use
some techniques which secular counselors would avoid. Since we
have already acknowledged the first of these conclusions, let us
consider the latter two.

Several years ago some researchers began using "sexual surrogate partners" to help counselees overcome sexual fears and develop more competent sexual behaviors. The Christian cannot use or condone such methods because they are considered morally wrong and contrary to biblical teaching. In like manner, nude encounter groups, the encouragement or endorsement of extramarital or premarital sexual intercourse, the development of self-centered goals and attitudes, the use of abusive language, or the encouragement of antibiblical values are among the procedures which must all be avoided. The Christian counselor must seek to be Christlike in his or her speech and actions, avoiding the appearance of evil, even if such techniques might be inclined to help the counselee. Like Timothy of old, Christian counselors must "in speech, in life, in love, in faith, and in purity" be "an example of those who believe" (1 Timothy 4:12 NIV). One cannot assume in counseling that the end justifies the means. The "means" or techniques must be consistent with biblical teaching.

This leads to some techniques which are distinctly Christian and may be used in Christian counseling at least occasionally. Prayer in a counseling session, the reading of Scripture, gentle confrontation with Christian truths, and encouraging counselees to become involved in a local church are the most common examples.

As with Christian assumptions and goals, therefore, Christian counseling techniques are often similar to those of secular counselors, but in some respects they are—or should be—unique.

DISTURBING ASPECTS OF CHRISTIAN COUNSELING

The recent blossoming of interest in Christian counseling could be seen as a healthy sign. No longer are we generally inclined to assume that "good Christians don't have problems," and no longer do we dismiss the need for counseling as a mark of spiritual and personal weakness. At times all of us face crises or develop problems for which counseling would be helpful. To meet these needs a number of Christian counseling approaches have been developed, some of which have been summarized in the preceding pages. Although their number and differences may create confusion, their creativity and even their existence has stimulated a continuing search for better and more biblically based ways to help people in need.

As the field develops, however, there are disturbing trends which should be recognized and which hopefully can be corrected. These trends include, but are not limited to, the following.

Competition and attitudes of superiority In their zeal to find a biblical approach to counseling, some writers and their followers have developed a superior attitude which implies (and sometimes states) that: "Ours is *the* biblical approach; other approaches are partially or totally wrong or at least non-biblical." Such an attitude assumes a self-righteous, hyper-critical, combative stance, and shows little love or respect for the work and understanding of other believers.

Surely no one counseling approach can claim to be the true and final answer to people helping. When we are convinced of error in the work of another, we should point this out and identify both apparent misperceptions and deviations from clear scriptural teachings. Mutual criticism and dialogue help to refine our approaches, but this should always be done in a spirit of gentleness (Galatians 6:1) and concern for others in the body of Christ.

Uncritical acceptance or rejection of secular psychology. Both of these trends are seen among Christian counselors. Many, steeped in secular psychology, have failed to recognize the humanistic, naturalistic assumptions upon which most psychological methods and techniques are built. Secular approaches are accepted, often uncritically, and then there is a search for Bible verses to "prove" that the theory is correct. Adams argues convincingly that this "baptizing of secular . . .

views, which has frequently characterized much that has been called Christian counseling, must be rejected. Instead, Christians must get back of these views and understand their basic antichristian presuppositions."[7] In somewhat picturesque language, Mowrer once proposed that "evangelical religion [has] sold its birthright for a mess of psychological pottage."[8] This is apparent in some of the preceding chapters, where the writers clearly begin with psychology and personal experiences and then refer to theology or the Scriptures when or if this seems relevant. For many the psychological cart has come before the theological horse.

But the solution to this problem is not to throw out psychology. Some evangelicals claim to do this in a sincere but misguided desire to have a pure biblical approach to counseling. Such approaches are never free of psychology, however. Psychological terms, methods, and concepts are "thrown out," only to be distorted and brought back under other names.

In the future, let us begin with our theologically based assumptions, and then learn what we can from modern psychology, accepting that which we perceive to be consistent with the teachings of Scripture. This is easier said than done, but we must consistently seek to evaluate psychology from a Christian perspective, avoiding the tendency to quickly and uncritically accept or reject psychological findings.

A psychological-theological dualism. Among some Christians there has been a tendency to divide human problems into the spiritual and the psychological, each of which gets unique treatment. Evangelism, helping people to grow spiritually, and confronting individuals with their sin are all part of spiritual counseling. Psychological counseling, in contrast, deals with issues such as depression, confused thinking, unconscious influences, and troublesome impulses.

By separating the spiritual from the psychological, this compartmentalism avoids the difficult issue of how theology and psychology can be integrated. It also rests on a questionable assumption about human beings: that spiritual issues can be restricted to a part of life. Surely we are whole persons, not individuals who can be carved into convenient categories. Most physicians realize that we cannot separate the physical from the psychological, and neither can we partition the spiritual from the rest of our human condition. Spiritual, psychological, and physical issues intimately influence each other. The sooner this is realized, the more effective will be our counseling.

An acceptance of selfism. In a perceptive and thought-provoking book, Paul Vitz has argued that selfism—the worship of the self—has become the dominant religion of our society; psychologists are its high priests. Self-actualization, self-fulfillment, self-help, and self-satisfaction are concepts which have replaced self-denial or self-sacrifice as important values.

> Selfism is now the standard position of much of the government bureaucracy that deals with social problems. It is certainly the controlling system in the so-called 'helping' professions—clinical psychology, counseling, and social work. . . .
> The relentless and single-minded search for and glorification of the self is at direct cross-purposes with the Christian injunction to *lose* the self. Certainly Jesus Christ neither lived nor advocated a life that would qualify by today's standards as 'self-actualized.' For the Christian the self is the problem, not the potential paradise. . . . Correcting this condition requires the practice of such un-self-actualized states as contrition and penitence, humility, obedience, and trust in God.
> To worship one's self (in self-realization) or to worship all humanity is, in Christian terms, simple idolatry operating from the usual motive of un-

conscious egotism. . . . Selfism is an example of a
horizontal heresy, with its emphasis only on the
present, and on self-centered ethics. . . . What is
excluded is the spiritual life of prayer, meditation,
and worship—the essential vertical dimension of
Christianity, the relation to God.***[9]

Vitz maintains that in the United States selfism began with
theologians Harry Emerson Fosdick and Norman Vincent
Peale. It continues in a popular form in the ministry of
Robert Schuller but is elaborated most carefully in the
writings of Erich Fromm, Carl Rogers, Rollo May, and
Abraham Maslow. If this anslysis is true it is not surprising
that selfism has been accepted into Christian psychology with
little awareness of its humanistic and harmful implications.
Such a view elevates self-actualization above biblical values
like duty, patience, self-sacrifice, and servanthood. In
counseling it is important to emphasize that we are valuable
creatures whom God loves, but the Bible also emphasizes a
giving, forgiving commitment to God and to each other.
Some Christian counselors appear to be forgetting this. They
are embracing a selfist approach, labeling it Christian
counseling, and failing to see its anti-Christian implications.

A lack of careful evaluation. Contemporary Christian
counselors freely provide demonstrations and personal
testimonies to indicate the success of their techniques, but
there are few if any carefully controlled investigations of
counseling effectiveness. It has been suggested that many
secular counselors and theorists have made "advances from
observations to conclusions with a maximum of vigor and a
minimum of rigor."[10] Personal experiences and stories of successful "cures" have appeared with abundance, but there is
little careful research to demonstrate whether a technique or

---

***Used by permission of William B. Eerdmans Publishers.
  See footnote 9.

approach is as effective as its advocates claim. Within recent years this has begun to change in the field of secular counseling,[11] but among Christians there are almost no scientifically respectable research studies of counseling effectiveness. Perhaps our acceptance of Christian testimonies has carried over to counseling. If some counselor, theorist, or counselee has positive experiences in counseling, we assume that there is no need for more rigorous research.

In fairness to Christian psychologists, we must recognize that quality research is both difficult and extremely expensive. It is difficult to formulate research questions concisely, to clearly define such variables as "improvement" or "effectiveness," to find representative experimental and control subjects, to make precise accurate measurements, and to control the variables (influences) apart from counseling which could confound the results. In addition, there is the serious question of whether traditional scientific methods can really test complex questions such as the effectiveness of counseling, the maintenance of these effects over time, the influence of counselor skill or personality, the effect of counselee motivation, the relative effectiveness of different approaches, and similar questions. In an earlier book[12] I proposed an "expanded empiricism" to deal with these issues, but the problems still are large and the costs excessive. It is not difficult, therefore, to understand why many people prefer to forget the research, to cite case histories, to find some biblical support for their conclusions, and to assume that their preferred therapy is therefore effective Christian counseling.

Until more creative, dedicated Christian researchers become involved in the careful testing of current theories, there is great danger that this field will "continue to exist in conceptual chaos" and in a technical psychological denominationalism which will confuse future generations of Christian counselors and adversely influence their counselees.

EVALUATING CHRISTIAN COUNSELING

How can Christian counseling be evaluated now and in the future? One might begin by seeking answers to the following questions:

1. *What are the underlying assumptions?* These are difficult to determine at times because they are not stated clearly. Nevertheless, counselors and writers invariably drop hints concerning their assumptions about God, the universe, human beings, epistemology, pathology, guilt, and related issues. Counseling methods and goals often (but not always) develop out of the underlying assumptions. What one does or teaches others to do in counseling usually is consistent with one's presuppositions. If you disagree with the beginning assumptions and especially if you believe that these are inconsistent with biblical teaching, this is a reason for caution in accepting the theory's conclusions and recommendations about counseling.

2. *What are the counseling goals?* These too are sometimes more implied than identified specifically, but they are an important part of any counseling approach. Perhaps there would be value in listing your personal goals for counseling. Keep the list available for later revisions. Then ask "Does this theory share my goals?" Remember that a theory with goals different from yours can be useful, but its methods must be accepted and used cautiously.

3. *What supports the theoretical conclusions?* Usually support for a counseling approach will fall into one of several categories: scriptural and theological support, empirical research, the support from established psychological thinking and insights, case histories, and the theorist's personal experience. It is suggested that the above categories are listed in order of importance. In evaluating Christian counseling we must find specific answers to the following questions. An approach which is supported by only one or two of these standards is of questionable validity, especially if support rests on-

ly with the last two questions.

a) Is the approach sound biblically and theologically? If the Bible is used, is there evidence of good hermeneutics?

b) Is there research evidence to support the theory?

c) Is the approach sound psychologically?

d) Are there successful case histories to support the approach?

e) Is the approach supported by the theorist's personal experience?

It will be noted that personal experience is placed at the end of the list. Experience is a shifting influence, and not the most solid basis on which to reach conclusions.

It should be stated, however, that "inner subjective feelings" do play a role in theory evaluation. Some people, for example, feel more comfortable with one specific approach and feel uncomfortable with other theories. It probably is wise to listen to such inner promptings in evaluating Christian counseling, providing such subjective experiences do not replace a careful consideration of the questions listed above.

4. *Is the approach practical?* This is largely a subjective question, but one which should be considered when counseling approaches are evaluated. A counseling system may be biblically based, psychologically sound, and logically organized, but if it is difficult to apply, the approach is of limited value. Some secular theories, for example, have confusing terms and techniques which are too complicated to use widely in practice. A similar danger is possible in Christian counseling. If an approach cannot be applied widely, its value is limited, regardless of the clarity with which it is stated.

5. *What are the qualifications of the writer or counselor?* Many of the best-known approaches to counseling and self-help have been proposed by people who have little or no formal training in psychology or counseling. This is not a unique issue for counselors. It would appear that many people in our society

distrust professionals and avoid their counsel. In seeking advice and information about health, diets, education, business decisions, finances, home repairs, theology, child-rearing, personal problem-solving, and a host of other issues, we turn not to experienced professionals but to untrained journalists, housewives, popular speakers, and neighbors. Perhaps this trend cannot be reversed, but it may result in considerable misinformation, extra expense, and personal harm.

It does not follow that the conclusions of these nonexperts are wrong. Tournier, for example, has no formal training in psychology, but he has read widely in the field and many of his conclusions are both valid and helpful. Surely, however, it is more logical to seek counseling advice from those who are trained and experienced counselors, just as it is wise to consult a physician concerning our physical problems, or to ask a trained pastor or theologian about our spiritual questions.

In evaluating Christian counseling, therefore, one might ask, "What qualifies this writer or Christian counselor to tell others how to counsel and/or solve their problems?" Ask if the Christian writer/counselor has formal training (and if so, in what field and at what schools), has counseling experience, is openly committed to Jesus Christ, and is showing evidence of spiritual maturing. These questions, especially the latter ones, are not easy to answer, but they are valid inquiries for those who are seeking to evaluate Christian counseling approaches.

6. *What are the disturbing aspects of the approach?* In the preceding section we discussed the superior, condescending attitudes of some counselors and writers, the uncritical acceptance or rejection of secular psychology, the tendency to divide psychology and theology into different and unrelated categories, the acceptance of selfism, and the lack of careful evaluation which characterizes many approaches. The prevalence of these and similar disturbing influences might lead you to be cautious in accepting any approach uncritically.

In all of our evaluations, however, it is well to remember

that no one approach is perfect or "right" for every counselor and counselee. In the future it is likely that new approaches will appear and old theories will fade in influence and popularity. This is healthy and reflects a growing discipline, but the Christian counselor must be alert to these different approaches, evaluating each as they appear, rejecting that which is nonbiblical and contrary to sound psychology, and then accepting that which can be of practical help to Christian people helpers.

FOOTNOTES

1. B. Narramore in *Psychology for Living*.
2. Ross S. Banister, "Directions" in *LifeStyles* (11500 Stemmons Freeway, Dallas, TX 75229), January-March 1979.
3. Gary R. Collins, *The Rebuilding of Psychology* (Wheaton: Tyndale, 1977).
4. Stanley R. Strong, "Christian Counseling in Action" in *Counseling and Values*, 21, February 1977, p. 101.
5. J. Adams, *Competent to Counsel* (Grand Rapids: Baker, 1970), p. 70.
6. *New International Version*.
7. Adams, op. cit., p. xxi.
8. O.H. Mowrer, *The Crisis in Psychiatry and Religion* (Princeton: Van Nostrand, 1961), p. 60.
9. Paul C. Vitz, *Psychology As Religion: The Cult of Self-Worship* (Grand Rapids: Eerdmans, 1977), pp. 107, 91, 93, 95.
10. M.B. Parloff, "The Family in Psychotherapy" in *Archives of General Psychiatry*, 1961, 4, p. 445.
11. See, for example, Sol L. Garfield and Allen E. Bergin, *Handbook of Psychotherapy and Behavior Change: An Empirical Analysis*, second ed. (New York: Wiley, 1978). This book summarizes and reviews several thousand research articles dealing with therapeutic effectiveness.
12. Collins, op. cit.

18

THE FUTURE OF CHRISTIAN COUNSELING

Gary R. Collins

What is the future of Christian counseling? Where are we going? What developments will we see in the years ahead? Will there be a merging of theories, or greater diversification? Will new methods be developed? Will the field continue to expand?

Only a few years ago, when the field was small and the number of trained counselors sparse, such questions were rarely asked. Today, however, great numbers of people are entering the counseling profession and many more Christians are acknowledging that "it is all right for a believer to have problems and to seek help." With this increase in interest there is an increasing demand for accountability. Like their secular colleagues, Christian counselors are being freed to consider whether their counseling is effective, how counselors should be selected and trained, and where this field might be moving in the future. We must make active efforts to determine the future direction of Christian counseling, since without such planning the field could explode like pellets of gunshot flying in all directions.

This concluding chapter proposes some directions for the future of Christian counseling. Written by the editor of this volume, the chapter is an expansion and revision of a paper entitled "Christian Counseling: Some Suggestions for the Future," presented at the South Florida Conference on Christian Counseling, Fort Lauderdale, May 1, 1977.

❖ ❖ ❖

In discussing the future of one's discipline, two approaches are possible. First, we can make predictions—crystal-ball-gazing about the direction we might take in the years that are ahead. Such prediction is of questionable validity, and, while it might be enjoyable, it probably serves no useful purpose. The second approach is, in my opinion, better. This is the approach which suggests proposals for the future. It is a perspective which sees value in looking periodically at where we are as counselors, where we have been as a discipline, and where we might go in the future.[1] This concluding chapter takes the second approach. It is more a proposal for the future than a prediction of what might be coming in the field of Christian counseling. The suggestions which follow are not meant to be the only issues to be considered, nor are the proposals necessarily the most important. Each of these must be considered, however, if we are to be effective counselors who are competent professionals but also true to our commitment to Jesus Christ and to the truths of the Scriptures.

1. *A Christian approach to counseling must clearly delineate its presuppositional foundations.* As we indicated in chapter 1, everyone involved in counseling has some presuppositions or assumptions which influence what takes place during the therapeutic process.

The *counselee,* for example, has assumptions about how the counselor will act and what the counselor will do. These assumptions determine, in large measure, how the counselee will act, at least in the beginning of therapy. When the counselee's assumptions differ from those of the counselor, this discrepancy must be dealt with at some time early in the counseling relationship if there is to be maximum therapeutic success.

The *counselor* also has goals and assumptions which influence his or her methodology. Rogers, for example, has goals and therapeutic techniques which differ from those of Wolpe, who in turn differs from Freudian analysts. The helper's presuppositions about such issues as the nature of persons, the ability of human beings to change, or the techniques for effective counseling can all influence therapy.

In addition, the *counselor-educator* has assumptions which influence how teaching occurs. Jay Adams,[2] for example, trains students using a team approach which involves the trainee observing as two counselors work with the counselee. This would be quite different from the more traditional approach to training, in which a counselor discusses tapes with a supervisor following an interview session. These differences in training undoubtedly reflect differences in assumptions about counseling that come from the trainer.

Finally, the counseling *researcher* is influenced by his or her assumptions. Behaviorists, analysts, and nondirective counselors each take a different approach to research in counseling. In each of these four examples—the counselee, counselor, educator, and researcher—all have presuppositions which determine at least to some extent how one works.[3]

Christian counseling must spell out its assumptions, since these will influence what goes on in therapy, in training, and in research. As Christians we must make a clear statement about the nature of persons (the extent to which we have free will or have our behavior determined, the extent to which our sinful nature influences behavior, and the influence of change that may come following the new birth, when one becomes a "new creation"). As Christians we must have a clear idea about the nature of God (is He a real Person or an illusion? Is He someone who exists independently, or is He the projection of a vivid imagination?). We must have a clear view of the nature of the universe (Is it created and held together by God's Son, as stated in Hebrews 1:1-3? Or is man alone in a universe indifferent to his fate, as has been suggested by Eric Fromm?). And we must have a clear understanding about the nature of epistemology. (Where do we get our knowledge about man and his behavior? Does it come from empiricism only, from logic, from the Bible, or from other areas? If we assume that the Bible speaks of human needs and human problems, solutions, values, and goals, do we accept some, none, or all of what the Bible says? As counselors we cannot stand aside and dispassionately watch the theologians "battle for the Bible," since our own view of Scripture has a significant impact on our approach to counseling.)

As a Christian counselor, I believe that psychology and counseling must be built on the assumption that man is created in the divine image, marred by the Fall, loved by a real God who exists, and able to be changed into a new creation by the act of confessing one's sin, commiting one's life to Christ, and experiencing the "new birth." As I have suggested elsewhere, truth can come from empirical methodology, from logical deduction, from analysis of fiction and other forms of literature, and from the Bible, God's inerrant Word.[4] Whether or not another Christian counselor agrees or disagrees with these conclusions, each of us must pause to delineate our presuppositional assumptions, since these influence what we do in our counseling, whether we realize this or not.

2. *A Christian approach to counseling must clarify its values.* George Albee, former president of the American Psychological Association, has argued that the Protestant ethic of hard work, belief in religion, and delay of immediate gratification is losing its influence in American society:

> With the death of the Protestant ethic, the decline of traditional religion, the rise of hedonism, the beatification of the pleasure principle, we have got, to mix a metaphor, a whole new ball game. With nothing left to believe in . . . it is little wonder that there is a growing and pervasive sense

of meaningless, nihilism, and purposelessness. Alan Wheelis and numerous other psychotherapists have described the growing and frantic contemporary search for identity. In the absence of a pervasive set of religious and moral beliefs, we see the inevitable rise of numerous new cults.[5]

Acording to Albee, we have now created a "self-indulgent society." It is a society in which we are more concerned about personal satisfaction than in feelings of empathy or respect for the rights of others. In this self-indulgent society, "we may feel less guilt but surely are doomed to be more anxious. The old existential questions have not been answered and the abandonment of traditional religions is leading to the search for new gurus with new answers."[6] This idea of a self-indulgent mentality has been critiqued in an insightful volume by Vitz [7] and discussed in the preceding chapter.

Recently this issue of values was discussed by the editor-in-chief of a large Christian publishing house. Among Christians in our society, there is much confusion about morality, the editor suggested. We are not sure how to react to the prevalence of X-rated movies, violence on television, questionable business ethics, or heavy petting. Some values are spelled out in Scripture (for example, the Bible clearly condemns overt homosexuality, sexual intercourse apart from marriage, and theft), but other issues are less clear. As a result, many Christians are involved in changing their personal values. Some practices which might have been considered sin only a few years ago are now considered acceptable behavior for believers. According to the editor, there needs to be something written to help Christians deal with the "gray areas" of life. These gray areas of values come up frequently in counseling, and Christian counselors must clarify their own thinking on such issues.

3. *A Christian approach to counseling must recognize the*

influence of culture. Several years ago Carkhuff suggested that empathy, warmth, and genuiness are basic variables in effective counseling.[8] Others have stressed the importance of rapport, individual differences, openness, the communication of body language, the therapeutic value of touching, and the significance of interpretations. All of this may apply effectively in the United States and Canada, but would it apply in other parts of the world?

Consider the Orient, for example. In certain Oriental countries people are less willing to talk openly about their problems than we are in North America. Counselors are expected to be more directive, and individuals in counseling are less willing to alter the environmental circumstances than we are in America.

Much counseling is cultural, and this must be considered in any therapeutic approach. Crosscultural counseling occurs even within our country, where a counselor of one socioeconomic class or age level often is called upon to counsel with people who are in a different socioeconomic class or in a different age level. It is probably true that most present counseling theory is middle-class, intellectual, limited in time, and focused on the verbalization of abstract concepts. Such approaches may be inappropriate in working with counselees who are members of a different culture or subculture.

We must consider, therefore, which of our techniques and concepts are culture-specific and which are not. A Christian approach to counseling undoubtedly will make room for the uniquenesses of a given culture, but counseling techniques and theories which are based on the Scriptures must be crosscultural in their application. Christian counselors have given very little consideration to crosscultural counseling, and any approach to biblically based counseling in the future must not neglect this significant area.[9]

4. *A Christian approach to counseling must constantly*

evaluate its methodology. Although some counselors would be inclined to disagree, most professionals who are Christians would not accept the fact that the Bible was written as a textbook of counseling techniques. In the field of homiletics there are various preaching methods, all of which are more or less consistent with the Scripture; in Christian education there are a variety of teaching methods which differ from one another but may be consistent with Scripture; likewise in counseling there can be a variety of methods which are consistent with the Scriptures but not necessarily derived from the Bible directly.

Consider active listening, for example. The Bible does not talk about this specifically, but Jesus showed an active involvement in listening. This is a technique clearly consistent with Scripture. In contrast, something like the use of sexual surrogates to help people with their sexual problems is accepted in certain areas of counseling but is not Scriptural and cannot be sanctioned by believers.

In any approach to Christian counseling, therefore, we must ask whether our methods are consistent with the Bible and with Christian ethics, whether our methods work to accomplish our therapeutic goals, and whether our methods are supported by empirical research. Applying this threefold criterion—is it scriptural, is it pragmatic, and is it empirical —we might eliminate some of the techniques which we are currently inclined to use but which are of debatable validiity.

5. *A Christian approach to counseling must consider how to select, train, and evaluate Christian counselors.* Counselor selection and education has become a major area of concern in the secular world. Numerous writers have criticized the ways in which potential counselors are selected, the irrelevance of their training, the gap between what counselors are taught and what they actually do in training, and the disappointing efforts at evaluating counseling effectiveness.

Most Christian counselors are trained in secular educational institutions and are taught models of counseling which are built on humanistic, naturalistic presuppositions. Within recent years, some Christian training programs have developed which challenge these non-Christian assumptions, but these training programs are few in number and are largely based on secular training models. Some Christian institutions have begun to offer graduate counseling degrees which are based on brief contacts with professors (short summer programs, for example, or periodic one-week seminars followed by independent study), and little or no supervised training. Such programs (which sometimes even claim to teach ''biblical counseling'') are of unproven effectiveness, are insensitive to state licensing laws for counselors, and offer proof to the counseling profession that many Christian counseling programs are second-rate ''shortcuts'' to a degree.

If Christian counseling is to be truly effective, professional Christian counselors and counselor educators must give careful attention and research study to the ways in which Christian counselors (including professional counselors, pastors, and lay people-helpers) can be selected, trained, and evaluated in the most effective ways possible. Perhaps we need our own standards for accreditation. This whole area of training is a needy but still largely untouched area in the field of Christian counseling.

6. *A Christian approach to counseling must acknowledge and influence the increasing influence of nonprofessional approaches to people helping.* Within recent years there has been an upsurge in lay approaches to counseling. Professionals may wish that this was not happening, but increasing numbers of persons who are untrained or only partially trained in counseling skills are helping their friends, relatives, and others to deal with the problems of life.

There are two basic approaches within the nonprofessional movement. The first is what we might term ''do-it-yourself'' counseling. Recently there has been some debate within the pages of *The American Psychologist* [10] on whether such self-help programs should be controlled or in some way licensed. Perhaps such control is impossible, but there is little debate about their presence, their general effectiveness, and their potential harm.

As we have seen in an earlier chapter, "do-it-yourself" counseling is especially common among Christians. Tim LaHaye has written books on depression, temperament analysis, and sex. Norman Vincent Peale and (more recently) Robert Schuller have talked about the importance of positive thinking. Numerous other well-meaning but sometimes untrained Christian writers have prepared books on such topics as marriage improvement and counseling, weight control, the reduction of depression, guilt, or anxiety, and a variety of other issues.

It should be remembered that these books and articles are the only help that some needy people will get or have the courage to consult. Professionals must recognize that there are people within the community who will never go for professional counseling and who thrive on simple answers, whether or not these anwers are supported by sound psychological and biblical analyses. Nevertheless, Christian counselors must not leave self-help programs to untrained popular writers and speakers. A Christian approach to counseling must attempt to develop solid self-help approaches to counseling and must help others to evaluate the approaches which are currently on the market.

A second aspect of the nonprofessional movement is the trend toward lay counseling. Research has demonstrated that peer counselors, besides being available and trusted, can also be very effective in helping people with their problems. [11] Several programs have been developed for the training of lay counselors, and both within and outside the church paraprofessional counseling is becoming an influential movement. [12]

There clearly is biblical precedence for lay people to bear one another's burdens, show compassion for one another, weep with those who are weeping, and help each other. The Christian counselor must recognize that such helping already is taking place apart from the professional. It is the responsibility of Christian professionals to develop, evaluate, and utilize training programs which will enable nonprofessionals to be trained as effectively as possible in lay people-helping skills.

7. *A Christian approach to counseling must consider the influence of religious experience.* Why are some Christians charismatics, fundamentalists, conservative evangelicals, or theological liberals? What are the effects of conversion? (Is it always positive, as William James suggested, or is it sometimes negative, as Leon Salzman has proposed?) Is conversion always of therapeutic value? Why is glossolalia psychologically liberating for some people but perhaps an evidence of pathology in others? What is the influence of prayer on the individual?

These questions are of crucial importance and have a great bearing on counseling, especially when we work with people who are religous. While there are many studies of religious experience, the subject is almost totally ignored in evangelical literature and rarely mentioned in relationship to counseling. As Christian counselors we must develop a greater understanding of religious experience (both Christian and non-Christian), including its influence on the individuals who experience religious phenomena.

8. *A Christian approach to counseling must give serious consideration to the prevention of problems.* Caplan's much-acclaimed book *The Principles of Preventive Psychiatry*[13] was a breakthrough volume in mental health and helped to launch the whole community psychology movement. The preventive psychiatry movement assumes that if we can change the culture we can prevent problems. As a result this

movement has attempted to reduce poverty, to remove discrimination, or to eliminate economic stresses, all on the assumption (undoubtedly valid) that many of these social conditions create the personal problems which subsequently are immobilizing.

In additon to this emphasis on communities, we must help invididuals to avoid problems before they arise or to arrest problems which might be developing. Such prevention does not occur in the counselor's office; prevention takes place in communities, in homes, in the schools, and especially in the church. Sunday school teachers and elders can spot developing problems and intervene before they get worse. Pastors who are involved in premarital counseling could also be involved in preretirement counseling, presurgery counseling, counseling with those who are facing death, and other forms of prevention. Church leaders must be helped to see the value of helping people by speeches, sermons, books, and articles, all of which can help individuals both anticipate and deal with their problems.

The Christian professional has a responsibility for stimulating this prevention through the church. It is our task to alert church leaders both to the possibilities of meeting human needs through messages and church programs, and to the building of caring churches where the body of believers supports, encourages, and bears one another's burdens. The Christian counselor should use his or her own skills to speak, to write, to lead groups, and to consult in ways which prevent new problems from arising and which prevent existing problems from getting worse.

9. *A Christian approach to counseling must put special emphasis on the family.* There is no secret that the family is in trouble. Divorce rates are increasing, family conflict is rampant, and concern for the family in our society is widespread.

The Christian counselor who is sympathetic toward the needs of the family cannot condone easy divorce and remarriage, the widespread destruction of life through abortion as it now exists, the prevalence of sexual intercourse outside marriage, or the practice of trial, gay, swinger, or open marriages. Divorce is sometimes inevitable, and sinful behavior is certain to occur, but we have some biblical standards for the family, standards which *must* be maintained. As counselors we can help our counselees learn, accept, and maintain these standards. We can also help people within the church to determine what are effective guidelines for family living.

A considerable number of books on marriage, family, and child-rearing have appeared within recent years. The prevalence of these books indicates that there is both a great interest and a great need in this area. Perhaps there is also a great confusion, so much so that a new understanding and emphasis on the family must be the cornerstone for Christian counseling in the future.

10. *A Christian approach to counseling must be research-oriented.* Within recent years a hostility toward research has developed within the American public.

> . . . the American public is growing increasingly dissatisfied with—even hostile to—research in psychology and the social sciences. We can speculate about the reasons for such hostility, but whatever the cause, social scientists are viewed with increasing suspicion and distrust by citizens and politicians alike. . . . The psychologist's job as a scientist is to search for data, principles, and laws that enlarge our understanding of psychological phenomena.[14]

It is interesting to note that in the midst of all this resistance to research, there is a turning to mysticism and various forms of parapsychology. Apparently

> . . . many people are turning, with an almost religious fervor, to mystical and occult beliefs. The

speakers most actively in demand on the college lecture circuit are those who are prepared to talk about astrology, voodoo, witchcraft, psychic forces, and the like. Today, possibly more than ever before, we find an uncritical acceptance of mystical ideas. Psychology has a special role to play in this regard. It is important that we try to keep the facts straight and not contribute to such irrational tendencies. . . . The best defense against a citizenry preoccupied with the occult is one that has an understanding of science, particularly psychology, and that can distinguish statements based on research from those that have no basis in fact.[15]

It is true that empirical research is not popular, but if we as Christians make statements unsupported by data, we are similar to the mystics who are criticized in the above quotations. The Christian counselor must avoid sweeping generalizations and testimonies of success unsupported by factual data. Such generalizations which characterize the contemporary mystical approaches are often also characteristic of the psychologically oriented theories proposed by well-meaning but psychologically naive Christian speakers, seminar leaders, and writers. In Christian approaches to counseling, therefore, we need research which supports our statements about how behavior changes and people grow.

11. *A Christian approach to counseling must be "body" oriented.* Doing things alone is the American way. We value rugged individualism, and perhaps this is nowhere more apparent than in dealing with our personal problems.

The Bible, however, does not emphasize this do-it-yourself growth, do-it-yourself Christianity, or do-it-yourself problem-solving. Instead, the Bible emphasizes body life. First Corinthians 12, for example, stresses that individual spiritual gifts and responsibilities are to edify and operate within the body of believers. In addition, Romans 12 stresses the importance of mutual support, encouragement, and practical people helping.

Following the Second World War, Maxwell Jones wrote a book entitled *The Therapeutic Community.*[16] Jones' approach, which for a time was very popular, emphasized the importance of treating people within the context of an environment where everyone was a therapist—the psychiatrist as well as the ward aide, the nurse, and the cleaning lady.

More recently, Richard Almond has produced a thought-provoking book entitled *The Healing Community,*[17] in which he advocates that the group can support, encourage, and model desired behavior. It should be remembered, however, that

> the assumptions of moral and milieu therapy were first stated in the Bible, although for some reason Christians have failed to follow the Scriptural model. As a result the church has neglected its role as a therapeutic or helping community. It has, instead, tended to become a listless organization where counseling is left to the pastor or a few laymen and where people in need of help are often ignored or rejected, especially if they are not active church members or if they show unusual mannerisms.[18]

Christian counseling may take place in the counselor's office, but to be truly Christian it must be backed up by a concerned body of believers supporting one another and caring actively for one another.

CONCLUSION

We who are Christians in the field of counseling have tremendous potential for the future. We cannot afford to be rigid, however. Instead, we must try to build approaches to people helping which clearly delineate our presuppositions and values; which are alert to the importance of culture and changes in methodology; which are concerned about selecting, training, and evaluating Christian counseling; which recognize and help those who are interested in nonprofessional approaches, religious experiences, and prevention; which have an emphasis on the family; and which are research-and-body-oriented. Perhaps these are the most important attributes of a Christian approach to counseling, but they *are* among the basic.

In all of this we must be flexible. Counseling is a growing, developing field, and it is easy to equate Christian counseling with biblical counseling and with the further assumption that ours is "true" counseling which cannot change or cannot grow.

All of us are fallible as human beings, and Christians probably will continue to develop a series of different approaches to counseling. We must be open to new findings in counseling methodology, to new understandings of Scripture, and to the new Christian counseling approaches which will appear in the future.

The road ahead is long, but the path to Christian counseling is both exciting and filled with possibilities. Hopefully, many more Christian counselors will have the courage and the creativity to carve out counseling orientations that really work because they are based on solid psychological research and on the divine biblical revelation of the holy, omniscient God.

FOOTNOTES

1. This is the approach taken by Marjorie K. Bradley in "Counseling Past and Present: Is There a Future?" in *Personnel and Guidance Journal*, September 1978, pp. 42-45.

2. J.E. Adams, *Competent to Counsel* (Grand Rapids: Baker, 1970).

3. B. Stefflre and K. Matheny, *The Fuctions of Counseling Theory* (New York: Tym Share Corp., 1968).

4. G.R. Collins, *The Rebuilding of Psychology* (Wheaton: Tyndale House, 1977).

5. G.W. Albee, "The Protestant Ethic, Sex, and Psychotherapy" in *American Psychologist*, 1977, 32, p. 159.

6. Ibid., p. 160.

7. P.C. Vitz, *Psychology As Religion: The Cult of Self-Worship* (Grand Rapids: Eerdmans, 1977).

8. R.R. Carkhuff, *Helping and Human Relations: Vols. I and II* (New York: Holt, Rinehart and Winston, 1969).

9. P. Pederson, W.J. Lonner, and J.G. Draguns, eds., *Counseling Across Cultures* (Honolulu: University Press of Hawaii, 1976).

10. I. Goldiamond, "Singling Out Self-administered Behavior Therapies for Professional Overview: A Comment on Rosen" in *American Psychologist*, 1976, 31, pp. 142-47; and G.M. Rosen, "The Development and Use of Nonprescription Behavior Therapies" in *American Psychologist*, 1976, 31, pp. 139-41.

11. R.R. Carkhuff, "Differential Functioning of Lay and Professional Helpers" in *Journal of Counseling Psychology*, 1968, 15, pp. 117-28.

12. See, for example, G.R. Collins, *How to Be a People Helper* (Santa Ana: Vision House, 1976); G.R. Collins, *People Helper Growthbook* (Santa Ana: Vision House, 1976); S.J. Danish, *Helping Skills: A Basic Training Program* (New York: Behavioral Publications, 1973); and G. Egan, *The Skilled Helper: A Model for Systematic Helping and Interpersonal Relating* (Monterey, CA: Brooks/Cole, 1975).

13. G. Caplan, *The Principles of Preventive Psychiatry* (New York: Basic Books, 1964).

14. R.C. Atkinson, "Reflections on Psychology's Past and Concerns About Its Future" in *American Psychologist*, 1977, 32, pp. 206-7.

15. Ibid., pp. 208-9.

16. M. Jones, *The Therapeutic Community* (New York: Basic Books, 1953).

17. R. Almond, *The Healing Community: Dynamics of the Therapeutic Millieu* (New York: Jason Aronson, 1974).

18. Collins, 1976, p. 132.

INDEX

A

Abortion, 348
Acceptance, 49, 68, 70, 71, 73, 173, 179, 211, 240, 262, 285
Adams, Jay E., 16, 24, 26, 151-164, 241, 268, 269, 270, 324, 328, 339
Adler, Alfred, 56, 66, 174, 211, 212, 219, 232
Advice, 19, 36, 74, 200, 270
Albee, George, 340, 341
Alcoholics Anonymous (A.A.), 245, 246, 247, 248, 262
Alcoholism, 61, 81
Almond, Richard, 350
American Association of Marriage and Family Counselors, 114,
American Psychological Association, 241, 340
Anger, 178, 298, 310
Anxiety, 62, 63, 127, 176, 177, 178, 233, 345
Apologetics, 22, 199
Aristotle, 321
Assessment, 12
Assumptions, 23, 25, 26, 35, 88, 100, 101-107, 109, 111, 115-117, 135, 172-182, 190, 214-216, 248-250, 276, 280-282, 318, 320, 321-324, 329, 333, 338, 339, 344
Attitude(s), 23, 48, 89, 102, 103, 152, 190, 193, 195, 210, 324, 328
Authority, 34, 47, 169

B

Bach, George, 296
Banister, Ross, S., 322
Behavior modification, 167, 319
Beliefs, 23, 152, 153, 158, 167, 190, 341
Berne, Eric, 99-112
Bible, 15, 16, 21, 34, 35, 38, 39, 48, 51, 68, 79, 101, 136, 137, 152, 153, 158, 162, 165, 172, 187, 189, 190, 202, 204, 223, 230, 231, 232, 238, 239, 263, 270, 275, 276, 296, 297, 298, 311-313, 314, 321, 322, 323, 328, 331, 334, 340, 341, 343, 349, 350

Bible Therapy, 297, 300
Biblical interpretation—see Hermeneutics
Birth control, 136
Birth order, 212
Body language, 342
Body of Christ, 44, 46, 203, 227, 229, 312, 318, 349
Boisen, Anton, 12, 207
Bollman, C.R., 300
Bonhoeffer, D., 50
Bonnell, John Sutherland, 15
Brain damage, 152
Brammer, Lawrence, 201
Brandt, Henry, 13
Brothers, Joyce, 273
Bruder, Ernest, 15
Buber, Martin, 73
Buchman, Frank, 245
Burden-bearing, 203
Bustanoby, A., 296

C

Calvin, John, 88
Caplar, Gerald, 346
Care, 174, 219, 229, 262, 292
Caring, 84, 85, 87, 88, 90, 148, 192, 230, 231, 347
Carkhuff, R.P., 52, 297, 342
Carlson, David, 51-54, 314
Carter, John, 45
Case histories, 307, 308, 333, 334
Cassette tapes, 76, 259, 268, 269, 303
Catharsis, 72, 236, 237
Catholic Approaches, 279-294, 301
Charge, 155, 156, 161, 162, 171, 194, 208, 213, 214, 216, 217, 218, 220, 309, 310, 324
Christian Association for Psychological Studies, 17
Christian Education, 320, 343
Church, 18, 83, 85, 86, 87, 91, 100, 101, 114, 133, 134, 161, 165, 182, 184, 203, 207, 208, 214, 215, 229, 241, 243, 251, 259, 261, 271, 272, 273, 274, 283, 286, 327, 347
Clinebell, Charlotte, 81
Clinebell, Howard, 22, 37, 81-97, 207